Negotiating the Complexities of Qualitative Research In Higher Education

Negotiating the Complexities of Qualitative Research In Higher Education

Fundamental Elements and Issues

Susan R. Jones ■ Vasti Torres ■ Jan Arminio

Routledge
Taylor & Francis Group
New York London

Routledge is an imprint of the
Taylor & Francis Group, an informa business

Published in 2006 by
Routledge
Taylor & Francis Group
270 Madison Avenue
New York, NY 10016

Published in Great Britain by
Routledge
Taylor & Francis Group
2 Park Square
Milton Park, Abingdon
Oxon OX14 4RN

Printed in the United States of America on acid-free paper
10 9 8 7 6 5 4 3

International Standard Book Number-10: 0-415-95055-4 (Softcover)
International Standard Book Number-13: 978-0-415-95055-8 (Softcover)
Library of Congress Card Number 2005034351

Library of Congress Cataloging-in-Publication Data

Jones, Susan R., 1957-
     Negotiating the complexities of qualitative research in higher education : fundamental elements and issues / Susan R. Jones, Vasti Torres, and Jan Arminio.
          p. cm.
     Includes bibliographical references and index.
     ISBN 0-415-95055-4 (pb : alk. paper)
     1. Research. I. Torres, Vasti, 1960-. II. Arminio, Jan L. III. Title.

Q180.A1J645 2006
001.4--dc22   2005034351

Taylor & Francis Group
is the Academic Division of Informa plc.

Visit the Taylor & Francis Web site at
http://www.taylorandfrancis.com

and the Routledge Web site at
http://www.routledge-ny.com

DEDICATION

To those from whom we learned
And those we hope to teach
In the circle of teaching and learning,
We dedicate this book

CONTENTS

PREFACE

The seeds for the idea of this book were planted through some admittedly bad behavior on our part—passing notes at a professional meeting. We were all members of an editorial board and were reviewing a number of manuscripts professing to utilize qualitative methodology. The subject of our notes revealed that all three of us were concerned about the methodological quality of many submissions. We wondered what we might do to improve the methodological goodness of qualitative work. It was important to us to engage this question by providing an accessible text that also illuminated the complex nature of qualitative research. This was a guiding principle that served as the foundation for this book. Another primary motivation for the creation of this book is that we believe that the ultimate purpose of conducting research is to create a pathway to greater good and social action. By this we mean that research ought to result in greater understanding of complex phenomena and that higher education can offer pathways to improved quality of life, particularly for those whose experiences and life situations are understudied and devalued in mainstream society. We wanted to make apparent how research can contribute to this goal.

Why is a book on qualitative research particular to the context of higher education necessary? First, due to their very nature, good qualitative studies can assist higher education in meeting learning goals and produce learning outcomes for students, especially those whose voices have been silenced or made difficult to hear within quantitative research. Also, higher education institutions play a critical role in preparing students as researchers. This occurs through classroom instruction as well as in research endeavors outside the classroom. To meet the accountability demands of stakeholders, the public and governing bodies are requiring higher education practitioners and institutional researchers to assess if educational goals are being met. Increasingly, such assessments are utilizing both quantitative and qualitative methodologies. Consequently, conducting sound assessment studies has important implications for institutions in their training of practitioners and scholars. Moreover, faculty members who conduct scholarly research, whether qualitative or quantitative, often use the higher education context as a setting for their work. Other texts have addressed assessment in higher education; our focus is on qualitative research, although we recognize that qualitative methods are often used in assessment work. As qualitative research becomes a more accepted means of conducting inquiry, it is critical that a common and clear understanding of the complexities that encompass qualitative inquiry exists so that more sophisticated research influences the developments and new initiatives in higher education. Here we offer insight into how these complexities are negotiated.

As we worked on this book, we realized that we were in fact mirroring the process of "working qualitatively." As coauthors working collaboratively to write a book, we brought to this process our own individual insights and experiences; we listened to each others' descriptions and perspectives, made decisions, and created a common understanding only after challenging and supporting each others' perspectives. We became much more reflective about our journeys as qualitative researchers and how the nature of the journey influences our work as researchers now. In fact, we structured the last chapter of this book through our own individual stories about our evolving understandings of what it means to work qualitatively.

We acknowledge that we came to this project from different life experiences, learned about qualitative research in different ways, and offered different interpretations of qualitative inquiry. Indeed, our own worldviews influenced all dimensions of this project—we referred to Jan as the "phenomenological mom" because her very being *is* phenomenological; Vasti was always very direct and to the point in her writing; and Susan took the long way around, using metaphors to tell her story. We have disagreed, negotiated, and settled on when and how to use terms such as *sample*, *rigor*, *validity*, *control*, and *goodness*. We navigated the tensions through our willingness to receive, sit with, and negotiate differing assumptions, biases, and opinions. We came to a better and deeper understanding of the taken-for-granted aspects of our previous work. However, what drew us together, and continues to sustain us, is a commitment to provide a useful text that presents the complexities of qualitative research, including its philosophical and theoretical foundations, and offers direction for good qualitative work. We did not want to write a simple book because we don't think qualitative research is simple at all. Instead, we hope to cultivate an appreciation for the complexity and ambiguity of this work and ways to think through the questions and tensions that undoubtedly emerge in the qualitative research process.

In acknowledging our differing worldviews, experiences, and training in qualitative research, those using this book may note that chapters are written in different voices and styles. This is most likely because, although we were all involved in the conceptualization and outline of each chapter and in the careful editing of every chapter as it was written, one of us took the lead in writing each chapter. We believe this approach is a strength of the book because it enabled us to bring multiple perspectives to bear in each chapter as well as to give the reader a glimpse into the great variety in writing styles and strategies associated with qualitative research. Writing the book in this way also enabled us to tap into our strengths and areas of research expertise as well as to stretch into new areas not treated as fully in other resources on qualitative research. We drew heavily on these other sources and do not view our book as the only book on qualitative research that a new researcher should read. Our goal is to help the researcher through the complexities of the research process—this, we believe, is new territory for an introductory text on qualitative research. However, many of the topics we cover are treated in greater depth in other works, and we highly recommend that those be read as well.

Although the conceptual approach to the book is one of negotiating complexities, the organizational approach is intended to mirror the process of designing a qualitative study. Chapters 1 and 2 focus on situating yourself as a researcher within an epistemological worldview and the research questions and methodological approaches that flow from that worldview. Chapters 3 and 4 take you through the process of identifying participants, or "sampling," and making connections between all elements of the research design. All the chapters in the book, and particularly these early ones, emphasize the importance of decision making in the research process. Every step of the way, the researcher is making decisions—regarding research questions, who is in the sample, what kinds of questions to ask in interviews, how to analyze data, and so on. Our approach is to emphasize the importance of intentionality in these decisions and the relationship of these decisions to chosen theoretical perspectives and methodological choices.

The remaining chapters emphasize issues we believe are important to consider in conducting qualitative research. Chapter 5 provides insights into issues of positionality and power, and how these dynamics influence our roles as researchers. Chapter 6 summarizes the elements required to conduct "good" research by examining criteria for goodness and trustworthiness that are used to judge the worthiness of qualitative studies. Chapter 7 provides an overview of issues involved in mixing methods, a topic rarely discussed in qualitative research texts. Although some purists may object to the inclusion of such a chapter, we believe that many researchers claim to mix methods by simply adding a few open-ended questions on the end of a survey. This does not constitute mixed methods research because there is no evidence of grappling with the complexity that comes with mixing methods. As a result, clarification about what it means to mix methods and how to manage the tensions is warranted. Chapter 8 addresses ethical issues inherent in the process of research, particularly in qualitative research, which typically involves the process of understanding others. Each of these chapters concludes with an exercise for readers to apply what was presented in the chapter to a research design. The final chapter, Chapter 9, illustrates our own learning about what it means to "work qualitatively." Here we offer our own stories about how we came to work as qualitative researchers and then provide a narrative analytic rendering of what can be learned from our stories.

We recognize the seemingly contradictory and ironic twist in a title that includes both the phrases *negotiating complexities* and *fundamental elements*. *Fundamentals* imply building blocks and neat recipes to follow, whereas *complexities* suggest ambiguity, challenges, and troubling taken-for-granted assumptions. Indeed, we are navigating in the space in between simplification and theoretical sophistication. We know there are trade-offs in our approach, but were guided in our work by an overarching commitment to produce a text that was useful and accessible to beginning qualitative researchers, while also engaging readers in the complex issues that emerge when conducting such research. We hope you will let us know how we have succeeded in this effort.

No book is ever produced as a completely solitary endeavor. In our case, we are far from solitude! Not only were we engaged in a highly collaborative process among the three of us, but we were also supported by others who provided feedback, proofreading, and general expressions of support. Two individuals read the entire book and provided very helpful critique and feedback: Anne Krabacher, a doctoral student in higher education and student affairs, and Patti Lather, professor and scholar in the area of qualitative inquiry, both at The Ohio State University. When we were trying to determine if we could make Chapter 9 work, Marylu McEwen from the University of Maryland provided a careful read and very useful feedback. Graduate students and colleagues read more of the book than they cared to but were very generous with their time and gracious in providing feedback and technical and logistical support. These individuals include: Danielle De Sawal and Ebelia Hernandez from Indiana University; Heidi Clark, Michael Penwell, and Kurt Kraus from Shippensburg University; Elisa Abes from Miami University; and Allen Delong from Bowdoin College. We also want to thank our three anonymous reviewers for their insightful and helpful feedback on the prospectus for the book and the entire manuscript. And to our colleagues from The Ohio State University, the University of Maryland, Indiana University, and Shippensburg University, we seek forgiveness for what we left undone while writing this book and give thanks for what we were able to accomplish with their guidance and support.

Susan R. Jones
University of Maryland

Vasti Torres
Indiana University

Jan Arminio
Shippensburg University

1

SITUATING THE RESEARCH: FIRST STEPS

Many beginnings are precarious. "The problem of the beginning is, in fact, the problem of the end. For it is with respect to an end that a beginning is defined" (Gadamer, 1960/1989, p. 472). How does a researcher negotiate the precariousness of beginning a study? How does one arrive at a completed, worthy qualitative study? We believe it is imperative that those who engage in qualitative inquiry address its fundamental and complex defining features. These features include situating the research in a grounding perspective; being congruent in the research design and in how one selects, interprets, and represents participants; making choices and managing the consequences of mixing methods; and, of course, meeting obligations of ethics and goodness (i.e., criteria for determining a worthy, well-designed, and well-implemented study). Negotiating these complex features determines the quality and worthiness of the research study, yet these features in particular are often overlooked by many researchers who attempt to conduct qualitative studies.

We begin this discussion by exploring the fundamental considerations of situating research. To situate a study means to "anchor" it (Jones, 2002, p. 463). This is a process that identifies a series of choices that include deciding upon an area of interest, a grounding perspective or worldview, a theoretical framework and perspective, a question, a purpose (e.g., research, assessment, or evaluation), and a relationship with the topic and participants. Studies that are not situated or anchored run adrift, ramble, become lost, and are without direction. In this chapter, the immediate considerations for negotiating necessary decisions to situate a study are explored and corresponding examples are offered, including the decision making of a fictitious researcher, "Michael," as he situates his study.

CONSIDERATION 1: SITUATING THE STUDY WITHIN A COMPELLING INTEREST

One of the first considerations in situating a study is to reflect upon what issue or topic is sufficiently compelling that causes "me" to want to contemplate more about it. What is it that presses upon me in a way that necessitates I understand it more? What unknown deters my practice, my community, my society?

The intent of qualitative research is to illuminate and better understand in depth the rich lives of human beings and the world in which we live. Hence, one's compelling interest must reflect this depth. Thoroughness and explicitness should be balanced with what Marshall and Rossman (1999) called the "do-ability" of a study (p. 9), or the feasibility that a study can be completed considering the resources available, purpose, and researcher competence.

Compelling interests that lead to unsettled questions are typically related to our life experiences. This is not to be avoided. Marshall and Rossman (1999) referred to this as the "want-to-do-ability" of a study (p. 10), and it is directly related to one of the central features of qualitative research, the researcher-as-instrument (Lincoln & Guba, 1986; Patton, 2002). Qualitative inquiry requires the researcher to become embedded in context and responsive to what is happening in that context. There often is, and should be, a relationship between the researcher and the researched. This reflects the passion that later becomes the research question. Critics of qualitative research often refer to this relationship as bias. The three of us believe this to be a strength of qualitative inquiry. We will address this criticism in depth later in this chapter and in subsequent chapters.

Let's look at an example. In one of his graduate classes, Michael studies campus environments. His reading assignments offer insight into his own experiences of being physically threatened and feeling unwelcome on campus. He finds that this literature supports and validates his feelings and experiences that safety is a broader notion than physical safety. In a subsequent class on research design, Michael feels compelled to study student safety on campus. Before deciding upon a particular question or its wording, however, Michael has much to think about, including his worldview about the generation of knowledge.

This brings us to consideration 2, and the question of how one's worldview about knowledge influences research decisions.

CONSIDERATION 2: SITUATING THE STUDY WITHIN THE RESEARCHER'S WORLDVIEW

Researchers often err in deciding upon a research question prematurely. Researchers must first consider their view about how knowledge is generated and the nature of reality. Jones (2002) noted that conducting qualitative research is both a blessing and a burden. Certainly the enrichment that researchers gain from the research process is one of the blessings, and, as Jones noted, researchers' responsibilities to those with whom they come into contact are significant. The "burden" comes in the need to understand the complexity of philosophy and theory upon which qualitative research and its associated traditions are founded. Negotiating these complexities may at times be burdensome. We encourage researchers to "lean" into these complexities. In fact, avoiding them would be irresponsible. Yet, this "leaning into" takes considerable study. Thelin (2003) noted the historical utilitarian and pragmatic aspects emphasized in American higher education. We believe these aspects continue to influence higher education through the reluctance of some practitioners and administrators to use theory to guide educational practice. Qualitative research is guided and influenced by theory. To engage in qualitative research is to pay attention to philosophy and theory. What differentiates this book from others, not particular to education, is that we assist the pragmatic user in negotiating the complexities of philosophy and theory for results that will be used in pragmatic ways. We begin by discussing worldview and what we believe are aspects of worldview including philosophy, epistemology, ontology, and theory.

One's worldview, or how a person perceives his or her relation to the world, is associated with one's culture and upbringing (Sue, Ivey, & Pedersen, 1996). Obviously one's worldview can be altered and matures through life experiences, but it also can house consistent values and concepts. It shapes one's philosophical grounding. In this book, we refer to *philosophy* as a system of fundamental principles that serve as a basis for action (Berube, 1995). Philosophy, the study and search for wisdom, is described as including the elements of logic, epistemology, ontology, ethics, and metaphysics (Brightman, 1964; Durant, 1961; Honderich, 1995). *Metaphysics* at one time referred to the study of the ultimate reality of all things including the study of existence (ontology) and the study of the nature of knowledge (epistemology). However, Heidegger (1926/1962) contested the notion of an ultimate reality of all things, a grand objective narrative, or representative understanding (Bronner, 1999). Heidegger wrote, "We do not know what 'Being' means. But even if we ask, 'What is Being'?, we keep within an understanding of the 'is,' though we are unable to fix conceptually what 'is' signifies" (p. 25). He stressed the necessity to "bring forward the entities themselves" (Heidegger, 1926/1962, p. 61).

One's worldview on the nature of existence and knowledge has implications for how one will embark upon a study. For example, believing that existence is an ultimate reality and knowledge a grand narrative, believing that existence is difficult to understand and that existence calls to itself rather than is represented, or believing other notions of existence and reality are important considerations in situating a study. "Ways of knowing are inherently culture-bound" (Lather, 1991, p. 2). Consider the traditional Russian wooden doll, where one very small doll is embedded within a small doll, which is embedded in a medium-sized doll, which is embedded in a larger doll; how data are analyzed and the ways in which data are collected are determined by a particular methodology, which is situated within a philosophical (that is, epistemological and ontological) stance. Often, this is referred to as the researcher's *theoretical perspective*.

Table 1.1 is an exercise to assist you in better understanding your epistemological and ontological worldview. It describes a series of belief statements listed in three columns. Circle those statements under the columns *A*, *B*, and *C* that are most consistent with your own views of knowledge and reality.

Is there a preponderance of circles in any one column? These statements indicate aspects of worldview that will influence views on research. There is also an activity at the end of this chapter that may help you identify philosophical differences and their influence on scholarship in higher education. Each column in Table 1.1 depicts a different view of knowledge and existence. We have depicted three views here, as have other scholars including Coomer and Hultgren (1989). However, Sipe and Constable (1996) noted four "vantage points or places to stand" (p. 162), and Lincoln and Guba (2000) indicated that four paradigmatic positions exist. Welcome to the complexities of qualitative research! Clearly, views of knowledge grounding research are dynamic and not to

Table 1.1 Worldview Exercise

A	B	C
Reality is a physical and observable event.	Reality is constructed through local human interaction.	Reality is shaped by social, political, economic, and other values crystallized over time.
The aim of research is to predict and explain, generalizing results.	The aim of research is increased understanding of complex human phenomena to alter existing power relations.	The aim of research is transformation and emancipation to promote a humanity capable of controlling its destiny.
Truth is universal and verifiable; findings are considered true.	Truth is an agreement between members of a stakeholding community.	Truth is influenced by history and societal structures.
The researcher can and should be objective.	Objectivity is impossible; rather, the researcher serves as an avenue for the representation of multiple voices.	The view of objectivity as a goal is harmful; rather, advocacy is the aim of research.
Good research is value free.	Values are a means of understanding.	Values are formative.
Researchers study a problem.	Researchers live a question with participants.	Researchers transform with a community by imagining and helping to create alternatives.
It is through the voice and jurisdiction of an expert that knowledge is gained.	It is through voices and acknowledgment of both participants and a researcher that knowledge is gained.	It is through theoretical perspectives of societal structures in conjunction with the people who are most affected that knowledge is gained.
The universe is human centered.		
History is progress.		

Source: Bronner (1999), Crotty (1998), Lincoln and Guba (2000), Maykut and Morehouse (2001), and Pinar, Reynolds, Slattery, and Taubman (1995).

be seen as discrete categories mutually exclusive of each other (Crotty, 1998). It is beyond the scope of this book to delineate the intricate differences of all the views on knowledge and existence. The point to take away is that these views bring with them assumptions that influence research questions, the purpose of research, and the interpretation of research findings.

Statements in column A are descriptive of views that knowledge and reality are universal and measurable. Terms associated with these views include *positivism* and *postpositivism* (Crotty, 1998; Lincoln & Guba, 2000), *empiricism* (Smith, 1993), *empirical/analytical* (Coomer & Hultgren, 1989), and *objectivism* (Crotty, 1998), with an emphasis on prediction. In column B, knowledge and existence are perceived and constructed through human interaction and emphasize understanding. The views represented in column B are often associated with the terms *interpretive* (Coomer & Hultgren), *constructivism* (Lincoln & Guba, 2000), and *constructionism* (Crotty, 1998). Column C depicts the purpose of knowledge as emancipation; meaning of the phenomenon of the study is imposed, imported, or translated by the subject (Crotty). Terms associated with these views include *subjectivism* (Crotty) or *subjectivist* (Lincoln & Guba, 2000) and *critical science* (Coomer & Hultgren). Experienced researchers will notice the absence of a column or columns portraying postmodernism, poststructuralism, and deconstruction. Such a clearly laid-out structure seemed at odds with the main tenets of these perspectives, so they are not represented here but will be discussed later in the chapter. We will return to a more in-depth discussion of these terms later. First, let's turn to the terms *qualitative* and *quantitative* and the worldviews they represent.

The statements in columns B and C are indicative of what is still commonly referred to as *qualitative research* or the *qualitative paradigm*. Crotty (1998) described the polar opposition of these terms as the "great divide" (p. 14). Since the 1980s some researchers have been moving away from these bipolar terms. Our dilemma here is whether to use terms that novices will recognize or to use contemporary terms. We will use the familiar terms, while encouraging the study and understanding of more current ones. The terms that one uses when referring to knowledge creation are themselves indicative of a worldview, a multidimensional one or one that can be simplified by two broad categories. A discussion on how the broad polarities of quantitative and qualitative research emerged will be helpful.

Thomas Kuhn (1970) used the Greek term *paradeigma*, meaning pattern or model, to refer to basic patterns that scientists use to interpret data. In this context, he defined *paradigm* as a model "from which

Figure 1.1

spring particular coherent traditions of scientific research" (p. 10). He went on to write, "In short, consciously or not, the decision to employ a particular piece of apparatus and to use it in a particular way carries an assumption that only certain sorts of circumstance will arise" (p. 59). He offered a number of examples of scientists whose work was ignored by the established scientific community restricting new understanding. Such scientists have included Copernicus, Galileo, Isaac Newton, and Albert Einstein. According to Kuhn, Copernicus did not discover more data, but rather he was able to imagine how the data might fit into a different pattern. Kuhn employed Joseph Jastrow's famous duck–rabbit picture* as a metaphor of the paradigm shift debate. He concluded that once the viewer has "seen" the new paradigm (or duck–rabbit), it is impossible to forget it. This opened the possibility of asking, "What would data look like from another perspective?" "What might the universe look like from the perspective of the sun rather than the earth?" and "What new insights can be offered by collecting data from a position of an 'emic,' or insider's view rather than the view of the authority observer?"

Through calling attention to the different ways of collecting and viewing data, the concept of a knowledge paradigm has created an overly simplistic distinction between new paradigm and old paradigm, between rational and mythic, and between quantitative and qualitative inquiry (Figure 1.1).

---

* There is some controversy as to who to credit for this drawing. Some, such as Kuhn, credit Ludwig Wittgenstein (*Philosophical Investigations*, 1953), but Wittgenstein himself credited Jastrow for the drawing published in *Harper's Weekly* in 1892.

Postmodern, poststructuralist, and deconstruction scholars attack this duality (Pinar, Reynolds, Slattery, & Taubman, 1995). Other dualities they oppose include fact versus fiction and myth versus reality. They also oppose and expose the construction of societal structures and distinctions such as kinship, the adolescent, and the gifted (Pinar et al.). These theorists will be discussed in greater detail later.

In situating a study within a worldview, researchers must become aware of the philosophical stances that inform their perspectives. Some beginning researchers say they embrace qualitative research while not truly understanding "what it is they claim to be reject-ing" or what it is they say they are embracing (Phallas, 2001, p. 10). Gaining knowledge through qualitative research has only recently become acceptable in research and assessment communities in the United States as compared to quantitative means. Hence, most students have been schooled in quantitative study design, but few have received formal training in qualitative research and the philosophy that grounds research.

As the differing views listed in Table 1.1 demonstrated, who we are as people encompasses our beliefs about the nature of reality, truth, and knowledge. These beliefs and theoretical perspectives define assumptions about the world and subsequently about the nature of research. Kezar (2004) wrote that researchers should know the philosophy of their worldview well enough to defend choosing it. She continued to write that researchers should

> engage in philosophical questions, write out assumptions about the issue to be studied, investigate one's own role as researcher, consider the purpose of the research from the tradition they are working in, [and] probe what they understand as the nature of reality and how knowledge is developed. (p. 43)

What terms should researchers use to illustrate assumptions? Before embarking further on situating one's study, it is necessary that we take a detour to discuss important terms and their definitions regarding qualitative inquiry.

Understanding Terms Necessary in Deciding How to Situate a Study

Crotty (1998) noted a lack of clarity and consistency in some of the fundamental grounding concepts of qualitative research. He wrote,

> Research students and . . . even more seasoned campaigners—often express bewilderment at the array of methodologies and

methods laid out before their gaze. . . . To add to the confusion, the terminology is far from consistent in research literature and social science texts. One frequently finds the same term in a number of different, sometimes even contradictory[,] ways. (p. 1)

To negotiate the complex fundamentals of qualitative research, we believe that it is important to be familiar with the terms *paradigm, epistemology, ontology, theoretical perspective, literature review/theoretical framework, methodology*, and *method*. However, these terms are sometimes defined and used differently by different scholars. Important fundamental concepts are listed in Table 1.2 along with definitions of notable research scholars. You will notice that some authors define terms similarly, some terms are defined differently, and some scholars refer to some of these concepts but not others.

Paradigm is rather consistently referred to as a set of interconnected or related assumptions or beliefs. It is also referred to as *worldview*. Related assumptions about the acquisition of knowledge are referred to as *epistemology*. Some scholars do not refer to epistemology, but those who do define it as the origins, theory, or assumptions about knowledge. Other scholars state what it is that epistemological questions illuminate, some scholars do not mention epistemology, and still others do not define epistemology in their recent works but did so in earlier works. Another set of related assumptions is associated with explanations or questions about the nature or structure of reality or existence. This is referred to as *ontology*.

Discussion about theory becomes more complicated because of its many uses. Defined as a set of interrelated explanations, theory guides a study, serves as a lens through which researchers view the world and subsequently their research, and is created from research. Glesne (1999) discussed levels of theories including substantive theories that have a low level of abstraction and provide a rationale for new studies, general theories that are used as a framework for discussing findings, and formal theory that helps form ideas during the beginning process of making meaning of data. Some scholars define theory, whereas others focus on its purpose in research or how to create theory. Still other scholars refer to theory created from previous research as informing researchers about a topic through the process of a literature review. What is consistent is that theory is made up of epistemological and ontological beliefs that span academic disciplines.

The inconsistent use of the terms *methodology* and *method* is of considerable concern to us. Some authors use the terms interchangeably, defining both as the means by which data are collected. Other scholars differentiate

Table 1.2 Various Definitions of Terms

Terms	Morse and Richards	Denzin and Lincoln	Crotty	Creswell	Maykut and Morehouse	Lincoln and Guba	Patton	Glesne
Paradigm	"Philosophical paradigms [include] feminism, postmodernism, and critical theory" (2002, p. 171).	The net that contains the researcher's epistemological, ontological, and methodological premises (2000, p. 19); assumptions that "re-present a belief system that attaches to a particular worldview" (1994, p. 2).	"Package of beliefs" (1998, p. 35).	"[W]orldview, a basic set of beliefs or assumptions that guide their inquiries" (1998, p. 74).	A set of overarching and inter-connected assumptions about the nature of reality (2001, p. 4).	Represents a distillation of what we think of the world but cannot prove; systematic set of beliefs (1985, p. 15).	A worldview, a general perspective, a way of breaking down the complexity of the world (1990, p. 37).	Refers to "modes of inquiry" (1999, p. 6); cites other authors in defining paradigm.

Epistemology	"[A]ssumptions [that] concern the origins of knowledge" (2002, p. 3).	"[H]as historically defined standards of evaluation" (1994, p. 6; 2000, p. 11); "specifies a set of questions" (2000, p. 18).	"The theory of knowledge imbedded in the theoretical and thereby in the methodology" (1998, p. 3).	"[T]he relationship of the researcher to that being researched" (1998, p. 74).	"Assumptions that concern the origins of knowledge" (2001, p. 3).
Ontology	"[C]oncern questions about the nature of reality" (2002, p. 3).	Explains the kind of being a human being is; answers the question "What is the nature of reality?" (2000, p. 19).	"Concerned with 'what is' the nature of existence, with the structure of reality" (1998, p. 10).	"[A]ddresses the nature of reality" (1998, p. 76).	"Concerns questions about the nature of reality" (2001, p. 3). "[N]ature of reality" (1999, p. 4).

(Continued)

Table 1.2 Various Definitions of Terms (Continued)

Terms	Morse and Richards	Denzin and Lincoln	Crotty	Creswell	Maykut and Morehouse	Lincoln and Guba	Patton	Glesne
Theoretical Perspective		"Set of propositions that are interrelated in an ordered fashion such that some may be deducible from others thus permitting an explanation to be developed for the phenomenon under con- struction" (Denzin, 1988,	"The philo- sophical stance informing metho- dology and thus providing a context for the process and grounding its logic and criteria" (1998, p. 3).	Provides "an explanation, a prediction, and a gen- eralization about how the world operates" (1998, p. 84).			"What distinguishes the discus- sion of theory . . . on qualitative methods is the emphasis on inductive strategies of theory development in contrast to theory generated by logical deduction" (1990, p. 66).	"The ultimate goal of this form of theorizing is to develop universal laws of human behavior and societal functioning" (Glesne & Peshkin, 1992, p. 19; Glesne, 1999, p. 22); differentiates low level (outcomes from previous studies) from middle range

	p. 49); "The ... researcher approaches the world with a set of ideas, a framework, theory, ontology" (Denzin & Lincoln, 2000, p. 18).		(explains a set of phenomenon) (1999, p. 22).
Literature Review	Under the heading "Using the Literature Review": "[T]heoretical context ... places the study in the context of the topic" (2002, p. 189).	"[H]ow others have approached similar concerns" (1990, p. 163).	"Reading about the studies of others. . . . [To] collect, scan, and read literature . . . can help find focus for your topic . . . can help inform your research design" (1999, p. 20).

(Continued)

Table 1.2 Various Definitions of Terms (Continued)

Terms	Morse and Richards	Denzin and Lincoln	Crotty	Creswell	Maykut and Morehouse	Lincoln and Guba	Patton	Glesne
Methodology	See method.	"[T]he specific ways questions are examined" (2000, p. 18).	"The strategy, plan of action, process, or designing behind the choice and use of particular methods" (1998, p. 3).	"[H]ow one conceptualizes the entire research process" (1998, p. 77).				
Method	"[S]hare the goal of deriving new understanding and making theory out of data" (2002 p. 13).		"[T]he techniques or procedures used to gather and analyze data" (1998, p. 3).	"[T]he most concrete, specific part [includes] essential steps" (2003, p. 153).	Sampling strategy and the people or settings that will make up the sample, data collection procedures for data analysis (2001, p. 65).		"Permits the evaluator to study selected issues in depth and detail" (1990, p. 13).	

Table 1.3 Various Definitions of Terms

Paradigm	Epistemology	Ontology	Theoretical Perspective and Framework	Methodology	Method
A set of interconnected assumptions that distinguish between worldviews	Assumptions about the acquisition of knowledge	Assumptions about the nature of existence	Perspective: philosophical (epistemological and ontological) assumptions that guide methodology Framework: suppositions and concepts (e.g., research and theories) that inform the phenomenon under study	Informed by epistemology, ontology, and theory, a process that grounds and gives direction to study design, implementation, data collection, data analysis, and interpretation	How data are collected

them, with methodology meaning the approach that guides how data are collected and analyzed. The exclusion of methodology from the discussion of qualitative research has consequences for the worthiness of a study. We believe that methodology is a central concept because it guides the research design. Without attention paid to methodology, the researcher lacks the means to appropriately design the study, analyze data, and make sense of findings. In addition, the reader has no context for understanding or judging the research findings. Examples of methodologies include ethnography, phenomenology, grounded theory, life history, narrative inquiry, and case study.

In response to the various definitions of terms, Crotty (1998) offered his own representation and definitions of important qualitative concepts. Like Crotty, we will offer our own representation, but one we believe to be appropriate in the pragmatic context of higher education.

The reader will notice in Table 1.3 that we have replaced the term *literature review* with *theoretical framework* to emphasize the importance of theory. We have differentiated theoretical perspective (assumptions about the nature of knowledge acquisition and existence) from theoretical framework (concepts and previous research that inform the phenomenon being studied). We have distinguished methodology (which guides research design) from method (the collection of data) while underscoring their relationship. Understanding and using these terms allow the researcher to situate his or her study.

Let's return again to Michael's thoughts as he continues to situate his study. Michael determines that his worldview is more consistent with an interpretive and constructivist view of knowledge. He believes that numbers cannot represent the experience of feeling safe or unsafe. He believes that an in-depth understanding about this phenomenon could best be accomplished through human interaction. As with all researchers, once he has contemplated his worldview, he must now further investigate his epistemological and ontological stance.

Epistemology and Ontology

In discussing epistemology and ontology, our aim is not to oversimplify what has occurred in the evolution of philosophy over several hundred years. On the other hand, we don't want to burden the reader with philosophical intricacies. Rather, we seek to sufficiently describe the philosophical differences so that the reader can acknowledge that epistemological underpinnings do influence the researcher and his or her research. What follows is a brief discussion of the primary epistemological and ontological frameworks that guide inquiry.

Put very simply, what is commonly referred to as *quantitative research* is based upon objective epistemology and the linked theories of positivism, postpositivism, and empiricism (Crotty 1998; Lincoln & Guba, 2000; Smith, 1993). According to Crotty,

> Objectivism is the epistemological view that things exist as *meaningful* independently of consciousness and experience, that they have truth and meaning residing in them as objects ('objective' truth and meaning, therefore), and that careful (scientific?) research can attain that objective truth and meaning. (1998, p. 6)

Objective Positivistic Empiricism

Objective claims are true or false independent of what anyone thinks or feels about it (Honderich, 1995) such that there is a clear distinction between fact and value (Crotty, 1998). According to J. K. Smith (1993), to be objective is to detach oneself from one's own interests and depict things as they "really are" (p. 30). Knowledge is what can be found and measured outside of us. Positivism is the optimistic notion that science leads to progress (Crotty, 1998; Lincoln & Guba, 1985). Postpositivism adds a note of uncertainty to scientific findings challenging that observer and observed are independent (Crotty, 1998, p. 29), whereas positivism views facts as ultimate truth that comes from measurements.

Empiricism is rooted in the idea that people can neutrally observe the world through the five senses (Honderich, 1995). According to J. K. Smith (1993), empiricism is the "solution to the knowledge-versus-opinion problem" (p. 5) in that humans have the capacity to not distort observations through the controlled scientific method. Through strict procedures, claims can be made and then judged based on evidence.

According to Denzin and Lincoln (2000) and J. K. Smith (1993), the most important aspect of objective positivistic empiricism is the belief that truth is universal and can be measured through observation and discovery, proving or disproving a hypothesis. Some of the components of objective positivistic empiricism were listed in column A in the exercise in Table 1.1. Philosophers most associated with this paradigm include John Locke (Woozley, 1964), who saw the minds of humans as blank slates "devoid of any ideas" (Smith, 1993, p. 27) from which they independently existed in the world, and Max Weber (1972), who believed that researchers and scientists can make a conscious decision to exclude their judgments.

Often stated in stark contrast to the epistemological and ontological views of objectivism, constructivism (Lincoln & Guba, 2000) is also referred to as and linked to interpretation or hermeneutics (the science and art of interpretation). Also referred to as constructionism, this view is that

> [a]ll knowledge, and therefore all meaningful reality as such, is contingent upon human practices, being constructed in and out of interaction between human beings and their world, and developed and transmitted within an essentially social context. (Crotty, 1998, p. 42)

Constructivism and Constructionism

Constructionism claims that "meanings are constructed by human beings as they engage with the world they are interpreting" (Crotty, p. 43). Sometimes deemed an epistemology (Crotty, 1998) while also considered a philosophy (Flew, 1984) constructionism and interpretation are concerned with the individual because knowledge is found within the individual. Constructivism seeks to understand individual social action through interpretation or translation. "Something foreign, strange, or separated by time, space, or experience, is made familiar, present, comprehensible" (Hultgren, 1989, p. 41). The aim is to understand aspects of human activity from the perspective of those who experience it (Hultgren). Kuhn (1962) believed that perception is symptomatic of all observation and that all knowledge is dependent on its context. Contrary to objective empiricism, all people, and therefore all researchers, bring with them a lived worldview. Heidegger wrote,

> We must rather choose such a way of access and such a kind of interpretation that this entity can show itself in itself and from itself. And this means that it is to be shown as it is *proximally and for the most part*—in its average everydayness. (1926/1962, p. 38)

Subjectivism

In subjectivist epistemology, meaning is not created from the interplay between humans, but rather meaning is "imported" (Crotty, 1998, p. 9) or brought into the study. For example, Hamrick (1998) used democratic political theory to increase understanding of college student activism. Democratic theory was not created through the interaction between the researcher and her students; rather, it was used as a lens to promote critique and analysis for the purpose of increased understanding, improved praxis, and ultimately liberation.

Unlike positivism and constructivism, subjectivist epistemology suggests that no one can interpret for others. It is only from an inside perspective that one can grasp meaning. Jürgen Habermas (1984) wrote, "What counts as fundamental is not the interpersonal relation between at least two speaking and acting subjects—a relation that refers back to reaching understanding in language—but the purposive activity of a solitary acting subject" (p. 279). Acting with others and engaging in discourse with them are the means by which there is understanding.

Because some people lack sufficient influence or power to have mastery over their own lives, or because people are afraid of losing the influence and power they have, their communication can be distorted by those with more power. Hence, Habermas believed that just because certain views exist doesn't make them valid (Coomer, 1989). It is through communicative action and discourse that findings are deemed sound.

Comparing Epistemologies

Several authors have created charts highlighting the differences noted above using a variety of comparative criteria (e.g., Coomer & Hultgren, 1989; Lincoln & Guba, 2000; Sipe & Constable, 1996). These charts are dynamic and illustrate a snapshot of current thinking rather than static definitions. The differences are most obvious at their extremes and do not represent "rigid or unchanging differences/boundaries" (Sipe & Constable, p. 153). We also have constructed a chart comparing epistemologies (see Table 1.4). The criteria we use are those we believe are most instructive in the context of higher education. Because we believe that higher education values utilitarian knowledge, we have selected the nature of knowledge, knowledge claims, and values as important comparative criteria. We offer the comparison chart as a summary of what we have previously discussed.

Experienced researchers will note the absence of postmodernism, poststructuralism, and deconstruction in Table 1.4. We concur with Crotty (1998) that postmodernism and poststructuralism represent theories, though we acknowledge that they are also considered paradigmatic stances (Sipe & Constable, 1996). We turn to theories next as additional aspects of worldview that inform the research process.

CONSIDERATION 3: SITUATING A STUDY IN A THEORETICAL PERSPECTIVE AND FRAMEWORK

In the chart noting our definitions of terms, we differentiated between theoretical perspective and framework. Here we will further clarify this distinction and the usefulness of each in situating the research.

Table 1.4 Comparing Epistemologies

	Positivism	Constructivism	Subjectivism
Nature of Reality (ontology)	Measure through observation	Outgrowth of human interaction	Perception can be flawed.
Values	Value neutral	Participant perspective	Passionate action
Relationship Between Researcher and Participants (researcher positionality)	Objective	Interpreter	Passionate participant
Nature of Truth	Universal	Individual	Purported truth can be flawed due to the oppressive nature of the world.

Source: Synthesized from writings of Crotty (1998), Lather (1991), and Lincoln and Guba (2000).

Theoretical Perspective

"Research cannot be conducted without the conscious use of underlying theoretical perspectives" (Broido & Manning, 2002, p. 434). A theoretical perspective is "the philosophical stance informing the methodology and thus providing a context for the process and grounding its logic and criteria" (Crotty, 1998, p. 3). It discusses how the "study fits into theoretical traditions in the social sciences or applied fields in ways that will be new, insightful, or creative" (Marshall & Rossman, 1999, p. 35).

There are a number of theoretical perspectives that give direction to research. Several are described below. We acknowledge that though some scholars refer to these theories as *movements* (Pinar et al., 1995), *philosophical approaches* (Bronner, 1999), and *paradigmatic stances* (Sipe & Constable, 1996), we agree with Crotty (1998) and Radhakrishnan (2003) and discuss them here as theory.

Theories most associated with quantitative research include positivism and modernism (Crotty, 1998). These theories seek to describe and predict human behavior that is then generalized to a larger population. However, some claim the demise of the foundations of modernism

(Crotty; J. K. Smith, 1993). According to Crotty, this demise came from the scientific community in research that demonstrated "uncertainty" and "limitation" (p. 30). Some philosophers also refuted the logic of induction itself. To subscribe to the scientific method assumes "a world in which the regularities we perceive today will remain unchanged in the future" (Crotty, p. 32). Other philosophers stressed "the absurd nature and the unpredictable in scientific knowledge" (Crotty, p. 38). In light of these revelations,

> Some [scientists and philosophers] have come to reject positivism and the objectivism that informs it and to adopt a constructionist view of meaningful reality. Others remain within the positivist camp but temper very significantly the status they ascribe to their findings. . . . This humbler version of the scientific approach . . . has come to be known as post-positivism. (Crotty, p. 40)

Many theorists, however, believe that postpositivism did not go far enough in moving away from the purported value-free structure of studying the world. Postmodernism is an interdisciplinary theoretical base attacking "any universal characterization of the individual" (Bronner, 1999, p. 189). It has also been described as a cultural, political, and historical movement (Pinar et al., 1995) "wherein no one owns the truth and everyone has the right to be understood" (Doll, 1993, p. 151). There are two other terms closely associated with postmodernism. They are *poststructuralism* and *deconstruction*. All three oppose structuralism. "While structuralism has sought to identify 'the system' that creates meaning, poststructuralism has sought to repudiate, dismantle, and reveal the variance and contingency of 'the system'" (Pinar et al., p. 453). Examples of structuralism would be reproduction theory (that schools reproduce the classist nature of society) and family systems theory. Poststructuralism contends that human reality has been constructed into hierarchical structures to achieve absolute certainty. Poststructuralism seeks not to substitute one absolute for another but rather to produce an awareness of the complexity of what was previously unpresented. Poststructuralism seeks to encourage ambivalence and multiplicity, exceed the boundaries of what can be imagined, expose dichotomies and illusions, and advocate for resistance to subjugation (Lather, 1991).

Deconstruction "disentangles the central threads running through the tapestry . . . of Western thought" (Pinar et al., 1995, p. 467). According to Pinar et al., "Heidegger invoked deconstruction to violate the everyday, the taken for granted sphere we construct and employ to evade the ontological facts of our fallenness, our being-toward-death" (p. 447). Deconstruction highlights the way in which "any system of reference is constituted as a fabric of differences" (Bronner, 1999, p. 193). One way of accomplishing this is by exposing the oppressive language and structure of a phenomenon under study. According to Caputo (1987), the work of destruction or deconstruction is deployed on two levels. In the first place, it must break through the commonplace described in terms of the present, in order to exhibit a deeper understanding. The deeper level Caputo referred to as a redical recovery. It is a recovery of the self.

Space does not allow for a thorough discussion of postmodernism, poststructuralism, and deconstructivism. Experienced researchers will note the brevity here. Scholars have described the relationship of the three, some of it in disagreement. Clearly, these concepts are continually being refined as they are lived. A gross simplification would be that postmodernism subsumes the other two, that poststructuralism is the left arm of postmodernism, that postmodernism articulates many of the ideas advanced by postructuralism and deconstruction (Pinar et al.), and that there are certain similarities in all three (Bronner, 1999). For an interesting metaphoric description of these theories, consult Sipe and Constable (1996) on how paradigmatic stances are like sports, colors, and famous people. The point is that these theories create a lens through which researchers can describe their perspectives of the phenomenon under study and the study itself. Researchers must become sufficiently familiar with theoretical perspectives so that theory can inform the perspective of their study.

There are other theories associated with the postmodern stance. These theories seek not only to abandon the limits and hegemony of positivism but also to replace it with justice promoting praxis. Critical theory is sometimes viewed as an epistemology (Coomer & Hultgren, 1989), a paradigm position (Lincoln & Guba, 2000), a paradigmatic stance (Sipe & Constable, 1996), and a theory (Crotty, 1998). *Critical theory* or *critical science* refers to the

> situation where human experiences are systematically repressed in a given society. . . . It views society as a human construction that can be altered through human understanding of taken-for-granted structures from the fiber of human life in the society. (Coomer, 176–177)

Habermas's notion of communicative action serves as a base for critical theory. He believed that communicative discourse is emancipatory. "With the concept of communicative action there comes into play the additional presupposition of a *linguistic medium* that reflects the actor-world relations as such" (1981/1984, p. 94).

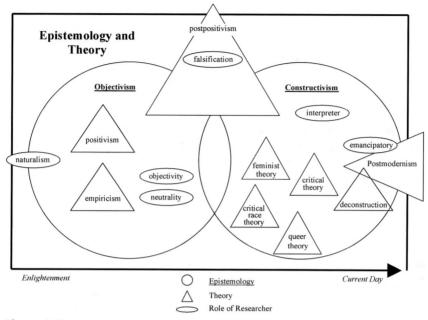

Figure 1.2

Still other theories within the postmodern view include feminist theory ("[V]ery simply, to do feminist research is to put social construction of gender at the center of one's inquiry"; Lather, 1991, p. 71), critical race theory ("[R]acism is an ingrained feature of our landscape, it looks ordinary and natural"; Delgado, 1995, p. xiv), and queer theory ("the ways the very homo/hetero distinctions [have] underpinned all aspects of contemporary life"; Gamson, 2000, p. 354).

Grasping these theoretical perspectives, their relationships to each other, and their relationship to epistemology is complex. We have tried to provide an instructive way to describe these complexities in Figure 1.2. What is noted here in this frame are epistemologies and theories that inform research along a chronological continuum from the Enlightenment to the current day. Postpositivism, poststructuralism, postmodernism, and deconstruction are depicted partly outside the frame because they all continue to be defined and refined and resist definition. Two epistemologies, objectivism and constructivism, are noted here as circles. Theories are indicated as triangles, and the role of the researcher or researcher positionality within the epistemology is noted within ovals. Theories associated within the epistemology of objectivism are positivism and empiricism. Postpositivism emerged from the postmodern protest of the notions of the supposed objective and neutral researcher and of truth emanating from exacting measurement. This is illustrated by the postpositivism triangle merging the objective and contructivist epistemologies. We note naturalism as the precursor to objectivism prior to the Enlightenment and the Age of Reason.

The constructivist epistemology is informed by poststructuralism, postmodernism, and deconstruction theories (also referred to as *schools* and *movements*). These theories are noted in larger triangles because they are more broad in scope and influence critical, critical race, feminist, and queer theories. Researchers in the constructivist epistemology are interpreters. Their role is to understand phenomena in an inventive way. The more closely the researcher is associated with poststructuralism, the more he or she seeks to emancipate society from its hegemonic structures through deconstruction (Figure 1.2).

In good qualitative studies, researchers identify the theoretical perspectives that guide their work. For example, in her article reporting on the Safe Zone project, Evans (2002) described her study as grounded in constructivist philosophy and stated that critical theory "undergirded" the study because the researchers viewed research as being able to contribute to the emancipation and empowerment of oppressed groups, a principle of critical theory.

Let us return to Michael. As Michael seeks to refine his compelling interest, he has many questions. He doesn't know where or how to start, and is feeling anxious about the research process. He worries whether he knows enough about his topic and research design to embark upon his study. He seeks out his advisor, who suggests that he look to theory for guidance.

Having done some preliminary reading about postmodern theory, Michael decides that feminist and queer theories offer guidance, not only on how he proceeds with his study but also about the phenomenon of safety itself. By using feminist theory as a lens, Michael is hoping that he might be better able to understand how gender plays a role in feeling safe. He also wonders how the coming-out process described in queer theory might illuminate the struggle with being truly present in a space that is hostile. How is it to come out as oneself in a place where safety is not expected? How is it to continually have to decide whether or how to come out with each new environment?

Theoretical Framework

Whereas theoretical perspective influences how the researcher will approach and design the study, and influences how the researcher will approach the topic under study in more abstract terms, the theoretical framework offers suppositions that inform the phenomenon under study. The theoretical framework links the unsettled question to "larger theoretical constructs."

Michael looks to campus environment theory to offer him insight into his study. This assists him in refining his question. He decides to use Moos's (1979) work in environment theory and Schlossberg's (1989) work on mattering and marginality to inform his topic. He reads campus environment theory (theoretical framework) simultaneously with feminist and queer theory (theoretical perspective). Both assist him in forming his question. As Michael proceeds, however, he will continually seek out literature to better inform his study. For example, in a study on White Being, Jan initially gathered information on White racial identity theory, White privilege, authenticness, and guilt and shame to better inform her compelling interest (theoretical framework) while simultaneously looking to Heidegger's notions on phenomenology to guide the design of the study (theoretical perspective) (Arminio, 2001; Arminio & McEwen, 1996). Later, when collecting data through conversations, Jan became aware of the influence that busing to achieve integrated schools had on participants in their meaning making of race. Coles's (1993) work on service and school busing offered revealing insight (additional theoretical framework) of the experience of entering other American cultures by bus. She used this literature to better inform her of her compelling interest after initial data had been collected. With insights from theoretical perspective and theoretical framework, Michael now seeks to frame his statement of purpose and research question.

CONSIDERATION 4: CHOOSING A QUESTION THAT PRESSES UPON US

[T]he path to all knowledge leads through the question.

Gadamer (1960/1989, p. 363)

It is from a compelling interest that those engaged in a study find unsettled questions. Gadamer noted that questioning is "more passion than an action. A question presses itself on us; we can no longer avoid it and persist in our accustomed opinion" (p. 366). Gadamer cautioned us to differentiate between a question and an opinion. A question is "not settled," whereas an opinion is. Several unsettled questions typically emerge from a compelling interest. Often, researchers contemplate a question that is either too broad or too narrow, or may generate several disparate unsettled questions from a compelling interest. A compelling interest offers the opportunity to dwell upon an unsettled question that should lead to a manageable study.

Factors of do-ability assist in determining which of the unsettled questions to undertake. Below are samples of compelling interests that led to research questions in studies that have been published. Note that the worldview of the researcher framed how the question was posed.

- A pressing interest in men's identity development led to the questions of "how college men internally experience externally defined gender roles" and how "conflicts related to socially constructed gender roles may impact men's identity development" (Davis, 2002, p. 510).
- An interest in understanding multiple leadership belief systems of organizational members at community colleges led to the question "How does positionality (i.e., gender, race, role within an organization, and field of study) relate to construction of leadership?" (Kezar, 2002, p. 563).
- To address the need "for a holistic picture of Latina/o doctoral student experiences. . . . The purpose of this study was to bring to the forefront the voices of Latina/o students in the process of attaining a Ph. D." (Gonzalez, Marin, Figueroa, Moreno, & Navia, 2002, pp. 541–542).
- Contemplating how to better understand dissenting students' efforts to change campus environments led to the question of how democratic political theory is useful in "helping student affairs professionals develop and sustain a campus environment that facilitates student exercise of democratic citizenship" (Hamrick, 1998, p. 449).
- A compelling interest in how interaction across dimensions of race, ethnicity, and social class through service learning influences the understanding of diversity led to the question "How do students and community participants come to understand diversity in the context of service learning?" (Jones & Hill, 2001).

As was noted in the discussion on deconstruction, the language one uses in describing a phenomenon illuminates its hegemonic structure. What are the implications of language in the research that educators conduct?

Implications for Language

The worldview of the researcher is communicated through language, whether explicitly or implicitly. A differing of opinion exists about whether those whose studies are grounded in a qualitative paradigm should use the same language of the "found world" (e.g., quantitative research; Smith & Deemer, 2000, p. 885) or create new language. Some scholars, such as Smith and Deemer (2000) and Smith (1993), believe that new language should be used that allows for "moving out from under the shadow of empirical-analytical expectations" (Arminio & Hultgren, 2002, p. 449). However, others, like Lather (1991), take terms from the positivistic paradigm and transform them to be applicable to other views of knowledge. For example, Lather offered a "reconceptualization of validity" (p. 66) appropriate for research that is openly committed to a more just social order by advocating for catalytic validity that "by far is . . . most unorthodox; it flies directly in the face of the positivist demand for research neutrality" (p. 68).

It is important that those engaged in research realize that the language they choose represents and communicates an epistemological worldview. For many of us, the language of objective positivism has been entrenched in our schooling to the point where we assume that words like *validity, reliability, sampling, correlation, rigor, significance,* and *comparison* have a universal use, but they can represent a particular research paradigm. As constructors of reality instead of solely being in contact with reality, researchers are responsible for understanding the implications of the language used.

Below are examples of language as represented by theoretical perspective:

Quantitative	Qualitative
Variable	Theme, category, multidimensionality
Correlate	Interpret, reflect, mutually shaping
Statistical significance	Profound, illuminating
Sample/subjects	Participants, co-researchers, co-travelers
Rigor	Goodness, worthiness
Validity	Trustworthiness, catalytic validity
Proof	Judgments, perceptions, textual rendering
Discovery, findings	Constructing, meaning making
Generalizations	Contextual findings, appropriations
Outlier	Unique
Mechanical	Morphogenesis
Objective	Tending to participants, indwell, human-as-subject

Bhaskar (1979) noted a poignant example of the implications of epistemology on language. Under Nazi rule,

1. Germany was depopulated.
2. Millions of people died.
3. Millions of people were killed.
4. Millions of people were massacred.

Bhaskar stated that though all four are true, only the fourth is a "precise and accurate description of what actually happened" (p. 76), because only the last implies that the deaths were a part of an organized campaign. "This point is important. For social science is not only about a subject matter, it is for an audience" (Bhaskar, 1979, p. 76). In the first three statements, we must question what is implicitly valued in the attempt to be value free. The fourth statement does not attempt at being value free. But which more adequately describes the event?

An example from the literature in higher education is found in the following: "Consequently, compared to their peers with highly educated parents, first-generation students are more likely to be handicapped in accessing and understanding information and attitudes relevant to making beneficial decisions" (Pascarella, Pierson, Wolniak, & Terenzini, 2004). How might this quote be viewed differently by the reader if it were said by a first-generation student rather than the researcher? How does the researcher's worldview promote the use of the word *handicapped* in this way? What language does one use about those with whom one is studying? How do these terms represent, re-present, and communicate the relationship? Kezar (2004) commented,

> A student tells me she wants to study the experience of graduate students in the United States who come from other countries. She wants to examine their experience in a foreign place. . . . [I ask her] what does it mean to use the term foreign? Is she comfortable with this term and its implications in her study? (p. 46)

What is communicated about the relationship between those being studied and the person conducting the study by the use of those words?

Words such as *illuminate, explore, discerning, meaning,* and *spirited* represent an openness to mutual construction and enlightenment (Arminio & Hultgren, 2002). Some interpretive methodologies such as hermeneutical phenomenology encourage "troubling" the language (Ellsworth, 1997) to better express what is intended. *Troubling the language* means that words are used in a slightly new or different way in order to challenge the status quo. For example, in an article on the question of criteria of qualitative research, Arminio and Hultgren asked, "How do we as phenomenologists understand our respons-ability to reframing criteria?" (p. 447). "Respons-ability" troubles the word *responsibility* by highlighting the notion of the ability to respond in the word *responsibility*. This may be considered a "play on words," but this play or troubling extends the "potential of words to spread understanding beyond accustomed boundaries" (p. 452). Jones (2002) also troubled the language to extend meaning potential in her title "(Re)Writing the Word: Methodological Strategies and Issues in Qualitative Research." She wrote,

> To (re)write the word, to engage in research that holds potential for getting closer to what is true about a particular phenomenon, for exhibiting true generosity, and for contributing to the elimination of inequality, those most fully engaged in qualitative research must recognize the complexities in the effort. (p. 472)

The use of "(re)write" emphasizes the importance of revising for deeper understanding that may be lost with the more commonplace use of *rewrite*.

Let us return to Michael and his efforts at situating his research. Michael has decided that his worldview is consistent with the constructivist and interpretive epistemologies because he has noticed how he learns through interactions with others. He believes that perception defines people's realities and believes that he is best able to learn about the experience of safety through interaction with others. He wants to "probe deep" with others about their experiences. He wonders how experiences of safety and feelings of inclusion relate. He refines his compelling interest into an unsettled question in language that represents and communicates his worldview: "What is the lived definition of campus safety for students who feel unsafe?"

CONSIDERATION 5: RESEARCH, ASSESSMENT, OR EVALUATION

For what purpose does Michael engage in this study? Another aspect of situating a study is whether the study is research, assessment, or evaluation. Upcraft and Shuh (2002) admitted that differentiating these may be seen as not very relevant. We believe it is for several reasons. First, by exposing the differences, we highlight the point that qualitative methodologies can be used in assessments and evaluations, not only in research. Although many institutions have institutional research offices, assessment tasks typically are add-on responsibilities to educators outside of such offices (Ewell, 2002). Furthermore, many staff and administrators in higher education believe they are conducting assessments when in fact they are conducting evaluations. Differentiating these data-gathering activities recognizes the burgeoning scholarship of assessment (Ewell).

Briefly, research concerns theory: forming it, confirming it, disconfirming it. Research assumes broader implications than one institution or program. Assessment, on the other hand, is more focused on the outcomes of participant programs, though this can be very broad as to include an entire institution. It does not infer individual student outcomes. The purpose of assessment is to guide practice rather than relate practice to theory. Evaluation is even more particular to a specific program and is concerned with the satisfaction, organization, and attendance of a program. As Figure 1.3 indicates, there is some overlap and the three are related. For example, a program may be based on a theory particular to adult student development. Outcomes of the theory-based program are assessed to determine if adult students are indeed gaining from the program what was intended. Using the assessment outcome data to change policy and practices related to the program is evaluation (Upcraft, 2003). The three are not mutually exclusive but rather have a dialectic relationship. Marshall and Rossman (1999) referred to this as the cycle of inquiry, which is depicted by the arrow in Figure 1.3. What is important to remember is that the means of conducting a study, whether for research, assessment, or evaluation

Research Assessment Evaluation

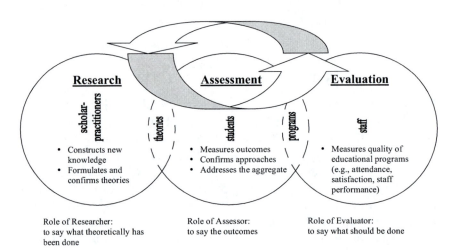

Research

scholar-practitioners

theories

* Constructs new
  knowledge
* Formulates and
  confirms theories

Assessment

students

programs

* Measures outcomes
* Confirms approaches
* Addresses the aggregate

Evaluation

staff

* Measures quality of
  educational programs
  (e.g., attendance,
  satisfaction, staff
  performance)

Role of Researcher:
to say what theoretically has
been done

Role of Assessor:
to say the outcomes

Role of Evaluator:
to say what should be done

Erwin, 1996
Upcraft & Shuh, 2002
Upcraft, 2003

Figure 1.3

(design, sampling, method for collecting and analyzing data), can be similar, but the purpose of conducting research, assessment, and evaluation differs.

Michael has decided to situate his study as research because he is seeking to consider how students experience safety in a broad sense, rather than particular to any one program or outcome. The purpose of his study is not to create or confirm theory; it is a priori. In addition, he seeks insight that is beyond a bounded context. He seeks to explore more than just satisfaction or dissatisfaction with safety or who is safe and who is not (evaluation), but rather the questions of what safety is, how it is experienced, when it is not experienced, and why. How do students negotiate being safe? How do they make meaning of safety? Michael now has articulated his compelling question and has determined that his purpose is research. He also must contemplate how it is that he will be with the participants of his research study.

CONSIDERATION 6: RESEARCHER POSITIONALITY

Positionality describes the relationship between the researcher and his or her participants and the researcher and his or her topic. Research paradigm, theoretical perspective, and methodology all influence those relationships. However, Fine (1994) believed that positionality does involve decision making on the part of the researcher, including the way in which researchers will represent or, more accurately, "re-present" (p. 110) participants. What is happening between the researcher and participants during the study? Researchers must address not only what is said but also what is not, not only what was said and quoted but also what is being protected from public view and why. Are researchers protecting the elite? Are researchers protecting themselves? Are researchers even conscious of what they include or exclude? Vasti stated that journaling and consulting with advisors during her research assisted in addressing these questions (Torres & Baxter Magolda, 2002).

This concept is so important to good qualitative work that it will be addressed in several subsequent chapters in more depth. For now, however, it is important for the reader to know that deciding upon the relationship of the researcher to the researched is one of the fundamental considerations that researchers must make as they embark upon their work.

Michael realizes that his experiences with feeling unsafe shape how he will engage with his participants. He also realizes that his role as researcher and graduate student; his gender, race, and sexual orientation;

and his status as a first-generation college student influence the relationship he will establish with his participants. He considers how to engender trust with his participants throughout the research process.

SUMMARY

Situating a study necessitates determining within what epistemology, theoretical perspective, methodology, and method the question will be explored. Not appropriately situating a study is a frequent mistake made by researchers who believe that qualitative research is simply interviewing a few people and noting common themes. The analogy below may help you differentiate the different phases of situating your study.

If you were to consider your study a journey, the fundamental elements would be the following:

- Destination: increased understanding about an unsettled question
- Territory to travel upon: epistemological worldview
- Map: theoretical perspective
- Specific routes to take: methodology (to be discussed in Chapter 2)
- Mode of transportation: method (also to be discussed further in Chapter 2)

There are several means and routes that will take you to the same destination. However, some routes are appropriate for some modes of travel. For example, you wouldn't travel very far by riding your bicycle on railroad tracks using an atlas as a guide. Yet, sometimes this happens when researchers frame a question not consistent with their worldview or use a method of collecting data that is not consistent with a particular methodology and not grounded in its founding philosophy. Apprentice researchers often find the notion that there are several appropriate ways to explore a question frustrating. Situating an unsettled question in a consistent epistemology, theoretical perspective and framework, and methodology is crucial because often during a project, questions arise that can only be answered when epistemology, theoretical perspective, and positionality are consistently grounded (Maykut & Morehouse, 2001). For example, in a study conducted by Jan, a participant shared a poignant story that appeared to be unrelated to the compelling interest (Arminio & McEwen, 1996). Yet, the story itself was compelling. As is customary with her chosen methodology, she convened a human science dialogue with other researchers knowledgeable of her methodology. Together, using the methodology as a guide, they determined how to appropriately use the story to illuminate the phenomenon under study.

Often, there are delays along the inquiry journey. They are not always negative. In fact, often delays or detours can lead to unexpected insight. When this occurs, and it will, researchers should use the map (theoretical perspective and framework) and specific routes (methodology) to continue.

EXERCISES

Two exercises are offered here to assist the reader in using the elements necessary for situating a study.

1. Below are long quotations from various philosophers upon which views on research have been constructed. Note the philosophical differences in these four quotes. Consider how these differences influence views on knowledge and research. All four describe a philosophical approach to language.

Language: A Look at Four Philosophical Perspectives

A.

Language is as old as consciousness—language *is* the first practical, real consciousness, existing for other people, and hence also for me; and language like consciousness, first arises from need, the need of intercourse with other people. (My relation to my environment is my consciousness.) Where a relationship exists, there it exists for me; the animal "*relates*" to nothing and altogether not at all. For the animal, its relationship to other ones does not exist as relationship. Hence consciousness is from the outset a societal product and remains such as long as men exist together. (Marx, cited in Padover, 1977, p. 72)

In like manner, the beginner who has learned a new language always translates it back into his mother tongue, but he assimilates the spirit of the new language and expresses himself freely in it only when he moves in it without recalling the old and when he forgets his native tongue. (Marx, cited in Padover, 1977, pp. 21–22)

B.

The guiding idea . . . is *that the fusion of horizons that takes place in understanding is actually the achievement of language.* Admittedly, what language is belongs among the most mysterious questions that man ponders. Language is so uncannily near our thinking, and when it functions it is so little an object, that it seems to conceal its own being from us. In our analysis of the thinking of the human sciences, however, we came so close to this universal mystery of language that is prior to everything else, that we can entrust ourselves to what we are investigating to guide us safely in the quest. In other words we are endeavoring to approach the mystery of language from the conversation that we ourselves are. (Gadamer, 1989, p. 378)

C.

With the concept of communicative action there comes into play the additional presupposition of a *linguistic medium* that reflects the actor-world relations as such. At this level of concept formation the rationality problematic, which until now has arisen only for the social scientist, moves into the perspective of the agent himself. We have to make clear in what sense achieving understanding in language is thereby introduced as a mechanism for coordinating action. Even the strategic model of action *can* be understood in such a way that participants' actions[,] directed through egocentric calculations of utility and coordinated through interest positions, are mediated through speech acts. In the cases of normatively regulated and dramaturgical action we even *have* to suppose a consensus formation among participants that is in principle of a linguistic nature. Nevertheless, in these three models of action language is conceived *one-sidedly* in different respects. (Habermas, 1981/1984, p. 94)

Only the communicative model of action presupposes language as a medium of uncurtailed communication whereby speakers and hearers, out of the context of their preinterpreted lifeworld, refer simultaneously to things in the objective, social, and subjective worlds in order to negotiate common definitions of the situation. (Habermas, 1984, p. 95)

D.

Words are sensible signs, necessary for Communication. Man, though he have great variety of thoughts, and such from which others as well as himself might receive profit and delight; yet they are all within his own breast, invisible and hidden from others, nor can of themselves be made [to] appear. The comfort and advantage of society not being to be had without communication of thoughts, it was necessary that man should find out some external sensible signs, whereof those invisible ideas, which his thoughts are made up of, might be made known to others. For this purpose nothing was so fit, either for plenty or quickness, as those articulate sounds, which with so much ease and variety he found himself able to make. Thus we may conceive how *words*, which were by nature so well adapted to that purpose, come to be made use of by men as the signs of their ideas; not by any natural connection that there is between particular articulate sounds and certain ideas, for then there would be but one language amongst all men; but by a voluntary imposition, whereby such a word is made arbitrarily the mark of such an idea. The use, then, of words, is to be sensible marks of ideas; and the ideas they stand for are their proper and immediate signification. (Woozley, 1964, p. 259)

[B]ut upon a greater approach, I find that there is so close a connection between ideas and words, and our abstract ideas and general words have so constant a relation one to another, that it is impossible to speak clearly and distinctly of our knowledge, which all consists in propositions, without considering first the nature, use and signification of language. (Woozley, 1964, p. 255)

Answers and References

A. Karl Marx: subjective (Padover, 1977)

B. Hans-Georg Gadamer: interpretive (Gadamer, 1989)

C. Jürgen Habermas: subjective (Habermas, 1981/1984)

D. John Locke: objective positivism (Woozley, 1964)

2. Note on a piece of paper your compelling interest of study. From that interest area, write questions that would inform you about your compelling interest. Which one "presses upon you"? Eliminate those for which you already hold a closed opinion. Eliminate those that are too narrow or specific and those that are too broad. Identify the epistemological framework in which your questions are best situated.

2
RESEARCH DESIGN

The temptation is great, we have found, for qualitative researchers to begin the research process with an idea of methods firmly entrenched in their minds. Comments such as "I am going to interview some Latino students about their experiences on this campus for my study," "We are observing classroom discussion patterns for our research on gender differences," or "I am analyzing all the reports focused on sexual harassment in the residence halls" are illustrative of a focus on methods in qualitative research. A common approach to research finds an individual with a compelling question in mind (e.g., "What is life like for Latino students on this campus?") that is then quickly connected to a particular method (e.g., "Well, I'll find out by interviewing some Latino students"). Although the researcher might learn some things from this strategy, it does not constitute good qualitative research practice because it promotes action without reflection on the larger epistemological and methodological frameworks connected to how one might investigate a particular phenomenon.

The overarching framework for a study includes articulation of all aspects of the research (e.g., epistemological and theoretical perspectives, and methodological approach and methods) and how they are interrelated. This framework is called the *research design*. In this chapter, elements of a research design are presented, guidance for how to make decisions about these elements is provided, and connections between the elements are explored. Because Chapter 1 focused extensively on epistemological and theoretical considerations, particular attention will be given in this chapter to methodology and methods.

DEVELOPING A RESEARCH DESIGN

Elements of a Research Design

The elements of a research design most typically include *epistemology*, which conveys philosophical assumptions about what constitutes knowledge; *theoretical perspective*, which is also philosophical in nature and informs methodological choices; *methodology*, which describes the general strategies of inquiry and governs the choice of methods; and *methods*, which refers to the actual and detailed procedures of and techniques for participant selection, data collection, data analysis, and reporting (Creswell, 2003; Crotty, 1998). Although these terms are frequently used interchangeably in the literature, they are conceptually distinct and integrally related to one another, and imply important decision points to be made in the research process (Jones, 2002). Crotty (1998) articulated well the nature of these questions and research decisions: (a) What epistemology informs the theoretical perspective of the area of inquiry? (b) What theoretical perspective lies behind the methodology in question? (c) What methodology governs our choice and use of methods? And (d) what methods do we propose to use?

The research process begins by identifying and understanding the assumptions a researcher holds about the phenomenon under investigation, how the researcher will come to know more about this phenomenon, and what might become known through the inquiry. This is central to the research design because how the researcher responds to these questions will then provide the guidance and direction for every other decision to be made. For researchers working within the qualitative research paradigm, regardless of methodological choice, certain characteristics of the design will most often be present. These include the following: Understanding emerges from an emic or insider's perspective, the researcher functions as the instrument of research, research occurs in natural settings and is context dependent, research is inductive in nature and emphasizes in-depth understanding, and research findings emphasize rich description of the phenomenon under investigation (Merriam, 1998; Stage & Manning, 2003).

However, how these more general characteristics are enacted and realized through the research process varies considerably depending upon one's epistemological and theoretical perspective, which then informs the choice of methodology and methods. For example, if one is interested in exploring the experiences of White students engaged in service learning, which route one takes depends upon one's worldview or beliefs about how one comes to know. One could design a survey of all the White students in the class that measures their White racial identity on a scale (positivist perspective-survey research); one could develop an interview guide that elicits student understanding and meaning making about their lived experiences as racial beings and how they come to see themselves as White in the service-learning context (constructivist perspective-phenomenology); or one could co-construct a design that places the researcher in the setting alongside the study participants for the purpose of unearthing power relationships, oppressive structures, and cultural norms that maintain the privileges of being White (subjectivist-critical ethnography).

The important point here is that attention and thoughtfulness must be given to these questions in order to develop a research design. Furthermore, evidence of researcher decisions regarding epistemology and theoretical perspective must be present in all elements of the research design. For example, as will be described in greater detail in this chapter, interviews function as a qualitative method in a variety of theoretical perspectives and for a diverse array of methodologies. However, interview questions in a critical inquiry should be worded very differently than questions in a phenomenological study.

Statements regarding the purpose of a study and the corresponding research questions should both reflect the philosophical underpinnings of a study and show congruence between the elements of the research design. In other words, readers of your work should never lose sight of your epistemological and theoretical perspective because it should be evident in all aspects of the research design. Table 2.1 provides several examples from published research that illustrate the connections between various elements of the research design.

Connecting Epistemological and Theoretical Perspectives with Methodological Approaches

As the examples in Table 2.1 demonstrate, the relationship between epistemological and theoretical perspectives to methodological approaches is an important one because it conveys *how* the researcher is grounding an investigation of a particular phenomenon and *what* the researcher

Table 2.1

Research Study	Phenomenon of Interest	Philosophical Underpinnings
Family Influences on Latino Identity Development	"The purpose of this study was to explore family influences on identity development of Latino/a first-year students."	"This study uses a constructivist epistemology . . . and grounded theory methodology" (Torres, 2004, p. 459).
College Men's Identity Development	"The purpose of this study was to explore conflicts related to socially constructed gender roles that may impact men's identity development."	"Consistent with the epistemological assumptions of constructivism is the phenomenological methodology employed in this study" (Davis, 2002, p. 510).
Student Understanding of HIV/AIDS	"The purpose of this study was to explore the development of students' knowledge, attitudes, and behavior regarding HIV/AIDS in the context of a university-community partnership."	"The approach of this study was constructivist case methodology. . . . [T]his theoretical framework was well suited to the study because the focus of our inquiry was on participants' construction of meaning and understanding about HIV/AIDS and the learning that occurs in a service-learning context" (Jones & Abes, 2003, p. 472).
Gay Male College Students	"The intent of this work is to highlight the experiences of queer students at Clement [University] as they struggle to gain a private and public voice."	"This work is based on an ethnographic study of gay and bisexual male students enrolled at Clement University" (Rhoads, 1994, p. 11).

is interested in exploring. These decisions never begin with an articulation of methods because nearly every method is appropriate within any methodological approach (Sipe & Constable, 1996). However, methodologies vary considerably in terms of their fit within certain philosophical traditions.

Most qualitative methodologies fit within constructivist/interpretive (with an emphasis on understanding and the lived experience), critical/subjectivist (with an emphasis on emancipation), or poststructural (with an emphasis on deconstruction) epistemological and theoretical perspectives (Crotty, 1998; Lather, 1992). A theoretical perspective may inform a range of methodologies (Crotty). For example, a researcher may utilize critical theory as a theoretical perspective but engage this perspective as either ethnography or phenomenology and design a critical ethnography or a critical phenomenological study. Although the choice of a theoretical perspective gives shape to the selection of appropriate methodological approaches, the decision about a particular methodology then provides the direction for decisions regarding methods. In the example given above, a critical ethnography would most likely rely upon extensive fieldwork and participant observation, whereas a critical phenomenological study would more typically engage participants in in-depth, unstructured interviews.

METHODOLOGICAL APPROACHES

Methodology is best described as a *strategy* that guides the actual research plan and "provides specific direction for procedures in a research design" (Creswell, 2003, p. 13). Once a study is situated in a particular philosophical tradition, which informs the methodology, the methodological approach becomes the rudder for all additional research decisions. A number of methodological approaches from which to choose exist in qualitative research. In addition to the approaches detailed in this chapter, other methodologies include narrative analysis, life history, participatory action research, and feminist inquiry. Although it is not possible here to provide a comprehensive description of each, what follows is a summary of several methodological approaches most prevalent in the higher education literature: grounded theory, phenomenology, case study, and ethnography. Examples from the studies referenced in Table 2.1 (and others) will be provided to illuminate the particularities and characteristics of each approach. Last, the connections between methodology and methods will also be explored. Books and resources for these methodologies must be consulted and studied before embarking upon designing research. However, the descriptions that follow should provide the reader with a beginning understanding of each methodological approach, key terminology and characteristics that should be present in the design of a study using each approach, and ample citations that point in the direction of the important literature with which a researcher would want to be familiar.

Grounded Theory

Grounded theory methodology was developed by two sociologists, Barney Glaser and Anselm Strauss, and explained in their pioneering book, *The Discovery of Grounded Theory* (1967). Each was raised in a different research paradigm (e.g., scientific and interpretive) that, when brought together, incorporated both the flexibility and structure characteristic of grounded theory. The purpose of grounded theory research is to develop theory that remains true to and illuminates the phenomenon under investigation (Strauss & Corbin, 1990, 1998) by studying the "experience from the standpoint of those who live it" (Charmaz, 2000, p. 522). As conceived by Glaser and Strauss, grounded theory methodology employs a systematic and structured set of procedures to build an inductively derived theory grounded in the actual data and informed by the area under study. The theory generated in grounded theory studies is typically not formal theory but *substantive theory*, which is "localized, dealing with particular real-world situations" (Merriam & Associates, 2002, p. 7).

The original conception of grounded theory as described by Glaser and Strauss (1967) is firmly rooted in positivist and objectivist notions of reality and a prescribed set of procedures. The credibility, utility, and efficacy of grounded theory were further advanced with the publication of Strauss and Juliet Corbin's text, *Basics of Qualitative Research: Grounded Theory Procedures and Techniques* (1990), which clearly delineates the methodology and methods of grounded theory. More recently, researchers are situating their grounded theory studies in a constructivist theoretical perspective that is more open-ended, flexible, and interpretive (Charmaz, 2000). More specifically,

> A constructivist approach to grounded theory reaffirms studying people in their natural settings. . . . A constructivist grounded theory recognizes that the viewer creates the data and ensuing analysis through interaction with the viewed. Data do not provide a window on reality. Rather, the "discovered" reality arises from the interactive process and its temporal, cultural, and structural contexts. Researcher and subjects frame that interaction and confer meaning upon it. The viewer then is part

of what is viewed rather than separate from it. (Charmaz, 2000, pp. 510, 523–524)

Even newer work in grounded theory seeks to "push grounded theory more fully around the postmodern turn through a new approach to analysis . . . called situational analysis," which "allows researchers to draw together studies of discourse and agency, action and structure, image, text and context, history and the present moment—to analyze complex situations of inquiry broadly conceived" (Clarke, 2005, p. xxii).

Let's return to our example from published research to further illuminate these distinctions in a researcher's approach to grounded theory methodology. Vasti made explicit her approach:

> This study uses a constructivist epistemology, which recognizes that the interaction between researcher and participants is necessary to understand the meaning of experiences shared during the research process (Charmaz, 2000; Lincoln & Guba, 1985). . . . Using constructivist grounded theory methodology, the "'discovered' reality arises from the interactive process" (Charmaz, p. 524) inherent within the interactions between participant and researcher, which is a central tenet of qualitative research. (Torres, 2004, p. 459)

This is a good example of the important connection between epistemology and methodology (and the appropriate use of methodological citations to create credibility for research decisions). The decision to lodge a study within a constructivist or objectivist framework brings consequences for how a question is framed, and for strategies of inquiry and particular methods, as does the choice of methodology. What follows is a description of some of the most important defining characteristics and methods of grounded theory methodology. The focus is less on data collection methods because a variety of methods are appropriate in a number of methodological approaches.

Constant Comparative Method of Data Analysis

The research process in grounded theory does not proceed in an orderly, sequential process. Instead, sampling, data collection, and data analysis occur continuously and in relation to one another. The strategies of the constant comparative method of data analysis and theoretical sampling make this relationship explicit. As the name implies, the constant comparative method engages the researcher in a process of constantly analyzing data at every and all stages of the data collection and interpretation process, and results in the identification of codes. Constant comparison in grounded theory involves the following:

- Comparing different people (such as their views, situations, actions, accounts, and experiences)
- Comparing data from the same individuals with themselves at different points in time
- Comparing incident with incident
- Comparing data with category
- Comparing a category with other categories (Charmaz, 2000, p. 515)

Strauss and Corbin (1990) identified three different levels of coding: open, axial, and selective.

Open coding describes the initial stages of data analysis and begins with the "fracturing of the data" (Strauss & Corbin, 1990, p. 97) and careful examination of the words used by participants to describe or convey experiences, understandings, or meaning. This typically involves a line-by-line examination and keeps the researcher close to the data, rather than imposing one's own ideas onto the data (Charmaz, 2000). Each word, phrase, or sentence is categorized and coded as a concept. Concept names are selected to accurately reflect and describe what the data conveyed. Charmaz cautioned against "pasting catchy concepts on our data" (p. 515) and instead recommended staying very close to the words participants themselves used. The number of codes generated will depend in part on the number of participants and data collection. Open coding in the study conducted by Vasti (Torres, 2004) included a line-by-line analysis of each individual interview transcript and resulted in the generation of over 1,000 in vivo (words used by participants) codes.

The next step in open coding involves the process of grouping concepts into categories and naming these. In examining the relationships between concepts, categories are generated that reflect greater complexity and level of abstraction. Categories are understood by the identification of their properties (or characteristics of a category) and dimensions (location of properties along a continuum) (Strauss & Corbin, 1990). Categories, then, are typically recorded with all the supporting concepts listed underneath. As categories are developed, they are compared with one another and evaluated by their properties and dimensions. The evolving and dynamic process of moving back and forth between categories results in movement toward integration of categories and identification of relationships among categories (Lincoln & Guba, 1985). Transcripts are frequently returned to during analysis to assure that the category names accurately conveyed the meaning of the particular phenomenon.

Because the study conducted by Vasti was multi-institutional and included 83 first-year Latino students, the next phase of coding in her study involved constant comparison among the individuals within each institutional context (Torres, 2004). This phase produced approximately 50 categories that "provided insight into environmental concerns as well as consideration of how the context influences students' interpretation of their experiences" (p. 461). Categories were also considered in relationship to existing research and theories related to the phenomenon of interest (e.g., ethnic identity development).

The next coding level, referred to as *axial coding*, involves reconfiguring data after open coding by "weaving the fractured data back together again" (Glaser, 1978, p. 116). These higher order categories begin to represent theoretical constructs in order to make explicit the relationships among categories (Strauss & Corbin, 1990). When categories are grouped by their conceptual relationship with each other, key categories are created. Axial coding also surfaces the *conditions* that give rise to categories (Strauss & Corbin, 1990).

In Vasti's study, axial coding is described as "connecting—or in some cases reconnecting—the data, which provided a more conceptually dense and elaborate explanation of . . . the phenomenon" (Torres, 2004, p. 462). The focus of this particular article, based upon a larger longitudinal study of the college experiences of Latino students, relates to one of the *conditions* integral to Latino identity development, family influence, and generational status. Discussion includes the influence of this condition on the *key category* of situating Latino identity (Torres, 2003).

The final level of coding, *selective coding*, involves "the process of selecting the core category, systematically relating it to other categories, validating those relationships, and filling in categories that need further refinement and development" (Strauss & Corbin, 1990, p. 116). Codes generated during selective coding "account for the most data and categorize them most precisely. Making explicit decisions about selecting codes gives us a check on the fit between the emerging theoretical framework and the empirical reality it explains" (Charmaz, 2000, p. 516). During this process, a story line is generated to capture the essence of what is happening in the study. This story line becomes the core category, which is "the central phenomenon around which all the other categories are integrated" (Strauss & Corbin, 1990, p. 116). Emerging theory, then, grounded in the data, is written from an analysis of the core category. In the example of Vasti's research (Torres, 2004), the core story is still being written and the emerging theory is being developed.

Theoretical Sampling

Sampling in grounded theory research mirrors to a certain degree the analytic process and is rarely a onetime event. In the early stages of the study, the researcher samples in a more open, expansive manner by focusing on the phenomenon of interest. As data analysis proceeds and the researcher begins to develop some hunches about what is going on in the data, sampling becomes guided by "concepts that have proven theoretical relevance to the evolving theory" (Strauss & Corbin, 1990, p. 176). As Charmaz (2000) noted, "We use theoretical sampling to develop our emerging categories and to make them more definitive and useful. Thus the aim of this sampling is to refine *ideas*, not to increase the size of the original sample" (p. 519). From a practical standpoint, this may mean returning to the same individuals to ask follow-up questions or seeking out new participants who can add depth to the concepts emerging as important. Furthermore, "Although we often sample people, we may sample scenes, events, or documents, depending on the study and where the theory leads us" (Charmaz, 2000, p. 518).

Because Vasti was interested in adding conceptual and contextual depth to her emerging theory, she employed theoretical sampling to accomplish these objectives (Torres, 2004). Theoretical sampling led her to include a diverse array of institutional types and student participants. Sampling decisions were informed by her earlier research on this topic and the ongoing development of an emerging theory to describe the phenomenon of interest. As her analysis progressed, sampling continued so as to enrich the emerging theory.

Phenomenology

Phenomenology is both a school of philosophy associated with the works of Hans-Georg Gadamer, Edmund Husserl, Martin Heidegger, and Maurice Merleau-Ponty, and a methodology (Arminio & McEwen, 1996; Merriam & Associates, 2002). Each of these philosophers created a slightly different school of phenomenological thought (e.g., Gadamer's work focused on the philosophical and historical; Husserl, on transcendental psychology; Heidegger, on hermeneutic phenomenology; and Merleau-Ponty, on existential phenomenology), but all share certain important constitutive elements (Crotty, 1998). Because most research in education represents hermeneutic phenomenology, or the science of interpretation, the focus here is on this approach. Martin Heidegger's development of hermeneutical phenomenology emphasized interpretation and understanding "whereby existential structures and then Being itself come into view" (Crotty, p. 96). His approach is rooted in philosophy and theology as contrasted with the more psychological and historical interpretations of Husserl. Gadamer, Heidegger's student, emphasized historical understanding and the need to fuse the past with the present to create a picture of the whole.

The philosophical foundation of hermeneutic phenomenology provides direction for phenomenological research, which focuses on the uniqueness of the lived experience or *essence* of a particular phenomenon. As such, phenomenology is always anchored in the *lifeworld* (van Manen, 1990, p. 7) of the individual and the meaning making associated with being-in-the-world. According to van Manen (1990),

> From a phenomenological point of view, to do research is always to question the way we experience the world, to want to know the world in which we live as human beings. And since to *know* the world is profoundly to *be* in the world in a certain way, the act of researching—questioning—theorizing is the intentional act of attaching ourselves to the world, to become more fully part of it, or better, to *become*, the world. Phenomenology calls this inseparable connection to the world the principle of "intentionality." (p. 5)

An important principle to grasp in phenomenological research is that this lifeworld is prereflective. That is, uncovering the essence of experience means surfacing the meaning or the structure of the experience itself, rather than providing a conceptualization of the experience, and it requires great thoughtfulness and caring (Heidegger, 1926/1996). van Manen (1990) explained this distinction: "Phenomenology . . . differs from almost every other science in that it attempts to gain insightful descriptions of the way we experience the world prereflectively, without taxonomizing, classifying, or abstracting it," and it "offers us the possibility of plausible insights that bring us in more direct contact with the world" (p. 9).

What does the research process look like in a hermeneutic phenomenological study? What does it mean to illuminate an aspect of the lifeworld *as we find it* (van Manen, 1990, p. 18)? Before turning to several important components of phenomenological research, it is important to acknowledge a central tension in this approach. That is,

> To *do* hermeneutic phenomenology is to attempt to accomplish the impossible: To construct a full interpretive description of some aspect of the lifeworld, yet to remain aware that lived life[,] is always more complex than any explication or meaning can reveal. (van Manen, 1990, p. 18)

Turning to our example from published research, Davis (2002) provided an explanation of his methodological approach:

> Consistent with the epistemological assumptions of constructivism is the phenomenological methodology employed in this study. Phenomenology addresses experience from the perspective of the individual and is based on the assumption that people have a unique way of making meaning of their experience. . . . This investigation is informed by a hermeneutic philosophical position. (p. 511)

Although much of what is written about phenomenology addresses its philosophical foundation, van Manen (1990), in his book entitled *Researching Lived Experience*, provided an explication of the methodological approach to hermeneutic phenomenology. He identified six critical research activities that are not intended to outline a series of steps to the research process, but rather are themes central to this approach that exist in a dynamic interplay with one another. However, these activities do provide the researcher with a guide for *doing* phenomenological inquiry. Each will be briefly described with reference to published research in order to bring the activities to life.

Turning to the Question

The integral process of "turning to the phenomenon" situates the researcher as an individual with an "abiding concern" (van Manen, 1990, p. 31), deep interest in, and questions about a particular phenomenon. The process of turning is central to phenomenology because it captures, and recaptures, the deep questioning so much a part of good phenomenological inquiry and an interest in understanding what something is like. It also helps the researcher most fully explore the nature and scope of the research project (van Manen, 1990).

Integral to the process of turning to the question is the idea of *bracketing* (Husserl, 1970). Bracketing describes "how one must take hold of the phenomenon and then place outside of it one's knowledge about the phenomenon" (van Manen, 1990, p. 47). Furthermore,

> The procedure [bracketing] has the purpose of allowing the life-world of the participant in the research to emerge in clarity so as to allow a study of some specific phenomenon within the life-world to be carried out. The researcher must suspend presuppositions in order to enter the life-world. . . . Two main categories of suppositions should be bracketed: those to do with the temptation to impose on the investigation of the life-world claims emanating

from objective science or other authoritative sources, and those to do with the imposition of criteria of validity arising outside the life-world itself. (Ashworth, 1999, pp. 708–709)

However, despite Husserl's claim that "bracketing out" is important to phenomenological work, others acknowledge that this is impossible. Instead, as van Manen (1990) suggested, "It is better to make explicit our understandings, beliefs, biases, assumptions, presuppositions, and theories" (p. 47), thereby exposing the "preunderstandings" that influence our interest in a particular phenomenon.

Often in the case of published research, the reader intuits the abiding concern in the focus of inquiry. Less often does a researcher make explicit the outcome of the discernment process in the narrative; however, all aspects of the research design serve as indication of the thoughtfulness, care, and depth of understanding characteristic of phenomenological questioning and inquiry. In Davis's article (2002), we learn of his interest in understanding the influence of socially prescribed gender roles on college men's identity. We also read something of his process of bracketing in his statements about negotiating his own preconceived notions about men's identity development in the collegiate context and letting his participants "speak for themselves" (Davis, 2000, p. 512).

Investigating Experience as We Live It

This activity guides the data collection process with an emphasis on getting at the core and structure of an experience, rather than a conceptualization of it. Phenomenological researchers refer to this as the abiding concern with basic experience, getting behind the experience itself, dwelling in the lived experience, and turning "to the things themselves" (Husserl, 1970). Because of the emphasis on the experiences of those individuals living them, phenomenological research focuses on the everyday and ordinary occurrences in human life and on generating thick description. This most typically is accomplished through in-depth conversations with a few participants. Numbers of participants tend to be small to allow for relationship building and in-depth immersion in a particular area of interest. Davis interviewed 10 male undergraduate students about what it is like to be a man on campus and how societal gender role expectations influenced the nature of this lived experience. He was interested in getting behind the more performative nature of gender identity to the experience of maleness itself (Davis, 2002).

Reflecting on Essential Themes

Phenomenological reflection and the writing process are central to this methodological approach because it is through these processes that the researcher approaches a grasp of the essential meaning of a particular phenomenon (van Manen, 1990). As van Manen elaborated, "The insight into the essence of a phenomenon involves a process of reflectively appropriating, of clarifying, and of making explicit the structure of meaning of the lived experience" (p. 77). This process then brings the phenomenological researcher closer to direct contact with the phenomenon as it is lived by those living it. This is accomplished by conducting thematic analysis. Unlike other qualitative data analysis, phenomenological themes are less descriptive *of* a particular phenomenon and more so as illuminations of the *structures* of the phenomenon.

How do phenomenological researchers uncover the structures of experience? How are themes identified? Drawing upon the etymological tracings of the word *analysis*, Arminio and Hultgren (2002) described thematic analysis as an "unloosening" that occurs only as the researcher spends "a great deal of time seeking to understand the text" (p. 456) and then illustrates interpretations with many examples from the text. This loosening process results in the uncovering of meaning that lies behind the phenomenon itself and what participants actually say about the phenomenon. Clarity of interpretation often comes as a result of phenomenological writing and rewriting. Another important characteristic of phenomenological research is the emphasis on the uniqueness of the essence of the experience, the *qualis*, or "whatness," and that "phenomenological description is always *one* interpretation, and no single interpretation of human experience will ever exhaust the possibility of yet another complementary, or even potentially *richer* or *deeper*[,] description" (van Manen, 1990, p. 31). Davis spoke to this in describing his research process:

> As we discussed themes, debated interpretations, checked biases, I feel we more deeply captured participants' lived experience. At the same time, I acknowledge that our description of these men's experiences was no more and no less than one (the investigation team's) interpretation. (T. L. Davis, personal communication, September 16, 2004)

The Art of Writing and Rewriting

Through the writing process, the researcher seeks to offer an interpretation of the essence of the particular phenomenon of interest. According to van Manen (1997), a phenomenological description "strives for precision and exactness by aiming for interpretive descriptions that exact fullness and completeness of detail, and that explore to a degree of perfection the fundamental nature of the notion being addressed in the text" (p. 17). This exactness and completeness come through writing and rewriting and eventually coming to a phenomenological response to the question "What is it like to be [a male college student]?" This writing process requires great thoughtfulness, attentiveness to language, and a constant back-and-forth between thinking, writing, formulating, reformulating, and rethinking. Van Manen (1997) described this well: "So phenomenology is the application of *logos* (language and thoughtfulness) to a phenomenon (an aspect of lived experience), to what shows itself precisely as it shows itself" (p. 33).

In Davis's research on college men's identity, the reflection and writing process produced five themes: (a) importance of self-expression, (b) code of communication caveats, (c) fear of femininity, (d) confusion about and distancing from masculinity, and (e) a sense of challenge without support (p. 514). The data analysis process is described, including the interplay between researcher and participants, and each theme is presented with illustrative comments from the participants themselves. One caveat about phenomenological research is worth noting. Because so much of the process depends upon writing, good writing skills and love of the written word are necessary.

Maintaining a Strong and Oriented Relation

This methodological component relates to focus and to maintaining an abiding concern throughout the research process. As van Manen (1990) noted, "To establish a strong relation with a certain question, phenomenon, or notion, the researcher cannot afford to adopt an attitude of so-called scientific disinterestedness. To be oriented to an object means that we are animated by the object in a full and human sense" (p. 33). Thus, what the phenomenological researcher "produces" from an inquiry also stands as an example of "the way we stand pedagogically in life" (p. 138) or a visible demonstration of what matters to the researcher. This stance then also influences how the researcher continues to move through the world and the kinds of commitments made. As such, phenomenology is considered a philosophy of action because deepened thinking leads to deeper action, results in pedagogic thoughtfulness, and reinforces personal engagement and the connections between research and life (van Manen, 1990).

In his phenomenological study, Davis reflected on the theme of maintaining a strong and oriented relation:

> For me, maintaining a strong commitment to the fundamental philosophical and methodological orientation helped in two

ways: first, our genuine interest (as opposed to scientific disinterestedness) as researchers helped us persist through the intense time demands of transcribing, interpreting, reinterpreting and analyzing data, and second, it helped us avoid what van Manen (1990) called "wishy-washy speculations." As an example, I recall reading several transcripts where men talked about going gambling, playing video games, and watching WWF. My first instinct was to dismiss these activities as non-developmental and non-important to the study. Our strong commitment to the phenomenological methodology, however, required us to remember that it was not our preconceptions, but the participants' lived experience[,] that was our focus. (T. L. Davis, personal communication, September 16, 2004)

Balancing the Research Context by Considering Parts and Whole

One of the tensions inherent in phenomenological research is the focus on the essential nature of a phenomenon, the *qualis*, while maintaining the overall orientation toward the structure that holds the constitutive elements. Negotiating this tension requires that the researcher keep an eye on the overall design and questions asked as well as the details of the results. As van Manen (1990) suggested, "It also means that one needs to constantly measure the overall design of the study/text against the significance that the parts must play in the total textual structure" (p. 33).

In relation to our example from published research, Davis reflected,

Balancing the research context by considering parts and whole meant for me in our research study that we constantly had to remind ourselves that *what* we were focusing on was how men construct their identities as men. In listening to participant voices we had to balance a tension between what they were revealing and what it was we were looking for. There were times, for example, that I became immersed in their stories (the parts) such that the focus of the study (the whole) became unfocused. (T. L. Davis, personal communication, September 16, 2004)

In phenomenological research, navigating this tension between the parts and the whole is an ongoing process that requires researcher attentiveness, reflection, and focus on the abiding concern that guides the research.

Case Study

Case study methodology is frequently used in higher education and student affairs research because many of our work environments represent "cases." The temptation becomes great, then, to simply identify a known group on campus (e.g., student organization, living-learning program, or service-learning class) and design a "case study." However, the term is often used incorrectly because researchers new to case study often refer to it as a unit of analysis rather than a methodology. In fact, both definitions are correct but appropriate in different contexts and serve different purposes. For example, Stake (2000) suggested, "Case study is not a methodological choice but a choice of what is to be studied" (p. 435), whereas Merriam (1998) described case study as an "intensive, holistic description and analysis of a single unit or bounded system" (p. 12).

What distinguishes case study methodology from other qualitative approaches is the intensive focus on a *bounded system*, which can be an individual, a specific program, a process, an institution, or a relationship. Implicit in the selection of case study methodology is the assumption that there is something significant that can be learned from a single case (Stake, 2000). Stake (1995), in his book entitled *The Art of Case Study*, clearly articulated the unique contribution of case study:

> A case study is expected to catch the complexity of a single case. The single leaf, even a single toothpick, has unique complexities—but rarely will we care enough to submit it to case study. We study a case when it itself is of very special interest. We look for the detail of interaction with its context. Case study is the study of the particularity and complexity of a single case, coming to understand its activity within important circumstances. (p. xi)

Case study methodology is "the preferred strategy when 'how' or 'why' questions are being posed, when the investigator has little control over events, and when the focus is on a contemporary phenomenon within some real-life context" (Yin, 1994, p. 1). Despite the seeming confusion about case studies, several defining characteristics exist and are highlighted, with illustrations from published research, below.

Connecting Case Study to Theoretical Perspective

Because case study is both a unit of analysis and a methodology without a presumed philosophical tradition attached to it, it is both common and important to see case studies described with an anchor in a particular theoretical perspective. For example, referring back to the published research (Jones & Abes, 2003), this case study is described as a "constructivist" one "because . . . the focus of our inquiry was on participants' construction of meaning and understanding about HIV/AIDS and the learning that occurs in a service-learning class" (p. 473). Similarly, a case study might be designed as a critical case study because the inquiry "keeps the spotlight on power relationships within society so as to expose the forces of hegemony and injustice" (Crotty, 1998, p. 157) or as a feminist case study because "to do feminist research is to put the social construction of gender at the center of one's own inquiry" (Lather, 1992, p. 5). This connection to a theoretical perspective both adds philosophical richness and depth to a case study and provides direction for the design of the case study research project. The case study methodology then becomes emblematic of the philosophical tradition and the particular unit of analysis.

Setting the Context

Although all qualitative research is naturalistic, or occurs in natural, real-world settings (Patton, 2002), setting the context for some studies is more crucial than for others (e.g., case study and ethnography) because the context is an integral part of the "case." Because cases are situated within a bounded system, understanding the relationship of the case to the bounded system is crucial. This process begins by situating the specific phenomenon of interest (the case) in a larger context by describing what that context looks like. This has implications for both the design of the case study research and how the results are presented.

In the example of the case study investigating student understanding of HIV/AIDS in the context of a service-learning class, the context of both the service-learning class and the community service organizations involved is provided (Jones & Abes, 2003). Great care is usually given in presenting this context in written form so that readers have a way of understanding both the boundaries of the particular case and the relationship of the case to a larger context. This typically occurs as the researcher introduces the case study methodology in a section entitled "setting the context," "description of the setting," or "context for the study." This section should be richly descriptive and provide the reader with enough details to create a picture of the larger context within which the case is nested.

Types of Case Studies

Case studies are also distinguished from one another depending on the purpose of the research. Merriam (1998) distinguished among *particularistic*, *descriptive*, and *heuristic* qualitative case studies. A particularistic case study focuses on a very specific phenomenon, which can be a situation, individual, program, or event, and as such is most useful in solving problems that emerge from daily life (Merriam, 1998). The emphasis of a descriptive case study is on the outcome of the investigation, which should produce rich description of a particular phenomenon, typically in narrative form. Heuristic case studies focus on understandings and insights gleaned from the case study investigation and lead to new meaning and rethinking about the phenomenon (Merriam, 1998).

Stake (2000) further delineated types of case studies, distinguishing between *intrinsic, instrumental,* and *collective* case studies. An intrinsic case study is used when the researcher is interested in understanding the particulars of one case—that is, "because, in all its particularity *and* ordinariness, this case itself is of interest" (Stake, p. 437)—rather than focusing on an issue or a more abstract concept. An instrumental case study is less about the case itself and more directed toward understanding of an issue. As Stake defined it, "The case is of secondary interest, it plays a supportive role, and it facilitates our understanding of something else" (p. 437). A collective case study focuses on several instrumental cases in order to draw some conclusions or theorize about a general condition or phenomenon (Stake).

Stake (2000) pointed out that rarely are these categories mutually exclusive or rigorously bounded. Indeed, in the example of published case study research we are applying here, the case study is described as

> a hybrid between an intrinsic case study . . . and an instrumental case study. As an intrinsic case study, the research focused on the uniqueness, context, issues, and story of the partnership. As an instrumental case study, the research explored issues related to developing students' understanding of HIV/AIDS in the context of service-learning, as well as creating and sustaining reciprocal partnerships. (Jones & Abes, 2003, p. 473)

Sampling

It is important for researchers using case study methodology to think through these distinctions because they guide not only the case study design but also significantly how the case study is interpreted, written, and presented. Because the single most defining characteristic of case study methodology is the emphasis on the bounded system or case, sampling, or identifying and selecting, the case is very important. A case is bounded if, and only if, it is clearly identifiable and limited in scope. Merriam (1998) suggested,

One technique for assessing the boundedness of the topic is to ask how finite the data collection would be, that is, whether there is a limit to the number of people involved who could be interviewed or a finite amount of time for observations. If there is no end, actually or theoretically, to the number of people who could be interviewed or to observations that could be conducted, then the phenomenon is not bounded enough to qualify as a case. (pp. 27–28)

Because of the focus on a single case, the selection of the case, or single unit of analysis, is purposeful, that is, it represents a phenomenon of interest to the researcher and can be "unique or typical, representative of a common practice, or never before encountered" (Merriam & Associates, 2002, p. 179). Identification of the particular case is both theoretically derived and then practically executed through the determination of specific sampling criteria. As with other methodologies, the selection of the case emerges from the theoretical framework, or the "structure, scaffolding the frame of your study" (Merriam, 1998, p. 45), because this provides the foundation for the particular investigation and leads to the purpose of your study. Once the purpose is clear, sampling criteria are identified that will most likely enable the researcher to get closest to the phenomenon under investigation. (Greater discussion of sampling is found in Chapter 3.)

Typical in case study methodology, sampling occurs on two levels: selection of the case and selection of the participants within the case (Merriam, 1998). Criteria for sampling in case studies are usually purposeful, with an emphasis on information-rich participants (Patton, 2002). In the example from the study on student understanding of HIV/ AIDS in the context of service learning, the case, or unit of analysis, is identified as the university–community partnership, studied through the perspectives of student and community participants (Jones & Abes, 2003). The case was bounded by the AIDS service organization affiliated with the service-learning class, students enrolled in the class who provided community service at the organization, and the faculty involved in teaching the class. In this particular study, then, all the students involved with the AIDS service organization were invited to participate in the study, as were all staff members and instructors. Data collection included interviews with students, staff, and instructors as well as observations by the researchers who were both well acquainted with the AIDS service organization through their own community service work there. These sampling strategy and data collection procedures provided the researchers with insight into all aspects of the case.

Ethnography

The disciplinary roots of ethnography come from the field of anthropology and have at their core an interest in cultural phenomena or cultural interpretations of a particular group of people. As defined by Tedlock (2000), "Ethnography involved an ongoing attempt to place specific encounters, events, and understandings into a fuller, more meaningful context" (p. 455). Given that methods associated with ethnography are often used with other methodologies, Merriam and Associates (2002) made this helpful distinction:

> Historically associated with the field of anthropology, ethnography has come to refer to both the method (how the researcher conducts the study) and the product (a cultural description of human social life). This dual use of the term has led to some confusion in what is called ethnography; that is, the mere use of data gathering techniques associated with ethnography does not result in an ethnography unless there is a cultural interpretation of those data. (p. 236)

Because of the primary emphasis on cultural understanding and interpretation, ethnographic research is characterized by extensive fieldwork, immersion in a particular setting, prolonged engagement and relationship building, and the generation of *thick description* to describe the people, processes, relationships, and space in that setting (Hammersley & Atkinson, 1983). These are the approach and the strategies needed when the researcher is interested in developing a localized and cultural knowledge of a particular phenomenon. Ethnography is a methodology that can be utilized when the researcher is interested in studying groups to which one belongs, or not, although each brings a different set of dynamics and challenges. Regardless, all ethnographic research is characterized by an interest in understanding in a holistic way the complex dynamics of a particular group or human society to "produce historically, politically, and personally situated accounts, descriptions, interpretations, and representations of human lives" (Tedlock, p. 455).

In our example from published research, Rhoads (1994) was interested in understanding the experiences of gay and bisexual male college students enrolled at Clement University. Rhoads anchored this ethnographic study in a critical theoretical perspective because of his interest in connecting localized knowledge and behavior to larger social structures. He wrote, "Critical ethnography requires exploration of the structural constraints associated with class, patriarchy, racism, and *heterosexism*, in the case of this study" (p. 45). This critical approach is reflected in all aspects of the research design and particularly in the analysis and interpretation of data. Several defining characteristics of ethnography are highlighted below with examples from Rhoads's study.

Access and "Getting In"

In order to effectively conduct ethnographic research, the researcher must become an "insider" in the community of interest. This means that the process of gaining access is very important. Although some may see gaining access as purely a logistical issue, Hammersley and Atkinson (1983) pointed out,

> The process of gaining access is not *merely* a practical matter. Not only does its achievement depend upon theoretical understanding, often disguised as 'native wit', but the discovery of obstacles to access, and perhaps of effective means of overcoming them, themselves provide insights into the social organization of the setting. (p. 54)

And gaining access is also not merely a matter of gaining permission to conduct research in the setting (Hammersley & Atkinson). Instead, the process involves self-reflection about the researcher's role as a "member" (either new or not) of this group, one's own identity in relation to the community under study, as well as knowledge development about the norms, values, beliefs, and behaviors of the group.

In his 2-year ethnographic study, Rhoads (1994) spent the entire first year studying the literature on gay, lesbian, and bisexual college students; reading the campus newspaper with particular attention to "gay issues"; and making initial contacts with staff members and students involved with gay, lesbian, and bisexual (GLB) student services. These initial contacts led to attending GLB student organization meetings and to introductions to additional students, typically referred to as *snowball* sampling or the use of *key informants* in qualitative research (Patton, 2002; Spradley, 1979). By the end of the first year, Rhoads was known by many of the GLB students on Clement's campus and regularly attended their meetings. In fact, it was not until year 2 that Rhoads explained his study to these students and invited participation. Although some may detect an ethical issue in working in the field for a year before disclosing his interests in their participation, nonetheless, Rhoads was immersed in the context and well versed on the culture before initiating the formal process of research. Through this relationship-building process, as well as time in the field, in the students' territory, Rhoads developed personal trust and credibility for his work.

Immersion and Participant Observation

The characteristic method for data collection in ethnography is participant observation, which necessarily involves extensive work in the field or, as it is referred to in ethnography, *fieldwork* (Hammersley & Atkinson, 1983; Patton, 2002; Spradley, 1980; Tedlock, 2000). Becoming immersed in the field and engaging as a participant observer are time-consuming processes and are not easily accomplished with a few observations or interviews. The role of the researcher in the field is also one that requires great thoughtfulness and raises complex issues involving ethics in the field, appearance, deception, and authenticity. As Hammersley and Atkinson suggested, "It is only through watching, listening, asking questions, formulating hypotheses, and making blunders that the ethnographer can acquire some sense of the social structure of the setting and begin to understand the culture of participants" (p. 89). Although this may be self-evident, an important distinguishing characteristic of ethnography is the primary emphasis on observation and listening, rather than asking questions through interviewing as is typical of other qualitative methodologies. Interviewing is also a method used in ethnography; however, the ethnographic interview may also be different in design from interviewing associated with other methodologies. Spradley (1979) identified three types of questions asked in the ethnographic interview: descriptive, structural, and contrast. The distinctions between these kinds of questions will be described below using the example of published research.

In Rhoads's study, both participant observation and ethnographic interviewing were utilized. To observe effectively, the researcher must be perceived as a participant in a particular culture, which is accomplished through immersion. Careful note taking and journaling are important parts of this process as the researcher records observations that are descriptive, sensory, reflective, affective, and interpretive. Rhoads's (1994) observations occurred over the course of an academic year and included attendance at all LGBSA meetings,

> queer dances, parties, and movie nights. . . . I participated in local protests and days of celebration such as National Coming Out Day, where I stood on the steps of the school auditorium with other queer students and allies. And I rode on the bus with students and staff to join the lesbian, gay, and bisexual march on Washington, D.C. (p. 49)

In short, he was fully immersed in many aspects of the lives of these students so he could participate firsthand in this culture.

Rhoads (1994) also utilized ethnographic interviewing and was attentive to the three types of ethnographic questions. Descriptive questions, or those used to access language and terminology of the culture, were reflected in questions such as "How do you identify in terms of sexual orientation?" Rhoads used structural questions, or those that enhance understanding of an individual's cultural knowledge, to ask participants, "What does coming out mean to you?" Finally, contrast questions, or those that emphasized an individual's meaning making concerning key experiences, were asked, such as "What does the term 'gay community' mean to you and how is it different from or similar to the term 'queer community'?" (Rhoads, pp. 49–50). Wording of interview questions is always important, particularly when the researcher is not a member of the community under investigation. Piloting of the interview protocol and revising questions after initial interviews are two strategies to assure the terminology is congruent with that of the culture studied.

Generating "Thick Description"

Good ethnographic research must generate "thick description" (Denzin, 2001; Geertz, 1973), which offers the reader entry into the culture as it exists. Thick description comes from the immersion of the researcher in the cultural context and from collecting data from a variety of sources. Thick description makes possible the opening "up a world to the reader through rich, detailed, and concrete descriptions of people and places . . . in such a way that we can understand the phenomenon studied and draw our own interpretations about meanings and significance" (Patton, 2002, p. 438). Evidence of this thick description comes in the narrative text written from the ethnographic research process. In addition to Rhoads's (1994) *Coming out in College: The Struggle for a Queer Identity* discussed here, Michael Moffatt's (1989) ethnography, entitled *Coming of Age in New Jersey: College and American Culture*, and Rebekah Nathan's (2005) *My Freshman Year: What a Professor Learned by Becoming a Student* are good examples.

Cultural Interpretation and Representation

Immersion in the field produces thick description, which is then analyzed and interpreted through a cultural lens. One of the primary interests in the researcher's interpretation is that participants' perspectives are accurately and fully represented. This is referred to as an *emic*, or insider (Patton, 2002), perspective. There is no one analytic strategy associated with ethnography; however, what is central to analysis is the cultural lens and interpretation. Geertz (1973) suggested that this emphasis on cultural analysis "is guessing at meanings, assessing the guesses, and drawing explanatory conclusions from the better guesses, not discovering the Continent of Meaning and mapping out its bodiless landscape" (p. 20). Rhoads (1994) applied Geertz's guidelines to his study and reported, "The emphasis in the data analysis and in the project as a whole was to make sense of an unfamiliar (unfamiliar to me) aspect of student culture. This is and was an interpretive process that is never-ending" (p. 56).

Few good examples of ethnographic research exist in the higher education and student affairs literature. Most likely, this is due to intensive immersion in the field and the extensive time required to complete an ethnographic study. Although many researchers may utilize ethnographic methods, such as participant observation, it is the prolonged engagement and cultural interpretations that distinguish ethnography from other methodologies. However, cultural understandings of both the student experience and campus environments are important and necessary in higher education and student affairs practice.

SUMMARY

This chapter connected epistemological foundations with methodological approaches, emphasizing the important characteristics that distinguish one methodology from another. Researchers must take care in situating each study in an epistemological tradition that serves as an anchor for other elements of the research design. One such element is sampling or participant selection, which is the focus of the next chapter. Sampling is much more than simply a technique for finding and interacting with participants. It, too, is reflective of methodological approaches.

EXERCISE

Write several statements that flow from your compelling interest that begin with "The purpose of this study is . . ." Continue to work at this statement until you believe you have a very clearly communicated focus for a study. Identify the methodological approach best suited for a study with this focus and 3–6 characteristics that define this methodological approach.

3
PERSPECTIVES ON SAMPLING

Participant selection, or *sampling*, as it has been called historically, is perhaps the most understudied and least understood dimension of the qualitative research process. Many researchers treat sampling as a purely procedural strategy that yields a pool of participants for a particular study. However, this approach fails to consider the relationship between sampling and other methodological elements. The purpose of this chapter is to make explicit the decisions involved in sampling in qualitative research and to explore the complexities of issues that emerge when considering these decision points. Particular attention will be given to sampling strategies, sampling criteria, coverage, and issues related to establishing diverse samples and researcher positionality. Intentional focus on these issues is important in any research project because poor sampling decisions directly impact data quality, credibility, and trustworthiness of findings (Marshall & Rossman, 1998).

Returning to the examples of published research from the previous chapter, the following statements about sampling strategies and participants begin to demonstrate the importance of sampling to the overall research design.

Seven institutions were selected to be part of the study. . . . Because the number of Latino students at each institution varied, a random sample was asked to participate at the institutions with more than 200 Latino/a freshmen, whereas all self-identified Latino freshmen were asked to participate at institutions with fewer than 200 Latino/a freshmen. Of those contacted, 83 students agreed to participate in the interviews held on their campus. (Torres, 2004, p. 460)

Participants in this study were 10 male undergraduate students who ranged in age from 18-21 years old. Five were in their last semester of their senior year, 4 were juniors, and 1 was a sophomore. All participants in this study were White and heterosexual. . . . Each participant was extensively involved in leadership of at least one of the following organizations: Interfraternity Council, Student Alumni Council, University Housing and Dining Services, or the Bureau of Cultural Affairs. (Davis, 2002, p. 511)

In this study, and typical of case study methodology, purposeful sampling was used at both levels. At the first level, the university-POHC partnership was selected because of its continued growth and apparent adherence to principles of good partnership development, as well as the many tensions that draw attention to the challenges of partnership development. At the second level, we sought individuals affiliated with POHC and the service-learning classes who have been directly or indirectly involved in the partnership, including students and instructors, as well as POHC staff. . . . The total sample of 15 for this case study included 8 students, 3 individuals associated with instructing the class, and 4 staff members of POHC. (Jones & Abes, 2003, pp. 473–474)

The universe for this research project includes all gay and bisexual men enrolled at Clement University. However, locating gay and bisexual male students is difficult because many are closeted. . . . I interviewed nearly every gay and bisexual male member of LGBSA—which amounted to about thirty of my forty research participants. . . . The rest of my interview participants were referred to me by members of the gay student community. . . . In an ideal world, my sample would be representative of the various class years, including graduate students. However, research is a series of compromises; and sampling equally across class year was one goal I was forced to drop. (Rhoads, 1994, pp. 53–54)

As the statements above suggest, decisions regarding sampling strategies are instrumental to a study not only because they result in participants for a particular study but also because they serve as further reflection of one's theoretical perspective, one's methodological approach, and the researcher's interpretive stance (Jones, 2002). On the face of it, sampling appears as a pretty straightforward process: identifying and inviting individuals to participate in research. In actuality, the process is of utmost importance to qualitative research designs because "[t]he strategy of participant selection in qualitative research rests on the multiple purposes of illuminating, interpreting, and understanding—and on the researcher's own imagination and judgment" (Glesne & Peshkin, 1992, p. 27).

LANGUAGE AND COVERAGE

The notion of sampling, regardless of paradigmatic orientation, suggests the identification of a subset of a larger phenomenon. However,

Nowhere is the difference between quantitative and qualitative methods better captured than in the different strategies, logics, and purposes that distinguish statistical probability sampling from qualitative purposeful sampling. . . . Not only are the techniques for sample selection different, but the very logic of each approach is distinct because the purpose of each strategy is different. (Patton, 2002, p. 46)

The random-sampling characteristic of quantitative research is intended to produce results that may be generalized to a larger population. By contrast, in qualitative research a sample is purposefully drawn with an emphasis on information-rich cases that elicit an in-depth understanding of a particular phenomenon. A common and persistent question asked by those not familiar with qualitative methodology is "How can you say anything about this topic if your sample is so small?" Qualitative researchers must have a good response to this question (suggestions for responses are offered later in this chapter). To respond, however, a researcher must understand the logic and purpose of qualitative sampling, and then convey the rationale behind sampling decisions. Some qualitative researchers avoid any pretense of quantitative language in describing sampling strategies, using terms such as *participant selection, conversation partners, co-travelers,* and *co-investigators*—all of which reflect a different conceptualization and purpose of the research design and approach. Because the word *sampling* is most prevalent in the qualitative research literature, we will use it in this chapter.

Sampling in qualitative inquiry is distinguished by *purposeful sampling,* that is, sampling for *information-rich* cases that hold the greatest potential for generating insight about the phenomenon of interest. "Information-rich cases are those from which one can learn a great deal about issues of central importance to the purpose of the research, thus the term *purposeful* sampling" (Patton, 2002, p. 46). This definition returns the researcher to the purpose of the study and research questions. Stated differently, in every study, what constitutes information-rich cases will depend on the phenomenon under investigation, the methodological approach, and the questions designed to illuminate understanding of this phenomenon. The researcher then must "seek out groups, settings, and individuals where and for whom the processes being studied are most likely to occur" (Denzin & Lincoln, 2000a, p. 370).

Although sampling in qualitative research focuses on information-rich cases, appropriate *coverage* of the phenomenon is also critical. *Coverage* refers to more than sheer numbers of participants (e.g., sample size, which will be discussed later in this chapter), and also relates to the relationship between one's methodological approach, research questions, data collection, and participant selection strategies. Morse and Richards (2002) referred to this as the "scope of a study" and suggested, "The scope of a study is never just a question of how many, but always includes who, where, and which settings will be studied; and what can be asked and answered" (p. 68). The implication is that participant selection must be intentional with consideration given to the relationships between how well participants are able to illuminate the phenomenon under investigation, the nature of the questions asked of participants, and the contextual influences on participant selection, data collection, and analysis. Too many qualitative researchers err on the side of convenience when considering these factors, deciding to limit participation based on time and resources. However, as Patton (2002) implored, "While convenience and cost are real considerations, they should be the last factors to be taken into account . . . convenience sampling is neither purposeful nor strategic" (p. 242).

Determining when a researcher reaches appropriate coverage is fraught with ambiguity when considered in the context of sampling. In fact, complete coverage of a particular phenomenon may be an elusive, rarely achievable goal. How, then, might the qualitative researcher address the tensions inherent in coverage? First, researchers need to take special care in framing the purpose of a study. Because there is a direct relationship between the purpose of a study, sampling criteria, and participant selection, if the purpose statement is too broad, then coverage will be more difficult (if not impossible) to approximate. A clear and succinct statement of purpose should give the reader some initial indication of who (or what) the researcher is interested in investigating and, hence, who would and would not be included as participants.

Second, once the research is conducted, it is important for the researcher to be very explicit about the kind of coverage achieved. This is preferred to the sometimes subtle (or not) suggestions that coverage was accomplished in interviews with five individuals (which, again, may be possible given the scope of the study) because the researcher interviewed them more than once. In fully describing the sample, the researcher makes clear who is in the sample (and who is not), and why they are there. Last, although Patton (2002) cautioned against using convenience as a leading criterion for sampling, the reality is that most researchers have some limitations on time and resources. Thus, coverage may nearly always be compromised by some dimension of convenience. This, then, becomes a limitation of a study and should be duly noted. However, this reality does not diminish the researcher's responsibility to achieve coverage because many of these research decisions depend upon the good judgment of researchers as they weigh the options available in light of the most efficacious scholarship.

Participant selection, then, in qualitative research is guided by the purpose of the study, methodological approach, and research questions, with particular attention to the selection of "cases" most likely to provide in-depth coverage and insight into the phenomenon under investigation. A variety of sampling strategies is available to accomplish this research goal. However, before a researcher makes decisions about *how* to create a sample or group of participants for a study, the criteria upon which the sample will be drawn, or *who* the researcher is looking for and *why*, must be determined.

SAMPLING CRITERIA

The identification of sampling criteria is central to sampling selection. *Sampling criteria* refer to those variables, characteristics, qualities, and demographics most directly linked to the purpose of the study and, thus, important to the construction of the sample. In other words, given the purpose of the study and primary research questions, certain characteristics must be present in the sample that are most likely going to elicit insight and greater depth of understanding about the phenomenon of interest. Sampling criteria, then, serve as the foundation for making sampling decisions and must be made explicit as the guide for selecting a sample.

Researchers must be able to defend why certain characteristics are important as selection criteria. For example, what is the rationale for a sample composed of only women—who are African American, attend one institution, are between the ages of 18 and 21, represent a diverse array of academic majors, and live on campus? These criteria are some of the ways in which researchers bound their samples, and each should reflect a specific and intentional decision made by the researcher. In our examples from published research, we learn something about the criteria utilized in constructing the sample by reading how the sample is described:

- Eighty-three Latino/a freshmen: 9 from community colleges, 17 from private colleges, and 57 from public urban university. Nine countries of origin; 79.5% first-generation college students; median age is 22; range is 18–52. (Torres, 2004)
- Ten male undergraduates, ranged in age from 18 to 21 years: 5 were in last semester of their senior year, 4 were juniors, and 1 was a sophomore. All were White and heterosexual; variety of majors represented. (Davis, 2002)
- All students who volunteered to participate in the study were selected to participate. In total, 8 students: 6 women, 2 men. Six were in their second year, one in her first, and one in his third. Diverse range of academic majors, all but one identified as White, and all identified themselves as heterosexual. (Jones & Abes, 2003)
- Forty participants, skewed toward upper-class and graduate students; 18% students of color; average family income was $64,600. (Rhoads, 1994)

Some of these characteristics contribute toward an effort in describing the sample and also imply what is important to the researcher and presumably central to an understanding of the study. Sampling criteria might include demographic information (e.g., race, ethnicity, gender, social class, or age), membership in an organization or community (e.g., fraternity, AIDS service organization, or residence hall), relationship to the phenomenon under investigation (e.g., perspective of a parent, advocate, recipient of a service, or director of a program), particular status (e.g., first-generation college student, honors student, award recipient, or new professional), or level of involvement (e.g., leader in a group, nonparticipant in community service, someone required to complete community service, senior student affairs administrator, or social justice educator), to name a few of the many possibilities. Often, in a study, the researcher is interested in participants who possess several sampling criteria simultaneously, such as African American fraternity men or White students involved in service-learning classes.

However, as the examples from the published research illustrate, the relationship between sampling criteria and the actual sample may not always emerge as a precise one. For example, if we return to Davis's (2002) study on "men's identity development," as described in the purpose of his study, we learn that his focus is on men, which presumably becomes a primary sampling criterion. However, when we read the description of his sample, we learn that his sample consists exclusively of *White* and *heterosexual* men. Sampling criteria that included diversity in race and/or sexual orientation may have produced very different findings. We might reasonably expect that the social construction of gender roles for an African American gay male, for example, would be considerably distinct from that of a White heterosexual male.

Similarly, in Vasti's study of "family influences on the identity development of Latino/a first year students" (Torres, 2004), the goal was to expand theory, so sampling criteria focused on institutional type. However, sampling criteria could focus on familial structures and/or countries of origin and, again, potentially yield different results. A sample that included single heads of households or students from one country of origin would be different from a study in which participants were part of a large extended family or were from a variety of countries of origin. The point here is not necessarily that one sample is better than the other but that making sampling criteria explicit, with appropriate rationale that can be traced back to the purpose of the study, is crucial because the makeup of the sample influences all other dimensions of the researcher design (e.g., data collection and analysis).

In addition to providing a rationale for why certain criteria are central to the study and utilized to guide sampling decisions, it is also important to define criteria when/if there might be any doubt. For example, if the criterion of *new professional* is identified, the researcher should make explicit whether this is defined by length of time in the profession (first 5 years of work) or in relation to receipt of a degree (within 5 years from completion of master's degree). In a study exploring the dynamics of lesbian identity, Abes and Jones (2004) discussed in their sampling section the decision to use the word *lesbian* while recognizing that this may not be the identity label used by some participants. Had the researchers chosen to use the word *queer*, for example, an entirely different group of interested participants might have emerged (E. S. Abes, personal communication, December 15, 2004). Terminology and defining terms and criteria are critical to the sampling process. So, too, is the decision making regarding sample size.

SAMPLE SIZE

The oft-quoted passage from Patton (2002) that "[t]**here are no rules for sample size in qualitative inquiry**" (p. 244) is typically offered as the strongest rationale for a small sample size one can provide. Patton went on to write, "Sample size depends on what you want to know, the purpose of the inquiry, what's at stake, what will be useful, what will have credibility, and what can be done with available time and resources" (p. 244). However, Patton's intent was not to give blanket permission to qualitative researchers to feel good about a small sample. Instead, he directed the researcher back to the purpose and significance of the study and suggested that these must be connected to decisions about sample size. For example, phenomenological investigations, with in-depth emphasis on a particular phenomenon, tend toward smaller numbers of participants, whereas an ethnographic study, by definition, must include perspectives from multiple sources in order to accomplish the cultural analysis and interpretation characteristic of this approach. Creswell (1998), in his summary of five qualitative methodologies, provided guidance about sample sizes that are reflective of these different traditions. Thus the methodological approach, coupled with the purpose of a study, provides both guidance and a rationale for sample size decisions.

It is important to point out that the language of sample size is grounded in a positivist perspective. The quantitative paradigm utilizes sampling procedures (as noted earlier in this chapter) and criteria regarding sample size that are anchored in randomization and generalizability. In quantitative investigations, typically the researcher identifies the population and sample at the onset of the investigation and then implements procedures to create this particular sample. The notion of sample size takes on different meaning in qualitative research. In thinking about the decision making surrounding sample size in qualitative investigations, the concept of *theoretical sampling*, taken from the literature on grounded theory methodology, is instructive. Strauss and Corbin (1998) defined theoretical sampling as follows:

> Data gathering driven by concepts derived from the evolving theory and based on the concept of "making comparisons,"

whose purpose is to go to places, people, or events that will maximize opportunities to discover variations among concepts and to densify categories in terms of their properties and dimensions. (p. 201)

Although some of this language is specific to grounded theory, the transferable ideas are that data gathering and sampling are guided by the goal of maximizing opportunities to uncover data relevant to the purpose of the study and that the sampling process interacts with data analysis. That is, as themes or concepts begin to emerge through analysis of data, the researcher identifies additional sites or individuals who hold the potential of yielding theoretically relevant data. Thus, sampling continuously evolves throughout the research process (Strauss & Corbin, 1998). The researcher continues to sample (and collect data) until these opportunities are maximized or until patterns in the data continuously emerge.

This concept related to maximizing data and sample size is called *saturation*. When themes or categories are saturated, then the decision to stop sampling is justified. Saturation occurs when the researcher begins to hear (or observe, or read) the same or similar kinds of information related to the categories of analysis. Lincoln and Guba (1985) referred to this as sampling

to the point of redundancy.... In purposeful sampling the size of the sample is determined by informational considerations. If the purpose is to maximize information, the sampling is terminated when no new information is forthcoming from new sampled units; thus *redundancy* is the primary criterion. (p. 202)

Sampling to redundancy may not always be feasible or realistic given constraints of time and resources. To navigate this tension, Patton (2002) suggested, "The solution is judgment and negotiation. I recommend that qualitative sampling designs specify *minimum samples* based on expected reasonable coverage of the phenomenon given the purpose of the study and stakeholder interests" (p. 246). The researcher then must take care to explain sampling decisions and to justify the sample size, as well as to identify the connections and limitations related to sampling and the findings of the study (Patton, 2002).

Once sampling criteria are identified and sample size given consideration, then the researcher must determine *how* to locate participants who meet the criteria. This is referred to as the *sampling strategy*.

SAMPLING STRATEGIES

The sampling strategy is the way to identify and secure the individuals, organizations, or research settings that reflect the sampling criteria. A sampling strategy is a method that implies a plan for identifying those who may shed light on a particular phenomenon. This plan is linked to the purpose of the study and methodological approach. A variety of strategies is available to the qualitative researcher, each serving a slightly different purpose. Patton (2002) provided an excellent description of these strategies and the purposes that each serves (i.e., pp. 230–244).

It is important to note that utilizing more than one strategy in a study may be appropriate. Participant selection in qualitative research, regardless of the methodological approach, is usually a fluid, flexible, ongoing process. Different from quantitative methods, the sample in qualitative approaches is rarely set and static before a study commences. Relating to the discussion of coverage, the researcher presumably continues to sample until appropriate coverage is achieved. Furthermore, as data are collected and the initial analysis is conducted, new insights about how the participant group should be bounded may emerge as the research process evolves. The issue of the flexibility needed in sampling is related to sample size and will be discussed later in this chapter.

In thinking about sampling strategies for a particular study, the researcher must focus on both selecting a strategy and then providing the rationale for why the strategy is most appropriate. Although no fixed rules exist for which sampling strategies attach to particular methodological approaches, there are clear differences among strategies such that some align more closely with certain methodologies than others. For example, in case study methodology the selection of a case suggests a focus on the specificity of a particular case; and in phenomenological research, with the appropriate emphasis on the lived experience of a particular phenomenon, participants must clearly reflect this phenomenon (e.g., intensity sampling). In an ethnographic study with emphasis on understanding cultural influences, the researcher must gain access to a diverse group of participants to provide in-depth perspectives on cultural dynamics (e.g., snowball sampling). However, the selection of the individuals within the case, or ethnography, may be selected by utilizing a number of strategies depending on the purpose of the study (e.g., maximum variation, negative case, or typical case).

To illustrate several of the strategies most typically utilized in higher education and student affairs research, let's return to our examples from the published research (see Table 3.1).

Table 3.1   Sampling Strategies

Purpose of Study	Sample	Sampling Strategies
To explore family influences on identity development of Latino/a first year students (Torres, 2004)	Eighty-three first-year Latino/a students from 7 institutions	Open sampling techniques were originally used to maintain a loose structure for determining the sample.
To explore conflicts related to socially constructed gender roles that may impact men's identity development (Davis, 2002)	Ten White, heterosexual, traditionally aged males—all involved in leadership of a campus organization	Participants were purposefully selected through snowball or chain sampling; exemplar cases.
To explore the development of students' knowledge, attitudes, and behavior regarding HIV/AIDS in the context of a university–community partnership (Jones & Abes, 2003)	One site (community service organization) and 15 individuals: 8 students, 3 instructors, and 4 staff members	Purposeful sampling was used at both levels, selecting the case and the individuals within it.
To highlight the experiences of queer students at Clement University as they struggle to gain a private and public voice (Rhoads, 1994)	Forty gay or bisexual men at one university, the majority of whom are juniors, seniors, or graduate students; predominantly White	Intensity sampling was used for 30 out of 40 participants as all male members of the LGBSA were interviewed; 10 were identified through snowball sampling or recommendations from the gay community.

What is most critical when considering sampling strategies is making the connection between the strategies utilized to generate a purposefully drawn sample and what it is the researcher wants to learn more about (e.g., the purpose of the study and research questions). This enables the researcher to identify the most appropriate sampling strategies for a particular study. For example, depending on the questions addressed in a study, a sample may be identified through the process of *maximum variation* in order to cast a wide net on the phenomenon of interest or through *intensity* sampling that suggests that the phenomenon of interest is intensely present (Patton, 2002).

Gaining Access

A related process, and one integral to sampling, is that of gaining access to participants for research and developing rapport. Simply identifying sampling criteria and strategies for creating a sample does not at all assure the actuality of a group of individuals who agree to participate. Marshall and Rossman (1998) pointed out that in a study seeking to illustrate maximum variation, "If the researcher cannot gain access to the site and to a range of groups and activities within it, the study cannot succeed" (p. 56). As Glesne and Peshkin (1992) described,

> Access is a process. It refers to your acquisition of consent to go where you want, observe what you want, talk to whomever you want, obtain and read whatever documents you require, and do all of this for whatever period of time you need to satisfy your research purposes. (p. 33)

Gaining access to participants or a particular field site is sometimes an easy process and sometimes fraught with difficulty—what makes the difference is the nature of the research project, the existing relationships the researcher has with those who can provide access, and the care the researcher has taken to know the context of the site and the participants within it (Glesne & Peshkin). Attention to several relationship-oriented processes will aid the researcher in facilitating access to participants.

Gatekeepers and Key Informants

One of the primary strategies for gaining access is through negotiation with gatekeepers and key informants. These are the individuals who know individuals and/or settings that meet the sampling criteria determined by the researcher. Gatekeepers and key informants typically hold some kind of formal or informal authority such that they may grant consent to enter a research setting (Glesne & Peshkin, 1992). Key informants may differ from gatekeepers because they are less likely to have authority to grant access, but once access is gained, key informants are integral to identifying the most suitable participants for a study because of their insider status. It is also useful to have key informants with insider knowledge to assist in identifying appropriate gatekeepers and those who can provide advice about politics involved, cultural considerations, or other dynamics likely to impact the researcher's request for access (Glesne & Peshkin). Key informants "are a source of information; literally they become teachers" (Spradley, 1979, p. 25). Furthermore, Patton (2002) defined key informants as "people who are particularly knowledgeable about the inquiry setting and articulate about their knowledge—people whose insights can prove particularly useful in helping an observer understand what is happening and why" (p. 321).

This distinction is clear in Rhoads's (1994) study of gay men in college. Gatekeepers for this study consisted of staff members at the university who were able to assist in gaining access to the LGBSA organization meetings and making contacts with several lesbian, gay, and bisexual students. Once *in* and visible within the queer student community, Rhoads began to develop relationships with several students, one of whom came to serve as a key informant. In this capacity, the informant provided access to additional individuals as well as reflections and reactions to the research process itself. For example, Rhoads explained the key informant's role in this way:

> Tito [the key informant] took me to a number of social events during the first year of my study and served as interpreter on many occasions when conversations and jokes went over my head. He also noted homophobic behaviors I exhibited. (p. 47)

Although key informants are crucial to providing access to participants to whom the researcher needs introduction, Patton (2002) noted that a potential danger in using key informants is an overreliance on their perceptions of what is going on as "truth" rather than as "necessarily limited, selective, and biased" (p. 321).

Gatekeepers may be approached through someone else who knows these individuals or through a request for communication from the researcher to the gatekeeper. Although the first strategy is advantageous because the researcher's credibility can be established by someone already known to the gatekeeper, in either case the importance of preparation cannot be underestimated. This means that the researcher must be able to provide a compelling case for the request for access that includes presenting a clearly thought out plan for the research, illustrating evidence of knowledge of the research site and participants, establishing credentials as a researcher, providing assurance of anonymity and confidentiality, and responding to questions and concerns the gatekeeper might raise (Glesne & Peshkin, 1992). The challenge in strategically negotiating access from gatekeepers is in figuring out how to gain entry while preserving the integrity of the study and the investigator's interests. The degree of difficulty involved varies depending on the purpose of the fieldwork and the expected or real degree of resistance to the study. Where the field researcher expects cooperation, gaining entry may be largely a matter of establishing trust and rapport. At the other end of the continuum are those research settings where considerable resistance, even hostility, is expected, in which case gaining entry becomes a matter of "infiltrating the setting." And sometimes entry is simply denied. (Patton, 2002, p. 310)

One of the best ways to provide assurance of your integrity as a researcher and to demonstrate commitment to the project and the potential participants (and, hence, to gain access to the site) is by spending time at the site, developing relationships and gaining insider knowledge. Marshall and Rossman (1998) referred to this as an ability to "blend in" (p. 58), and Glesne and Peshkin (1992) as "logging time" (p. 34). As Glesne and Peshkin went on to explain,

Just being around, participating in activities, and talking informally with people gives them time to get used to you and learn that you are ok. This approach leads to better data than one in which a superior [e.g., vice president for student affairs] requests a subordinate [e.g., students] to cooperate with you. (p. 34)

In the example of published research conducted by Jones and Abes (2003), focusing on student understanding of HIV/AIDS in the context of a university–community partnership, both researchers were very familiar with the site for the research (an AIDS service organization) because each was a regular volunteer with the organization. As a result, access to the site was easily granted because of the relationships the researchers developed with the staff and clients at the AIDS service organization and because of their insider knowledge of the context for the research. The ability to develop insider knowledge and to become visible and known at the site is closely connected to another important sampling-related issue, that of developing rapport and trust with participants.

Establishing Rapport and Developing Trust

The presence of rapport and trust is integral not only to securing participants for a study but also to sustaining participation over time. In fact, the relationship between researcher and participants is one of the hallmarks of qualitative research; however, this relationship can be neither presumed nor taken for granted. Establishing rapport and developing trust take time, care, and persistent attention throughout the research process. The presence of rapport suggests the development of a relationship characterized by reciprocity and mutuality. However, what makes rapport in the context of qualitative research potentially problematic is that rapport is needed primarily so that the researcher can accomplish certain results. As Glesne and Peshkin (1992) suggested, "In qualitative research, rapport is a distance-reducing, anxiety-quieting, trust-building mechanism that primarily serves the interest of the researcher" (p. 94). In other words, if a researcher is able to establish rapport, then participants will feel comfortable responding to researcher questions or observations. However, Glesne and Peshkin noted, "Rapport is a necessary but not sufficient condition for obtaining good data; researchers partake in the opportunities it enables by virtue of other skills" (p. 94).

The foundation upon which rapport sits is "the ability to convey empathy and understanding without judgment" (Patton, 2002, p. 366). This suggests the importance of trust and respect in a researcher–participant relationship, which must be present in all aspects of the research process. Although not writing specifically about qualitative research, Noddings's (1984) work on *caring* is particularly instructive in thinking about trust and respect in the context of research. Noddings suggested that when we care or are in a caring relationship with another, then we are *feeling with* that person:

> I do not "put myself in the other's shoes," so to speak, by analyzing his [sic] reality as objective data and then asking, "How would I feel in such a situation?" On the contrary, I set aside my temptation to analyze and to plan. I do not project; I receive the other into myself, and I see and feel with the other. (p. 30)

A researcher's ability to care, to receive the other into him or herself, is the backbone of trust and respect. Such a relationship communicates to one's participants a genuine regard for them as individuals and a deep commitment to understanding their experiences. Noddings's notions about caring in relation to the research process dovetail with Patton's (2002) suggestions about the importance of both rapport and *neutrality* in qualitative research. He explained this distinction as follows:

> Rapport is a stance vis-à-vis the person being interviewed. Neutrality is a stance vis-à-vis the content of what that person says. . . . Rapport means that I respect the people being interviewed, so what they say is important because of who is saying it. . . . Neutrality means that the person being interviewed can tell me anything without engendering either

my favor or disfavor with regard to the content of her or his response. I cannot be shocked; I cannot be angered; I cannot be embarrassed; I cannot be saddened. Nothing the person tells me will make me think more or less of the person. (p. 365)

Although there are no recipes for the establishment of trust and respect in the context of qualitative research, what follows are a number of specific strategies and qualities that may contribute to the creation and maintenance of trust and respect:

- Convey your interest in the project with your initial invitation to participate as well as your knowledge of the phenomenon under investigation.
- Be clear in the expectations you have of participants, and consider the question of why someone would want to participate in such a study—are there meaningful incentives you might offer?
- In addition to incentives, consider the question of how you might develop reciprocity in the context of the research process—what might participants get out of their involvement in your research?
- Recognize that methodological approach influences the processes of gaining access and building rapport. For example, in a critical inquiry, participants play an integral role in conceptualizing all aspects of the study design.
- Tune in—and adjust accordingly—to the culturally relevant norms, behaviors, appearances, language, and values of participants. This means learning about and developing an insider's view of the context and culture you are investigating and exploring. As Glesne and Peshkin (1992) pointed out, this may cause researchers to amend more typical (to them) speech patterns, expressions of beliefs, or behaviors.
- Be sensitive to the impact of your presence in the research setting. However unobtrusive you might feel, the mere presence of a researcher may be cause for anxiety, attention, or scrutiny.
- Consider the relationship between your own socially constructed identities (e.g., race, ethnicity, age, gender, sexual orientation, social class, religion, and ability) and those of your participants, and consider what difference these might make in your ability to establish rapport and trust (this will be discussed further later in this chapter and in detail in Chapter 5).
- Pay attention to the physical environment when interviewing or observing participants. Are they in a natural setting? Or a place of their choosing? Eliminate any potential distractions that may influence your ability to be with the participant.

- Make sure that your active listening and observation skills are strong. Effective interviewing is crucial to good research and depends upon very strong listening skills.
- Rapport and trust are also built by the ability to ask good questions. This requires practicing (typically through pilot studies), then following up with appropriate probes that demonstrate that you heard the initial response and stimulate further reflection or insight about the phenomenon.
- Rapport and trust must be sustained throughout the research process. One way to navigate this is through involving participants in member checking of data and, most importantly, your interpretations from the data. In other words, have you told their story in a way they recognize, deem true, and find meaningful to them?

ISSUES RELATED TO AN INTEREST IN A "DIVERSE" SAMPLE AND RESEARCHER POSITIONALITY

Related to decisions about sampling and criteria used to identify participants for a study is growing interest in a "diverse" sample. This interest has necessarily evolved out of a needed commitment to inclusion in research designs by representing in samples those whose life experiences and stories have previously been excluded or marginalized through the research process (Jones, 2002). However well intentioned and important these efforts are, creating a diverse sample requires careful and thoughtful attention to the issues of researcher positionality and to not unwittingly further marginalizing particular voices through a "tokenism" inherent in the sampling process. The issue of researcher positionality is discussed in further detail and greater depth in Chapter 5. However, researcher positionality is also connected to sampling in important ways that are rarely addressed in the literature, particularly related to the creation of a diverse sample and to researching within, or outside, the researcher's own community or social identities. These two specific considerations, as they connect to sampling and participant selection, will be addressed in this chapter.

The question of researcher positionality, or the connection between the researcher's socially constructed identities and those of participants, is a complicated one because it necessarily illuminates issues associated with what constitutes a "diverse sample" and researching within—or outside—the researcher's own community. Fine (1994) referred to this negotiation as "working the hyphens" of *self-other*, with "the hyphen that both separates and merges personal identities with our inventions of Others" (p. 70). Fine elaborated,

> By *working the hyphen*, I mean to suggest that researchers probe
> how we are in relation with the contexts we study and with our
> informants, understanding that we are all multiple in those re-
> lations. . . . Working the hyphen means creating occasions for
> researchers and informants to discuss what is, and is not, "hap-
> pening between," within the negotiated relations of whose story
> is being told, why, to whom, [and] with what interpretation, and
> whose story is being shadowed, why, for whom, and with what
> consequence. (p. 72)

The importance of working the hyphen by qualitative researchers is
apparent when examining what constitutes diverse samples in qualitative
studies. Far too often, this diverse sample is created by including one
of this and one of that, as if to suggest that the voice of disability, for
example, is heard by the presence of one individual with a disability. In
an article exploring an approach that suggests that only gays and lesbians
can speak to sexuality or that race is only salient for African Americans,
Maynard (2000) wrote that such an approach not only encourages "benign
description" but also misses the critical point that "these things structure
all our lives, no matter how invisible they might be in experiential terms,
[and] we are not excused from confronting them because we are not
members of a particular oppressed group" (p. 99).

Maynard's (2000) caution reminds researchers that central to qualitative investigations is the need for researchers to position themselves in
relation to the phenomenon under investigation (why do I care about
this topic?), the methodological approach (what assumptions do I carry
about how knowledge is constructed?), and participants in the study
(how might who I am and where I come from influence what I know
and what I hear and observe?). These questions are addressed more fully
in chapters that follow, but it is important to note here that researcher
positionality can also influence sampling decisions because of the sociocultural conditions that pattern the life experiences of researchers and
participants in both similar and distinctive ways.

Again, Fine (1994) framed this issue well: "The social sciences have
been, and still are, long on texts that inscribe some Others, preserve
other Others from scrutiny, and seek to hide the researcher/writer
under a veil of neutrality or objectivity" (p. 73). Applying this to higher
education research, a White researcher, for example, interested in the
experiences of female students participating in a math and science
program specifically designed for women might miss the fact that
this "special program" consists of 99% White women. Because she is
not conscious of her own White racial identity, she fails to see how

this potentially influences both her research decisions and outcomes. Similarly, many well-educated researchers investigating first-generation college students continue to describe students' lives and notions of family support from a deficit model. Not surprisingly, those researchers who are first generation themselves offer a very different portrayal of this phenomenon (e.g., Delong, 2003). Many examples exist where researchers claim to investigate the experiences of men or women, but fail to explicate any racial, ethnic, and cultural background information that may make a significant difference about what might be said about the experiences of particular individuals in the findings. These examples suggest the important relationship between researcher positionality and the creation of a "diverse" sample.

Because many researchers are interested in creating diverse samples, researcher positionality is connected to the issue of researching within and/or outside one's own community. Researchers may embark upon a project that takes them out of their own identities or communities with a naïve assumption that this should not or would not make a difference. I do not want to suggest here that sampling outside of one's own community is not possible but, more so, that great attentiveness and discernment be given about the implications of such work. Furthermore, attentiveness is also required when a researcher's participants are similar to his or her identity dimensions because similarity or commonality may be presumed when that is not the case.

A poignant example of the relationship between sampling and researcher positionality is offered by two researchers who engaged in a collaborative project investigating the school experiences of Mexican children (Merchant, 2001; Zurita, 2001). Zurita, a Mexican American woman, connected with her participants in a way that Merchant, a White woman, could not. Researching within Zurita's community elicited great anguish about her role as a researcher and her unwitting perpetuation of social inequality by simply documenting unjust conditions rather than working for change. Merchant described her intellectual awareness of the influence of her racial identity and tendency to speak for the other, but noted that this "was not enough to prevent me from lapsing into culturally biased patterns of research" (p. 15).

SUMMARY

What these examples from research suggest is the importance of examining the complex dynamics at work when participants in a study mirror, or do not mirror, the social identities of the researcher. The realities of researching within and/or outside the researcher's own community influence criteria identified for sampling, sampling strategies and approaches, access to participants, and the rapport and trust developed between researcher and participant. Most typically, when sampling and participant selection are discussed, the processes are situated as though they exist outside of any kind of sociocultural context. In fact, each dimension of "sampling" discussed in this chapter is patterned and influenced by this context, as well as the researcher's positionality within a sociocultural reality. Not to acknowledge the role these dynamics play in all aspects of the research design, including sampling and participant selection, is to perpetuate an "Othering" that results in a distancing between self and other, researcher and participant. Careful attention to the dynamics of sampling and participant selection works to connect sampling criteria and strategies to the purpose of the study and to the development of relationships that are the anchor of good qualitative research.

EXERCISE

Look again at your statement of purpose. Identify what the statement of purpose tells you about your sample. What does your methodological approach tell you about your sample? List who should be in your sample—what sampling criteria can you defend? What differences are important for you? Are these differences reflected in your list? Then, from your selected methodology, identify the appropriate "unit of analysis." After identifying the unit of analysis and from the above list, develop more specific criteria for selection of participants as well as any other considerations that flow both from the statement of purpose and from the methodological approach. What are the potential influences of your own positionality and social identities in your sample selection? How will you appropriately "work the self-other hyphen"?

4
CONTINUITY AND CONGRUENCE
IN THE RESEARCH PROCESS

The assumption that simply stating the method (interview) and providing the results (analysis of themes) will lead to a thorough and worthy research process, as illustrated in previous chapters, is erroneous. It is important to understand that collecting and analyzing data are not the only aspects of a strong qualitative study. Attention to issues of continuity and congruence in the research process also promotes integrity in the qualitative research process. It is the responsibility of the researcher, as the instrument of the research, to maintain continuity and congruence throughout the research process. This involves assuring consistency between all elements of the research design as well as making appropriate methodological decisions that complement one another.

Congruence in the research process embodies issues of commensurability among all the elements in the research study. Commensurability relates to the relationship between all elements of the research design. Continuity is the ability of the researcher to be consistent throughout the research process (Lincoln & Guba, 2000). This chapter helps the researcher assure an intentionally created research project that maintains congruence between theoretical perspective, methodological approach, method, and proposed analytical strategies. Although this may seem like a logical task, maintaining congruence and continuity creates difficult decisions in the qualitative research process.

In order for the reader to understand the intentional connections between the elements of qualitative research, this chapter begins with a short review of the necessary connections. This will be followed by a series of research decisions that should be considered during the process. Examples from published research studies will be used to illustrate research decisions.

REVIEWING THE ELEMENTS
OF THE RESEARCH DESIGN

In the first chapter of this book, the process of situating the research was illustrated through explanations of the research paradigm, epistemology, and theoretical framework and perspective. The researcher must identify his or her worldview and acknowledge what influences her or his view on how knowledge is created. If the researcher identifies with two paradigms, then a decision must be made about potential congruence among the paradigms. Although it is possible for a researcher to conduct a study that is commensurate with more than one paradigm, it is imperative that the researcher intentionally consider whether or how the different paradigms correspond (or are commensurate) to each other or if they are too different to use in one study. In considering the question of commensurate paradigms, Lincoln and Guba (2000) stated, "From our perspective, [the answer] has to be a cautious yes" (p. 174). Whereas some paradigms may have complementary epistemological beliefs, others may have conflicting beliefs. Understanding the underlying tenets of the paradigms is critical to maintaining congruence in the research design. Chapter 1 of this book detailed some of the underlying beliefs and proposed that reflecting upon these beliefs is a good starting point for considering commensurability among paradigms. Reading the original philosophical works that influence each paradigm is an additional essential part of the research process and helps the researcher develop a more sophisticated understanding of different paradigms.

Chapter 2 offers an in-depth explanation of the relationships between methodology and method. Congruence between methodology and method requires the researcher to be reflective about the self as the instrument of the research. One of the techniques recommended to assist in this reflective process is the continued use of a journal in which the researcher chronicles information about the self and the research process. Lincoln and Guba (1985) referred to this as a reflexive journal that contains information about the human instrument (self) as well as the rationale for decisions regarding methodology. Being able to intentionally reflect and justify decisions is a major component in maintaining congruence between methodology and method. In July 2000, Vasti wrote the following excerpt (edited for clarity) in her research journal about her longitudinal study:

> Going in-depth into the 2nd year interviews and I'm back to the question of how to treat the data? Last year I decided to look at the interviews as a whole. When I do that with this set—I keep going back to the individual first year interviews. Perhaps I will try to focus on the emerging categories instead of figuring out if there is fit with previous data. This way I can do the analysis of the interviews [method] and then once I'm done I can go back and say—is this consistent or does it add to what emerged in the first year? I think this will be more consistent with grounded theory. I could also switch and code for process—but I think it is too early in the process. (V. Torres, personal communication, July 2000)

Chapter 3 on sampling illustrated the level of "control" researchers have over the research process. By *control*, we are referring to the decisions the researcher makes about size, coverage, and diversity of the sample, as well as his or her relationship with the participants. *Control* is a word that is often misunderstood in research. Control is about determining what voices will be heard and how one sees the "self" as the instrument of the research. Sampling decisions are not a means of control but rather contribute to the congruence between the chosen paradigm, theoretical framework and perspective, methodological approach, and method. Sampling decisions are an aspect of reflexivity (Lincoln & Guba, 2000). Embracing and understanding the underpinnings of research decisions are important in maintaining congruence and understanding the false lure of control. The following are examples of research decisions that arise in attempting to maintain congruence within the research design.

DATA ANALYSIS DECISIONS

To maintain congruence and continuity, it is necessary to consider issues that may arise during the research process. In our experiences the issues that arise often surprise the researcher. Therefore, considering these issues before they arise will help the researcher see the connections and interrelationships among research decisions. It is important to realize that previous research decisions affect future decisions throughout the research process. The connections among the elements of research make it critical to see all decisions during a research study as interrelated.

Of the various facets of research, the analysis is perhaps the most pivotal. It is here where the researcher struggles to make meaning of the data collected. This requires "a radical spirit of openness" to new potential (Crotty, 1998, p. 50). How data are analyzed must be considered in light of previous research design choices. A common error occurs when data analysis techniques are considered separately from methodology, epistemology, or paradigm choices. The analysis of data should be tailored to honor the philosophical assumptions inherent in the research strategies chosen (Creswell, 2003).

Because certain data analysis techniques are appropriate for certain methodologies, the topic of data analysis is a complex one. Entire books are dedicated to the analysis function of the research process (e.g., Dey, 1995; Miles & Huberman, 1994). Space limitations here do not allow a thorough discussion of data analysis. However, to not address analysis in a book on the complexities of conducting qualitative research would be deficient. Some qualitative methodologies provide specific structure about how analysis should be conducted, whereas other methodologies offer less structure in analysis techniques. Therefore, we are offering some very general information regarding analysis, mentioning a few strategies of analysis to demonstrate the wide variety, and then providing examples of three specific strategies of data analysis that are guided by different methodologies.

It is through analysis that the text or data are undone to bring insight about the phenomenon under investigation. The word *analysis* stems from the German word *analusuein*, meaning to unloose or undo (Hoad, 1986). This unloosening allows for discovery of what is "hidden in the text" (Crotty, 1998, p. 92). Methodology directs how data are "unloosened" and what is done to the data afterward to generate understanding. Generally, qualitative traditions range from the deeply interpretive that offer meaning beyond what is said (such as phenomenology) to methodologies that offer requisite structure in analyzing what is said (such as grounded theory). The former is artful and poetic, and somewhat playful in how the text is unloosened, themes uncovered, and interpretation generated, whereas the latter offers a more systematic interpretation of the data (Arminio & Hultgren, 2002).

Data can be gathered through a number of approaches including structured and unstructured interviews, conversations, document review, observations, visual realities (e.g., film and photos), first person life histories, biographies, and focus groups. Oral data are transcribed and become text.

To begin the analysis, the researcher must spend a great amount of time and effort repeatedly listening to, reading, or watching the data or text. In doing so, the researcher notices descriptive, common, or unusual ideas, phrases, and words, and their meanings. These are often highlighted or noted in the text margins, thus becoming detached from the larger context (later to be reattached). Qualitative work enables analysis and interpretation of the text to be more fluid to reflect a state of emerging rather than one of being focused only on fixed categories. This fluidity in the "unloosing" can be frustrating, but it is this process that allows for the voices of the participants to be heard and for new understandings to emerge.

The researcher must search the text for what Ryan and Bernard (2000) referred to as the "basic unit of analysis" (p. 780). Methodology determines the unit of analysis. Common units of analysis include themes, codes, and categories or "trajectories" (Mishler, 2000). Next, the researcher must consider the relationship of these trajectories. In general, the researcher works between different trajectories looking for patterns.

In order to provide a broad understanding of what is involved with analysis, we will look at some common aspects of the analysis process.

- From a phenomenological perspective, the researcher might describe the process like this: The unloosening of the data at this stage is referred to in the word *analysis*. From these unloosened bits of datum, the researcher begins to identify "parallel trajectories" (Mishler, 2000, p. 129) or noteworthy elements and formulate the relationship of these trajectories to each other and to the larger context. The nature of these trajectories is determined by the chosen methodology. In phenomenology, these trajectories become themes. This process is also referred to as a *hermeneutical circle*, whereby analysis is created through the relationship of the parts to the whole meaning of the text (Kvale, 1987).
- From a grounded theory perspective, the researcher might describe this same process like this: The initial line-by-line analysis of data constitutes a microscopic analysis of the text. From this microscopic view emerge many possible codes that are then taken into consideration in the open-coding process (Strauss & Corbin, 1998).
- From an autoethnography perspective, the researcher might describe this same process like this: The researchers first look "outward on social and cultural aspects of their personal experiences; then they look inward" (Ellis & Bochner, 2000, p. 739).

One way to begin to recognize the relationship of these trajectories is to consider how these trajectories are similar or different. What boundaries might help explain differences? Do some differences appear to be extreme? Beyond these polarized relationships, the researcher could look for spatial relationships (Hodder, 2000). What are the metaphorical or analogous relationships of these trajectories (Ryan & Bernard, 2000)? What relationship is there in regard to strength or direction? Is there a puzzle (Silverman, 2000)? How are power and privilege evident in the trajectories? How might the researcher's own story be intruding upon this story (Fontana & Frey, 2000)? It is important that multiple meanings of trajectories be considered (Hodder).

Hodder (2000) suggested using two complementary ways of analyzing language: representational and presentational. Representational data analysis assumes that words are meant to capture thoughts, beliefs, knowledge, and feelings. This answers what was said and what thoughts are represented in the language that is used. Contrarily, in presentational analysis the language itself becomes the locus of study. This answers "how" it was said. In Jan's (Arminio, 2001) study of race-related guilt, participants described a feeling of shame about White racism (representational view) but used the word *guilt* in describing it (presentational view). Both illuminated the phenomenon. The complementary nature of these two views not only illuminates meaning but also demonstrates how the meaning is communicated.

The critical point here is that the analysis must go beyond merely making lists (Silverman, 2000) or reporting on what was said or observed; data are also interpreted. By examining how points are linked, or failed to link, the researcher begins to illuminate beyond simplistic understanding.

Methodology provides direction as to how abstract or concrete the interpretation of the data should be. The more richly networked the association of trajectories, the thicker the description and the more subtle the interpretations (Hodder, 2000). It is through thick description that particular and complex phenomena can be understood through interpretation. Interpretation tells the audience when, why, and under what conditions the units of analysis occur (Ryan & Bernard, 2000).

In some methodologies, models are created to illustrate the interpretation of the units of analysis. These models could include "concentric circles, each circle corresponding to a different level of influence" (Ryan & Bernard, 2000, p. 783). In other methodologies, constant comparison and key quotes are used to illustrate and exemplify the analysis. These quotes allow the reader "to understand quickly what it may have taken the researcher months or years to figure out" (Ryan & Bernard,

p. 784). The bringing back together of the data into their contextual whole is often referred to as the *hermeneutic circle* (van Manen, 1990) or *hermeneutic whole* (Hodder, 2000); in grounded theory, it would be considered axial coding (Strauss & Corbin, 1998). Examples of this process are seldom mentioned in the final product that presents the findings, but it is a critical process to reflect on. In Vasti's longitudinal study (Torres, 2004), the open-coding process created hundreds, even thousands, of potential codes. In the axial-coding process, these codes are grouped by similarities and differences into potential categories that provide more depth into the conditions that influence the phenomenon. The interpretation of trajectory relationships such as similarity, difference, analogy, and metaphor is mutually dependent upon the larger context (Hodder, 2000). Interpretation allows the reduced data to be brought back into the larger context. It is here in this larger context that the purpose of the research becomes realized, in improving educational practice.

In order to provide further examples of how methodology guides analysis, three methodologies and analysis strategies will be examined. First, a phenomenological process is explored; then grounded theory; and, finally, case study analysis is considered.

Phenomenological Analytic Process

In phenomenology a theme is most commonly understood to be an element that occurs frequently in a text or describes a unique experience that gets at the essence of the phenomenon under inquiry. Structures of experience are the units of analysis. Themes are understood as structures of experience (van Manen, 1990). More thoroughly, a "theme is the experience of focus, of meaning, of point. As a researcher reads over an anecdote, he or she asks, what is its meaning, its point?" (p. 87). Themes are "intransitive" (p. 87) because they lead the researcher to greater understanding but also to other paths. How is it that the researcher can encounter themes? According to van Manen, theme is the desire to make sense of something, as well as the sense the researcher is able to make of something. This occurs only when the researcher is open to something hidden and embedded in the text of life as it is experienced. It is through the process of finding, naming, and elaborating a theme that understanding of the phenomenon is heightened.

In the phenomenological study entitled "Voices of Gender Role Conflict," Davis (2002) identified five themes: importance of self-expression, code of communication caveats, fear of femininity, confusion about and distancing from masculinity, and a sense of challenge without support. These were common elements found throughout the text of participants' transcripts. However, what made these elements themes is described in the first line of Davis's description of his first theme. He wrote, "Contrary to the popular image of the inexpressive male, participants felt that self-expression and communication were very important to them" (p. 514). What made *importance of self-expression* a theme was not only that it was a common element throughout the tapestry of men's lived experience, but also that it contradicted the stereotype (oppositional relationship) of what was expected from men. The expressions used by these men were influenced by feelings of safety and were learned as appropriate ways of interacting with other men. Davis's openness to this relationship of difference, the lived experience of the men in his study from the experience Davis expected, allowed the illumination of this theme.

Grounded Theory Analytic Process

The process of analysis for grounded theory is systematic and structured. At the core of grounded theory is the researcher's need to constantly compare the emerging codes and categories with the data that have been collected or need to be collected. Through this process, the researcher may identify that additional participants need to be included in the sample in order to provide more richness to the understanding of the emergent theory. In constructivist grounded theory, there is recognition that knowledge is created mutually by the researcher and participants, while working toward an interpretive understanding of the participants' perspective and meaning (Charmaz, 2000). Chapter 2 of this text provides good examples of analysis in grounded theory.

Beginning stages of analysis in a grounded theory study begin by careful reading and rereading of transcripts. Key phrases and words are underlined in a line-by-line reading. In this microscopic phase, these words and phrases are then listed as possible codes in what is referred to as *open coding*. At this stage of the analysis a researcher can have several hundred, possibly as many as one thousand, possible codes that need to be reviewed for commonalities, differences, and relationships. From this phase of analysis, the researcher enters axial coding to pull the data back together into categories with conditions that describe aspects of an overarching category. Each condition within the category has a dimension that describes the continuum of possible aspects within the condition. As coding categories emerge, they are linked together in a theoretical model (Strauss & Corbin, 1998).

Case Study Analytic Process

The first step in case study analysis is identifying the unit of analysis. Case studies can involve a focus on multiple organizations, with each organization as a unit of analysis, or one organization with many members, making the embedded unit of analysis each individual member of the organization (Yin, 2004). The next step is to determine the theoretical perspective that guides the case study. Analysis using case study methodology can follow ethnographic, narrative, phenomenological, or grounded theory analysis techniques. Case studies can also use general analysis techniques used in qualitative research (Merriam, 1998). For this reason, it is important to acknowledge the theoretical perspective used in the case study and state that the analysis will be consistent with that perspective. Otherwise the researcher must justify why a more general approach to analysis will be used with the case study. Because examples of phenomenology and grounded theory analysis were previously illustrated, this section will focus on a general analysis technique to illustrate the analytic process.

Wolcott (1994) described the three primary categories for organizing and presenting qualitative data as description, analysis, and interpretation. Depending on the purpose of the study, the researcher can use one of these categories or all of them in some combination. The descriptive category considers "what is going on" through observations made by the researcher. The analysis category considers "how things work" by identifying features and systematic descriptions of relationships among data. And the interpretation category considers "what is to be made of it all" by providing a sense of meaning about data in the case study (Wolcott, p. 12). The three categories are not mutually exclusive, but the distinctions among them are helpful when the researcher wants a certain emphasis when organizing and presenting data.

DECISIONS ABOUT THE USE OF PREVIOUS RESEARCH

In order to maintain consistency with the previous chapters in this text, let's clarify the use of terms. *Theoretical framework* refers to previous research studies, or existing research, on the topic of interest. The review of literature is a common element of research and illustrates the understanding the researcher has toward the phenomenon of interest by providing an overview of the existing research. Most, if not all, journal and dissertation guidelines require the inclusion of a literature review. With this overview also comes an analysis of previous research designs and how the present methodology compares with previous studies. In many cases, the review of literature is expected to illustrate the researcher's knowledge about the topic and to justify the rationale for the present study (Hittleman & Simon, 2002). The issue that is seldom considered when conducting a literature review is how previous research or theories should or should not influence one's current perspective or the research design. For example, tension can result when researchers who see themselves as constructivist, who believe that meaning is constructed as a result of the interaction between humans and their world (Crotty, 1998), utilize previous literature conducted from a positivistic epistemological belief. The question that emerges is whether the previous literature informs the gathering and analysis of the data or suggests a more constructivist or open stance. The use of previous research is the process of linking "our research—and ourselves—with others" (Wolcott, 2002, p. 94). Too strong an emphasis on previous research can be viewed as having an *a priori* (presumptive) theory that has specific implications for the research design and analysis techniques used in the subsequent study.

The central issue in the process of linking one's own research study with the work of other researchers is how a researcher can use previous research to enhance, but not constrain, emerging findings. In grounded theory, this is referred to as *balancing one's theoretical sensitivity* (Glaser & Strauss, 1967/1999). Theoretical sensitivity is the depth of insight (knowledge of existing research) a researcher has about his or her area of research that allows her or him to make sense of emerging categories. Although a researcher would need to have sufficient theoretical sensitivity to conceptualize and formulate aspects of the study, there is also a need to not constrain possible new interpretations as a result of having this previous knowledge. Concerns about the use of previous research may not seem evident until the study is underway and issues arise about interpretation. For example, if a researcher is unable to separate what is known in the existing research from what might emerge from the data, a tension will emerge surrounding whether the study is confirming existing research or adding to the body of knowledge through a different lens. As a result, decisions about how to use previous research can be complex and at times difficult.

The approach that seems natural to many researchers is to treat the process of learning from previous research as independent from the linking of elements within the research design (paradigm, epistemology, theoretical perspective, methodology, and method). This tendency does not address the potential influence that previous research can have on understanding the phenomenon under consideration. Wolcott (2002) suggested that researchers select when links should be made to previous research and intentionally explain these choices to the reader. Examples of selecting when to link previous research with the present study would be to state its influence on the present study or to use previous research in making sampling decisions as necessary in grounded theory (Strauss & Corbin, 1998). In some cases, the linking of previous research may not occur until the discussion of the findings. Whatever choices researchers make, the key is to make them explicit with sufficient explanation for the audience to understand the approach selected.

The placement of theory in a qualitative study (e.g., in the beginning as a literature review or later after the findings) indicates the role that theory is playing in the study (Creswell, 2003). Researchers who expect to create theory use an inductive approach to theory building and are likely to consider existing theories toward the end of the study. The interplay between theory and the data must be considered as an influence, but not as a barrier to emerging conditions. Whether using theories *a priori* or *tabula rasa* (i.e., not at all, such as in a blank slate), it should be clearly stated how theory influences the study and what influence this decision has on the phenomenon under consideration.

In the study by Vasti (Torres, 2004) cited in Chapter 2 on the familial influences on the identity of Latino college students, several examples are given of explicit statements explaining how previous research influenced the theory-building process and the analysis of data. The first statement below is in reference to existing literature and is found in the introduction as part of the organizational statement for the article: "Because grounded theory methodology was used in this study, the review of literature is provided to illustrate the theoretical sensitivity that existed to help me conceptualize and formulate the theory that emerged from the data" (Torres, 2004, p. 457).

In this statement, Vasti made clear that theoretical sensitivity influenced the research process and her decisions. This statement also indicates that the existing literature did not guide the analysis process. The second example is found in the research design section of the article:

> An accepted process within grounded theory methodology is to consider the fluid nature of grounded theories as sets of concepts that can be elaborated and moderated to provide greater understanding of conceptual relationships (Strauss & Corbin, 1998). The existing research (Torres, 2003) is limited by a singular context and requires further exploration of the concepts demonstrated. The longitudinal design of this study supports the central process of constant comparison between data analysis and collection that is needed to create conceptually dense theory. (Torres, 2004, p. 459)

This statement introduces the process of theory building and how this study is linked to a previously published study (Torres, 2003). The statement also indicates why the theory building needed to continue and explains the researcher's decision to expand to multiple contexts. In the analysis section of the article, Vasti explicitly stated the process used and at what point the existing research was compared with the expanded sample. By providing in-depth information about the process and research decisions, Vasti justified the choices within the methodological literature while also maintaining congruence with previous research decisions.

The use of previous research can also influence the interpretation of the findings. An example of explicitly stating the influence of existing research in the analysis and interpretation phase can be found in a study of Black college students' faith development. This study was grounded in Afrocentric philosophy and influenced by hermeneutic theoretical perspectives. Stewart (2002) wrote in her analysis and findings section,

> Although Fowler's (1981) and Parks' (2000) faith-identity typology theory is presented as a means of interpreting and understanding the students individually and collectively, the faith-identity typology was not used as an a priori framework; rather, in the midst of the interviews, I searched for more literature related to the area of faith and spiritual development. The faith-identity typology stood out as being the most responsive to the stories that the students were telling me. (p. 584)

This statement clarified the process the researcher considered in regard to looking at existing research as well as clarifying its use and placement within the study.

In the first example, Vasti (Torres, 2004) used an inductive approach to existing theories and provided information about previous research because it was an expected portion of a research article and reviewers of academic journals would be expecting to see a review of literature (Creswell, 2003). In this case, the audience was considered as part of the writing process, and therefore, a short review of the literature was provided. In the second example, Stewart illustrated the interplay between data and existing theory that allowed propositions to be considered while also keeping a particular framework in mind. The key is to not let existing research become the mold for the data collection in the current study, but instead to maintain the fluidity of the interplay (Lather, 1986). This constant interplay is difficult to maintain and critical to congruency of the study.

DECISIONS ABOUT DATA COLLECTION AND THE ROLE OF THE RESEARCHER

Most researchers enter the data collection phase with excitement about the interesting information they will gather from their participants. What is seldom addressed in the research methodology literature is the evolving relationship between researcher and participant and issues that can arise regarding congruence and consistency. With the exception of the feminist methodology, phenomenology, and autoethnography, few researchers share their own reactions to the data collection process in their writings. The role of the researcher in the data collection process is an inherent aspect of the paradigm, epistemology, and methodology chosen. Although typically treated as an implicit dimension of a research project, the role of the researcher must become an explicit part of the design and presentation of results. The specifics of this relationship evolve as the data are collected and the relationship with the participants is explored rather than just conceptualized.

During the data collection process, these dimensions inherent in the researcher–participant relationship move to the foreground and present potential concerns that were not previously considered. The qualitative research literature refers to these issues using terms such as *subjectivity* (Peshkin, 1988), *objectivity* (Strauss & Corbin, 1998), and *trustworthiness* (Lincoln & Guba, 1985). Most of the literature in qualitative research encourages some degree of involvement with participants as a way to increase trust and rapport, yet the literature cautions the researcher to "also step back and see their [researchers'] own stories in the inquiry" (Clandinin & Connelly, 2000, p. 81). The tension between building rapport and maintaining appropriate distance to see the researcher's own story requires constant attention. This challenge was experienced by Vasti (Torres & Baxter Magolda, 2002) in her longitudinal study of Latino/a students in college. As a response, she chose to talk to a qualitative research mentor and eventually wrote about her experiences in a journal article (Torres & Baxter Magolda, 2002). In this article, Vasti explored how her own ethnicity and similarity of experiences to those shared in the students' stories caused her to reflect on herself as the instrument of the research. Having a false sense of control over the process (meaning that she was assuming that she could refrain from feeling such connections) gave way to an understanding of how the researcher can and should respond to these feelings during the research process. Researcher subjectivity is greatly influenced by the researcher's view of knowledge (epistemology) and the process used to create knowledge (methodology).

Feminist researchers embrace the development of a relationship with participants as a way to gain greater engagement and understanding into the phenomenon of interest (Reinharz, 1992). Generally accepted within the feminist research literature is the idea that "personal experiences [are] a valuable asset for feminist research" (Reinharz, p. 258). Most qualitative researchers look for research topics that stem from their own personal experiences. If a researcher is using a feminist theoretical perspective, then the issues involved with the researcher–participant relationship would always be at the forefront of the research process. This is also consistent with phenomenological approaches to research.

Congruence and consistency in the research design must include the role of the researcher and how the researcher understands the relationship between participants and researcher. In her book *Knowing and Reasoning in College: Gender-Related Patterns in Students' Intellectual Development*, Marcia Baxter Magolda (1992) chose to write the first chapter of the book about the research process she used and her own evolution toward understanding the creation of knowledge. In this chapter, she illustrated the evolving role of the researcher as well as explained how her perspective evolved from seeing her participants as the objects of her research to co-creators of knowledge in the analysis phase of her longitudinal project. When she began her study, she did not articulate her epistemology; rather, she focused primarily on conducting longitudinal interviews with students (method). In the data analysis stage, she began to experience dissonance between what her chosen analysis technique illustrated and what she heard from the student interviews. Although Baxter Magolda had statistical differences between men and women, the student interviews did not illustrate this difference. This is how she began resolving her dissonance: "My reconciliation of the students' stories with my computer printout occurred at a time when I was also exploring two other bodies of knowledge: naturalistic or constructivist inquiry and postmodern feminist literature" (Baxter Magolda, 1992, p. 14). This separate exploration of the "self" within the context of this research study created a "shift from assumptions of objectivity, generalization, and cause-effect relationships to assumptions of subjectivity, context-bound, and jointly shaped relationships" (pp. 15–16). This shift illustrated her movement toward a constructivist epistemology and greater congruence between the elements of her study. Later, Baxter Magolda admitted that at the onset of her study she was concerned with "treating participants fairly and ethically" (Torres & Baxter Magolda, 2002, p. 481), and after 15 years of sustained interaction her relationship has evolved toward the mutual construction of knowledge between researcher and participants.

Another example of this tension between self as a researcher and the participants can be found in Davis's (2002) study of men's identity. In the data analysis section of this article, Davis reported this tension:

> One of the greatest difficulties I had in analyzing the data was negotiating the Self-Other dynamic. . . . For me, this meant being aware that I might try to make the interview data fit my

preconceptions (Self) rather than allowing the participants (Other) to speak for themselves. I am drawn to the study of gender and men due to my own curiosity about the impact of gender on men's development, but I also have political, social, and cultural views related to this topic. I also clearly have biases associated with my own development as a White, heterosexual, Italian American male. (p. 512)

In this text, Davis explicitly stated his own role in the research and the influence his role had on the research process. Later, in the data analysis section of the article, Davis shared with the reader the techniques he used to manage this tension. The techniques he selected were consistent with his epistemology and methodology, thus maintaining congruence and consistency in the research process.

QUALITATIVE DATA ANALYSIS (QDA) SOFTWARE

The use of computer programs can also pose issues with maintaining congruence. Some qualitative researchers believe that in order for the researcher to truly function as the human instrument, the analysis cannot be assisted by computer software. It is important to understand that the role of the researcher is the critical instrument in the analysis process and that qualitative data analysis (QDA) programs can only assist, not take the place of, the researcher. If using computer software, the researcher must consider and be explicit with the reader regarding how such usage is consistent with the selected methodology.

Computer programs created for qualitative research are most often used in two ways: data management and theory construction (Richards & Richards, 1994). As data management tools, computer programs can assist in retrieving coded data in an orderly fashion. As a theory construction tool, the use of computer programs is more controversial (Denzin & Lincoln, 2000a). One of the major criticisms of these programs is that they impose a false sense of rational and linear relationships on data. This creates the impression that patterns exist within the data that were in fact created by the software and not the researcher. Greene (2000) expressed several reservations about qualitative software in grounded theory research with one illustrating the congruence between epistemology, methodology, and analysis technique. She stated, "These software packages appear more suited for objectivist grounded theory than constructivist approaches" (p. 520). Weitzman (2000) pointed out that QDA software can help with the data management, but the program does not analyze data for you. Qualitative data analysis software raises false hopes because researchers are lured into thinking they can do quick analyses, which presents the danger of prematurely closing in on theoretical ideas (Weitzman).

There are no clear-cut answers for how, when, or whether to use qualitative data analysis programs. However, there are several issues that are often presented for researchers to consider:

- Familiarity with the data: Using QDA software would not make this better or worse, but it does change how a researcher goes about getting familiar with data. The act of going back to the transcripts creates a familiarity with data that can be lost when using a software program that manages data for the researcher. The researcher's ability to "know" the data is critical to formulating and understanding relationships. Giving up that closeness to the data may influence the congruence and consistency of the process.
- Adapting methodology for the software available: Because the individuals developing software programs bring their own assumptions and theoretical frameworks, there is a possibility that the program selected may be based on different assumptions from those of the researcher. Most QDA programs will specifically state the methodologies they serve, yet these instructions may not address issues of paradigm or epistemology.
- Influence of software on the worthiness of the research: This issue can be interpreted both ways; software can diminish worthiness, or software can increase worthiness. Computer programs can find coded passages more quickly, thus allowing the researcher to see all possible building blocks of any code, but the program can also miss a passage if it was not coded to overlap with other codes (Weitzman, 2000).

The important issue to remember is that the researcher must understand and justify when and why the software was used. The quality of the study is based on how the researcher handled issues of congruence and consistency throughout the research process.

DECISIONS DEALING WITH TRUSTWORTHINESS

It is important to acknowledge that congruence and consistency are impacted by how researchers establish confidence in the research findings. This is trustworthiness (Lincoln & Guba, 1985). Although a more thorough treatment of the concept of trustworthiness can be found in Chapter 6, it is important to acknowledge here that an aspect of establishing the trustworthiness of a study is to ensure continuity and congruence among all the elements of the qualitative research process.

The process of establishing trustworthiness within a research study includes intentional behaviors that promote congruence. Perhaps the most critical aspect of congruence includes the ability to authenticate the findings with participants through member checks. The member-checking technique provides participants with the opportunity to react to the findings and interpretations that emerged as a result of his or her participation. In Vasti's and Jan's research (Arminio, 2001; Torres, 2004), the member checks also elicited more data regarding specific examples to illustrate the themes that emerged from the analysis. Through this technique, the researcher is able to complete the circle of authentication with participants by allowing them to provide input into the research process. If the circle is not completed, then there is lack of congruence with other elements of the research process. This technique is particularly important when there are social identity differences between the researcher and the participants. The member-checking process also raises issues about the desirability and plausibility of "verification of data" (Talburt, 2004). For example, in phenomenological studies, claiming factual accuracy is not as important as uncovering meaning that may be hidden for participants. However, the participants' ability to authenticate the findings is the primary means for assuring that the researcher understood and deepened the meaning of the experiences that represented the participants.

RECOMMENDATIONS TO CONSIDER

One of the most difficult aspects of conducting qualitative research is recognizing that there is no simple recipe to follow in order to ensure good research. Instead, each researcher must consider his or her decisions as issues arise within a study. For this reason, these recommendations are provided as a series of tools rather than answers:

- Chronicle research decisions: Many researchers use a research journal to help them remember the process of making decisions as well as the actual decisions. Journals can also provide a venue for reflection about the research decisions and prompt further questioning of subsequent issues that can emerge.
- Read original texts about paradigm, epistemology, and methodology: By reading the original text instead of secondary sources, the researcher integrates her or his own interpretation of these philosophical aspects. In addition, go back to these texts

periodically throughout the research process to force yourself to question your own understanding as it is emerging in the research process. Remember, this book is a secondary source. In all good research, secondary sources can be useful tools to begin the research process, but primary sources should always be used to make sure the researcher gains firsthand knowledge from those authors who first conceptualized an epistemology or theoretical perspective.

- Intentionally question research decisions: At each phase of the research process, take a moment to articulate (to yourself and someone else) how this phase fits with the previous choices made in the research process.
- Use a research auditor or mentor: Talking through research decisions with a more experienced researcher can help you think through ideas and provide different insights.
- Purposefully embed techniques to assist you as a researcher: For example, if the researcher and participants do not share similar social identities, what techniques will the researcher use to ensure that the voices of the participants were authentically understood? The inclusion of these techniques should be made intentionally and explicitly during the research design phase of the study.

SUMMARY

A qualitative researcher can anticipate dealing with some issues of congruence and continuity, but he or she must also be prepared to recognize the tensions that can unexpectedly arise during the process. Because the qualitative process usually includes human interaction, it would be impossible to predict all potential decision points. In this chapter, we have presented decisions and issues that are common in our experiences. It is our hope that in considering these decision points, the reader will be able to both anticipate and prepare for surprises that can occur during the qualitative research process.

EXERCISE

Write the identified epistemology, methodology, sample, and analysis techniques you will use with your collected data. Draw a diagram that depicts the relationship between these research elements. Depict how the epistemology, methodology, sample, and analysis connect and overlap. Make sure you note in your research journal how you see this analysis technique being consistent with your epistemology and methodology. What characteristics of your analysis are specific to the methodological approach?

5

INTERPRETATION AND REPRESENTATION: THE INFLUENCE OF SOCIAL IDENTITIES ON THE RESEARCH PROCESS

One of the issues that must be integrated into all phases of the research design, in order to maintain congruence in the research process, is the influence of your own social identities and the social identities of participants on the research process. This influence is particularly apparent in the interpretation of data and the way in which research participants are represented in the presentation of findings and discussion. The element of power is inherent in the relationship between the researcher and participant and gets played out in the interpretation and representation of participant stories. Power relations are present as a result of one's position as an authority or through race, gender, and social class privilege. Research may be seen as a mechanism of power without careful scrutiny about how power influences all aspects of a research design and particularly in regard to interpretation and representation. Because of how power operates in U.S. society and the pervasive nature of power, those conducting research both within and outside their own communities and social identities are influenced. This power element requires that the issue of social identities be carefully considered so that researchers recognize their own role and not "hide behind the alleged cloak of neutrality" (Weis & Fine, 2000, p. 34).

Social identities "are those roles [e.g., parent] or membership categories [e.g., race, ethnicity, or others] that a person claims as representative" (Deaux, 1993, p. 6), and they are distinguished from personal identity, which refers to traits, behaviors, and characteristics (Deaux). Social identities include gender, ethnicity and/or race, social class, sexual orientation, religion, or disabilities. When a research project includes interaction with individuals who belong to one, or more, of these social identities, it is critical to consider the impact this may have on the project and decisions the researcher must make. Researchers must pay attention to the role of social identities within the context of any research study. In addition, researchers should understand their own position by examining what social statuses they possess (either visibly or unconsciously) that illustrate power or privilege and they should recognize how their own social identities might be perceived by those with differing social identities.

Feminist researchers use the term *standpoint research* to refer to research that focuses on "women's experiences in everyday life as it is familiar to them" (Madriz, 2000, p. 838). At the core of feminist research is the belief that there is no one truth or authority (Reinharz, 1992). This core belief is the basis for acknowledging the influence of one's own identity and sociocultural history on the research process. An example of this would be when a researcher positions herself according to her race or ethnicity, indicating that it is an important element in the research process. For example, Ayala (2000) stated, "The second voice speaks through standpoint theory, where I position myself as a Latino researcher whose interpretations stem from theory and biography" (p. 102). A researcher's position indicates the influences that come from his or her own social identities. Acknowledging one's position in the context of the research helps the audience understand the influence of social identities on the research process.

Interpretation of data and representation of participants are linked to the concepts of positioning and standpoint. The notion of understanding one's own position (or standpoint) also describes taking into account the experiences and social identities of the researcher and those being studied, while considering how societal structures have constrained marginal, oppressed, or dominated groups (Durham, 1998). Understanding one's standpoint and position before entering into a research project is imperative so as to guard against hearing, seeing, reading, and presenting results that conform to the researcher's experiences and assumptions about self and other, rather than honoring the participants' voice in the study. A researcher must understand his or her position and power within societal structures in order to attend to her or his potential biases. Researchers must also guard against assuming their experiences are similar to those of their participants. Without reflection on the influence of social identities in the research process, interpretation and representation become more about telling the researcher's story and less about staying true to the words and stories of participants. Lincoln (1997) made this point well:

> Research participant's (subject's) words were used to provide evidence of some point which researchers wished to make (indeed, I have chosen particular quotations from my research respondents for exactly and precisely the same reason—to buttress some point of my own interpretation, not necessarily a point of theirs). (p. 43)

It is important to clarify whose story is being told and to clarify for the reader how the participants' words are being interpreted.

This chapter will focus on the intense work in which a researcher must engage when designing a study and collecting and analyzing data involving individuals whose social identities are different from or similar with the researcher's identity. The potential issues that can emerge are described by Duneier (2004) as he began an ethnographic study:

> Though there were also differences between our social classes (I was raised in a middle-class suburb, whereas most of them grew up in lower- and working-class urban neighborhoods), religions (I am Jewish and most them are Muslim or Christian), levels of education (I hold a Ph.D. in sociology and attended 2 years of law school, whereas some of them did not graduate from high school), and occupations (I am a college professor of sociology and they are street vendors), none of these differences seemed to be as significant as that of race. Actually, the interaction between race and class differences very likely made me uneasy, though I was unaware of that at the time. (p. 206)

In this statement Duneier acknowledged differences, but also recognized that he was unaware of his own uneasiness at the time he began his study. Although it is naïve to think that differences in social identities will not influence a qualitative study, Duneier's admission of unawareness demonstrates the taken-for-granted assumptions about differences and commonalities in the research process. This chapter seeks to help researchers become more cognizant of the issues that arise as a result of differences.

In order to explore the nature and influences of social identities on the research process, four areas will be discussed: (a) researcher position or the interaction with the same or different social identities, (b) power relationships and their influence on persons oppressed by social power structures, (c) the evolving role of the researcher in qualitative research, and (d) reflexivity.

RESEARCHER POSITIONALITY

How a researcher positions him or herself within a research study is critical to understanding the lens used to interpret the data. Ayala (2000) referred to this as "voicing my position(ality)" (p. 103). She described her voice in this manner:

> I write as a Latina, embodying what Hidalgo (1998) calls an "overlapping insider/outsider status." This affects how I interview, what I find, how I interpret what I find. An insider to the community of respondents I am interviewing, I share the Latino cultural citizenship. . . . My outsider status stems from the stretch of our educational, national, and generational differences. (p. 103)

In a description of her positionality, Ayala is clear how her insider status impacts the research process (approach to interviewing and the interpretation of the data), but she also makes clear what makes her an outsider (education, nationality, and generation). In this quote, Ayala illustrated the process of working the hyphen (Fine, 1994)—she is both an insider (by virtue of having similar ethnic identity) and outsider (by virtue of education and generational status), making it important to understand both insider and outsider perspectives and to actively engage in reflection that promotes an appreciation between both. Understanding both positions is important to the research process and allows the researcher to work the hyphen in different ways depending on the issue at hand and the research context. Without this understanding, the researcher's bias dominates the interpretation and analysis of the research process.

Another example of understanding the researcher's positionality is relayed by Merchant (2001), who is White, in her story about working with a research assistant (Martha) from another ethnicity (Mexican) on a project looking at immigrant Mexican students in a rural high school. Merchant reflected,

Because I am a Euro-American, the teachers saw me as "one of them," whereas they construed Martha's ethnicity as oppositional to theirs. The extent to which ethnic subjectivities conditioned not only the teachers' and administrators' response to Martha and me, but our interactions with them, was complicated by the fact that our study focused on the experiences of newly immigrated, limited- and non-English speaking Mexican students in the school. (p. 5)

This acknowledgment of differences in perception and positionality ultimately led Merchant to shift her stance and clarify that her focus during the research study was on understanding and not advocacy. This decision not only was difficult but also impacted the research process as well as the researchers. She acknowledged, "The majority of my interactions with Agriville staff were conditioned by perceptions of shared identities that were revealed as the year progressed" (p. 15). Perhaps even more moving is her admission "that I 'understood' their 'oppression'—when in fact, I could not" (p. 15). Despite her grasp of the literature about White researchers in contexts different from their own and her intellectual knowledge about the tendency of White researchers to speak for the other, she realized that was "not enough to prevent me from lapsing into culturally biased patterns of research" (p. 15). Although this understanding of herself as a researcher is important, Merchant came to understand,

Although I believe that it is essential to continue examining the ways in which my race and ethnicity, subjectivities, positionalities, and views of research shape not only my motives, but my actions, I am convinced that self-reflection is not enough. (p. 17)

Conversations between researchers and their participants or trusted advisors, held earlier in the research process, could prevent the dynamics that emerged during their study. These dialogues, however, are difficult and require trust, respect, and openness (Merchant, 2001). Later in this chapter, you will see how the positionality of Merchant's research assistant, Martha Zurita, who is a Mexican American, impacted her involvement in the research and reflections upon that process.

In feminist cross-cultural research, caution is offered about comparisons with one's own societal status. Feminist research encourages researchers to study their own experiences. In essence, it is virtually impossible for feminist researchers to avoid making comparisons between their own culture and the culture under study (Reinharz, 1992).

The response to this dilemma is to encourage women from within the culture under study to collaborate with the researcher on the research project so that voices of insiders and outsiders are included in the process. Although intragroup belonging is helpful in understanding different cultures, it is by no means a simple task to be an insider either. When Vasti began her longitudinal work with Latino/a college students, she considered being an insider (Latina) as an advantage in her approach to the research. What she did not expect was the personal reaction that occurred as a result of being an insider. In an article focused on the process of research, Vasti wrote,

> I found myself wanting to be a practitioner rather than a researcher. This desire arose as students told me their stories; some of them resembled my own story. Because this study is on a predominantly Anglo campus, this was the first time several of the freshmen felt comfortable talking about their conflicting feelings and the struggles they were experiencing around the choices they were forced to make about their culture of origin and the environment in which they live at college. (Torres & Baxter Magolda, 2002, p. 479)

These conflicting feelings and reactions caused Vasti to question her stance as a researcher and whether or not she was tending to the students or being more focused on maintaining her role as a researcher. Over time, Vasti established a rapport with the participants in her study that allowed her to explore issues seldom mentioned in the literature. Yet this rapport comes with responsibility to interpret the students' voices in a way that is authentic to their experiences. This demonstrates that even when ethnicity and culture are taken into account, the researcher can still experience difficult situations.

One of the elements that is most influenced by differences (and commonalities) in social identities is the analytic and interpretive process. The interpretation of the data is inevitably impacted by our own experiences and worldview. This reality requires that special attention be given to how our own and the participants' social identities influence what is said and what is understood.

For example, in a recent thesis chaired by two faculty members, both of whom identified as members of the gay, lesbian, bisexual, and transgendered (GLBT) community, a graduate student explored the experiences of undergraduate students who identified as allies to GLBT students. The researcher considered herself an ally. This identification and positionality as both researcher and ally influenced how she understood what her participants said and how she interpreted their stories.

One of her participants told a story about a friend who occasionally told gay jokes. However, the participant rationalized this by suggesting that the friend didn't tell jokes in front of gay people and really didn't mean to be offensive. Because the researcher so wanted to tell the positive story (her story) of ally behavior, she did not deal with this comment in the initial stages of analysis. Because she was, in essence, writing about her advisors' social identities, they were able to engage the researcher in conversations about what really constitutes ally behavior. The differences in interpretation are critical to understanding the phenomenon under study and impact whose story is really being told. The result was a much more nuanced and complex analysis and interpretation of her data that emphasized the situational nature of ally behavior, rather than starting from the premise that her participants were always engaging in ally behavior (Gribbin, 2005).

Other examples might include the study of women without considering the sociohistorical forces that influence societal views of women. Using theoretical perspectives that are focused on majority White students and imposing that perspective on students of color is a frequent, and misguided, decision that some researchers make. All of these examples illustrate the importance of understanding how the researcher's social identity can impact the study and representation of the other. This understanding is critical to reflexivity, which is a necessary element of the goodness in the research process. Goodness requires researchers to recognize themselves, their relationships with those involved in the study, and their relationship with the topic itself. This occurs through reflexivity.

POWER RELATIONSHIPS

Within the qualitative research literature, much has been written about the relationship between the researcher and participants. The literature refers to this relationship between the knower (researcher) and known (participant) as having an evolutionary process that goes from a separateness orientation (objective) to an orientation where inquiry is a form of interaction that influences both the knower and the known (co-construction of knowledge) (Lincoln & Guba, 1985). One area not always discussed in this literature is the existence of power differences in the self-other relationship. Ely (1991) referenced the process of "becoming the other" as an attempt to see research from the lens of the participants (p. 49). Lincoln and Guba (1985), in addition to Ely, acknowledged the role of the researcher, but seemed to minimize the inherent impact of power differences within the research process by suggesting the response should be to handle the situation. Weis and Fine (2000) more accurately referred to this process as working the hyphen between self (researcher) and other (participant). As quoted in Chapter 3,

> Working the hyphen means creating occasions for researchers and informants to discuss what is, and is not, "happening between," within the negotiated relations of whose story is being told, why, to whom, [and] with what interpretation, and whose story is being shadowed, why, for whom, and with what consequence. (Fine, 1994, p. 72)

"Coming clean at the hyphen" (Fine, Weis, Weseen, & Wong, 2000, p. 123) is especially critical in understanding how the researcher talks about the other or speaks in place of the other. In other words, interpretation of data and representation of participants are integrally linked to scrutiny of researcher positionality and standpoint.

Privilege and power must be acknowledged in the research process in order to appropriately work the hyphen and understand, to the best of our abilities, the experiences of participants from different social identities. Racism, sexism, and other isms are part of the fabric that makes up the national identity of the United States and can only change when the power hierarchies are changed (Torres, Howard-Hamilton, & Cooper, 2003). In many cases, researchers do not analyze their positions of power and privilege or recognize their own actions as oppressive (Ladson-Billings, 1998). Consequently, researchers must acknowledge the potential position of power they hold as researchers and as a result of their social identities. Researchers must then work through the messiness of understanding the influence these different positions have on the research process and their role as researchers in perpetuating the inequalities and oppressions.

One example many researchers take for granted is the use of the informed consent form and the power imbalances this form represents between researcher and participant. Weis and Fine (2001) came to the understanding that "[t]he introduction of an informed consent form requires analysis as much as that which is routinely and easily considered data" (p. 42). Fine elaborated that rapport can be unraveled when this form (informed consent) is given to the participant because what the form actually sets out is the differential power relationships between researcher and participant. Although many researchers downplay the differences, we believe it is also important to acknowledge the potential power differences as part of the research process. Chapter 8 provides further discussion of the role and ethics of the informed consent form.

In his study, Duneier (2004) reflected on his experiences and acknowledged that one cannot

> begin with the assumption that special rapport or trust is always a precondition for doing successful fieldwork. And don't be so presumptuous as to believe that you have trust or even special rapport with the people you are trying to write about, even when it seems you do. (p. 209)

This statement articulates the reality that researchers must face when working from a position of power and privilege, particularly in making decisions about how to conduct the study, what to ask participants, how to interpret and represent what they hear from participants, and what implications will be suggested. All of these decisions are made by the researcher and ultimately must be made explicit to the audience in order for those hearing or reading the research to know how a particular phenomenon was investigated and the influences that arose as a result of the interaction between the participants and the researcher. It is important for researchers to understand their positions and wrestle with what it means to experience events, situations, or interactions differently than the participants in the research study. Not seeing the differences dismisses the participants' sense of identity and can interfere with understanding the experiences being studied.

Because there are so many ways in which researchers can unintentionally exert power, this chapter can only skim the surface of these possibilities. For this reason, the lens of critical race theory (CRT) will be used to understand the intensity of inherent power roles. Because understanding and interpreting the experiences of others are central to qualitative research, CRT can be a powerful tool. The lens used by CRT can help researchers understand the impact of social differences in all methodological approaches. CRT has its origins in legal studies, where scholars attempted to illustrate how legal doctrines helped create and support the class structure in the United States that legitimizes racism (Ladson-Billings, 1998). Researchers utilizing CRT are "interested in studying and transforming the relationship among race, racism, and power" (Delgado & Stefancic, 2001, p. 2). A main tenet of CRT is that race is central to the analysis of institutions and societal standards (Parker, 1998). CRT can be used as a theoretical perspective that guides and influences the methodology of a study. Even if you do not plan to use CRT in your study, the principles of CRT are useful for understanding the dynamics of interpretation and representation in qualitative research. CRT "provides a framework to understand the centrality of racism in schools and university settings" (Parker, p. 49). At the core of CRT are three concerns:

(a) the deconstruction of structures that oppress, (b) the reconstruction of value for every human being, and (c) the construction of equal power among all involved (Ladson-Billings). Though some researchers attempt to carry out "color-blind" studies, CRT advocates that to deny race, ethnicity, and other social identities is to perpetuate a myth of equality that is not reality for all individuals (Parker). For this reason, it is crucial to understand the reality of socially constructed identities and create a design that enables participants within a qualitative study to express their own reality. This is central to understanding and interpreting participants' experiences (Ladson-Billings).

One of the consequences of not enabling participants to express their own reality is that researchers may impose their own experiences (privilege) on the words, behaviors, or experiences of the participants. When Vasti began her longitudinal study on the experiences of Latino/a college students (Torres, 2004), she used a research team as inquiry auditors during the analysis phase. During this process, a White research team member would interpret a behavior by using the norms of the majority White societal status rather than understanding the status of the participant. One example that emerged early on in the study is the understanding of autonomy. For many Anglos (Whites), autonomy entails separation from parents and independent thinking that is not influenced by parents (Erikson, 1968). Within many Latino cultures, separation from parents is not culturally acceptable and independent thinking is seen as making one's choice within the context of the family. These two interpretations of autonomy and the types of decisions that first-year Latino/a students relayed in the interview created many challenging and value-oriented discussions among the research team. These discussions allowed each of us to explore our biases and worldviews. The discussion and reflection process demonstrates how the three concerns of CRT—(a) the deconstruction of structures that oppress, (b) the reconstruction of value for every human being, and (c) the construction of equal power among all involved—can be addressed. The deconstruction of structures that oppress occurred when the White person's value of autonomy was inferred, but confronted by members of the team who are not from the majority culture. The reconstruction of value for every human being occurred when those involved entered into a dialogue. The construction of equal power among all involved occurred when multiple interpretations of autonomy were considered.

Ladson-Billings (1998), in her writings about CRT, emphasized the process of integrating the shared history between the researcher and participants as part of the analytic standpoint within studies using CRT.

The shared history between individuals from similar backgrounds allows for an understanding of the common culture and ongoing struggles that are inherent in the oppression of nonmajority participants. She also cautioned, "To the extent that Whites (or in the case of sexism, men) experience forms of racial oppression, they may develop such a standpoint" (p. 11). This is important to note regardless of the philosophical or theoretical framework an individual chooses; her caution speaks to the interpretive ability of one who does not share the same lived experience. Not having a similar lived experience causes a different set of tensions that a researcher must consider and work through. In the example above, the White research team member may have come to understand her culturally biased assumptions about what autonomy is by connecting her own experiences of being misunderstood with how she misunderstood Vasti's Latino participants. The use of inquiry auditors is one of the techniques recommended to establish trustworthiness in the research process and, in the example provided, illustrates how issues of trustworthiness are connected to positionality and standpoint. Trustworthiness is one of the elements of goodness and is discussed in more detail in Chapter 6.

Although this section discussed several examples dealing with researchers from outside the groups (outsider) studying the other, it is also important to recognize that issues can emerge for researchers from the same social identity (insider).

EVOLVING ROLE OF THE RESEARCHER

The previous examples illustrate the dynamics of social identities and positionality that occur during the research process. In the Merchant (2001) example, her stance in the research was reexamined and her reflections allowed her to recognize her own limitations in understanding the issues involved in researching an ethnic group different from her own. Vasti's reflection about her interaction with the participants in her study illustrated that "[p]erhaps the most significant impact of this study has been my own evolution as a researcher" (Torres & Baxter Magolda, 2002, p. 480). Vasti acknowledged that to assure the quality of the research, she must balance her own interpretations with the voices of the participants, allowing students to create their own meaning from their experiences instead of imposing her meaning on the experiences of the students.

As researchers, we must make choices about how to approach our research, and many of these choices can conflict with our own identities. Zurita, the research assistant working with Merchant, faced a different type of dilemma in her reaction to their research at a rural high school

(Zurita, 2001). Zurita's participation in the study caused her to rethink her responsibilities as a researcher studying her own ethnic community. She learned that she could not sit by and "study" oppressive and unjust situations, but instead needed to function as an advocate and intervene in the research because she understood the experiences of the immigrant Mexican students. Her conflict was that by participating in the research, she was also allowing these students to fail because she knew their needs were not being met and was not taking steps to work against the inequalities she witnessed. In reflecting on her experiences, she admitted that she learned a great deal about being a Mexican researcher. She described the impact of her positionality by acknowledging,

> The process of conducting research is not the same for everyone, and this process is shaped, in part, by the researcher's race and ethnicity in ways that are only now being made explicit. Educational researchers can teach you how to take field notes and code and analyze data, but do they tell you how to deal with the interpersonal issues that result from the intersection of your research activities and your race or ethnicity? Oftentimes, professors and other researchers act as if the research site is a lab—straightforward and controlled. It may be that easy for some researchers, especially those who claim that race does not matter. Those of us for whom it is a factor, however, have to fend for ourselves, despite our disillusionment when we realize things are not as clear-cut as we have been led to believe. (Zurita, p. 31)

These issues raised by Zurita are at the heart of understanding the influence of social identities on the research process. Each researcher has to reflect on and acknowledge these influences as part of the process in order to truly work the hyphen of "self" and "other."

Reflexivity

How one responds to those involved in the study and the topic itself is probably the most elusive but important criterion of goodness or worthy research. Ballard (1996) poignantly stated,

> We have critiqued the research method as if it were the foundation of our work. It is now time to look at the ghost in these research machines, that is ourselves. This means focusing on research as an essentially human activity and as therefore embedded in personal, social, cultural, political, historical, spiritual and gendered bodies and contexts. (p. 103)

An intent of qualitative work, as discussed in Chapters 3 and 4 and to be discussed in Chapter 6, is to provide an avenue for previously silenced voices to be heard. However, in the process of listening and describing, these voices are interpreted. hooks (1990) reminded us that as a researcher,

> I want to know your story. And then I will tell it back to you in a new way. Tell it back to you in such a way that it has become my own. Re-telling you. I write myself anew. I am still author, authority. I am still the colonizer, the speak subject, and you are at the center of my talk. (pp. 151–152)

To meet the criteria of goodness, researchers "must not portray themselves as experts of others' experiences" (Arminio & Hultgren, 2002, p. 455). Rather, increased knowledge arises from dialogue between researcher and participant (Gitlin, 2000). Yet, how we negotiate and manage this self-other relationship influences trustworthiness because "self and other are knottily entangled" (Fine, 1994, p. 72). As the previous example of Merchant (2001) illustrated, this can be especially worrisome in studies that require crossing distinct cultural perspectives.

Built into the research design should be an articulation of researcher assumptions. In the written report, researchers must address how or whether their assumptions changed during the research process. Also, how the researcher recruited, came to know, and think about the participants must be explicit in the explanation of the research design (Lather, 2003). This takes the form of what is referred to as *reflexive subjectivity* (Lather, 2003) or *reflexivity* (Glesne, 1999; Smith, 1993; Smith & Deemer, 2000). Regarding reflexivity, Gergen and Gergen (2000) wrote that researchers must seek

> ways of demonstrating to their audiences their historical and geographical situatedness, their personal investments in the research, various biases they bring to the work, their surprises and "undoings" in the process of the research endeavor, the way choices of literary tropes lend rhetorical force to the research report, and/or the ways in which they have avoided or suppressed certain points of view. (p. 1027)

Researchers must include in their research design ways in which they will demonstrate to their audience how they situate themselves historically and geographically, as well as their personal investment in the research. This often occurs in either the introduction or the end of the literature review when a researcher informs the reader about how he or she came to see the research questions or why one is compelled to study this question.

SUGGESTIONS ABOUT THE IMPACT OF SOCIAL IDENTITIES ON THE RESEARCH PROCESS

Throughout this chapter, the constant focus is on being aware of your own lens and position in order to understand your own reaction and the reaction of others to differences. In qualitative research, the researcher is the interpreter of the data, and one of the elements of goodness is to consider one's positionality. This is at the core of trustworthiness (establishing confidence in the findings) and methodological stance. The following suggestions are offered to assist researchers in making connections between their own social identities and the influence of these identities on the interpretation of data and representation of participants in qualitative inquiry.

- If this chapter is the first place you heard of the concepts of privilege and power in research, then you need to do much more reading on these issues. Being naïve or ignorant about these issues can potentially harm participants of a study. As a researcher, it is your responsibility to do no harm.
- Make sure you understand what social identity groups you belong to and which ones you do not. For example, if you are from a privileged group, it is critical that you explore why you would consider studying a less privileged group. Only through understanding your own privilege can you begin to understand the lack of privilege others have.
- Articulate to yourself and others why you are choosing to do research on a population that is different from your own social identity. Make sure you are the best person to conduct this type of research. The act of talking/writing/reading about this decision will allow you to reflect and hear/read yourself speak/write about the issues and promote discussion about your own identity and the identity of participants.
- Make sure you reflect on how your own identity may interact with different social identities and how you will respond to that interaction. Do not assume you will be trusted—that assumption illustrates your privilege and power, not understanding and empowerment.
- Insert into the research design elements to ensure that you are conducting a good study. Chapter 6 provides more insight into these elements and how to incorporate them into the research

design and process. Your positionality and lens influence the goodness of the entire process and the level of respect given to the voices of the participants.

- Acknowledge that there are multiple perspectives to any issue, and work to hear and understand those perspectives. Techniques that can be used include who you choose as a peer debriefer or inquiry auditor. Care should be given to this choice. Convenience is not sufficient reason.

SUMMARY

In this chapter, we attempted to bring to the forefront the importance of understanding differences, similarities, and one's own social identities. Part of understanding one's own social identities is to reflect on the privileges that come with any one identity and how that is perceived by others, most notably participants in a study. Throughout this chapter, examples are provided about the insider and outsider perspective, as well as how those perspectives can sometimes blur together. It is our desire to promote more responsible researchers who are aware of their own influence and actively take steps to understand others.

EXERCISE

Identify and list the social identities you possess. Adjacent to this, identify the privileges and stereotypes of these social identities. Reflect on how these identities will interact with the proposed focus of your study and the sample of participants you want to research. Be very specific in identifying the potential issues that may emerge as you research within and/or outside of your own social identities. Ask a colleague from a different social identity to look at your list and make any suggestions. Identify and list ways to ensure that differing interpretations will be respected within the research process. You may want to use the bulleted points above as beginning suggestions.

6

ENSURING GOODNESS OF QUALITATIVE RESEARCH

The stimulus for this book and some of our previous writing came as a response to our judgments about some of the qualitative manuscripts we reviewed in the higher education literature. For example, we read published manuscripts written by researchers masquerading their quantitative studies as qualitative work. Authors of one manuscript indicated that data from "phenomenological interviews" were used to conduct a statistical analysis. Likewise, it would also be inappropriate for researchers to claim that a study is grounded in phenomenology when there is nothing phenomenological about the research approach or method of collecting and analyzing data. Furthermore, several books exist about general research and assessment, written by experienced and reputable quantitative researchers who write "add-on" qualitative research chapters with little of the important grounding information on epistemology, ontology, theoretical perspective, and methodology. When we asked faculty and staff members about their dissertation research, some indicated they conducted a qualitative dissertation. When probed with the question "What methodology did you use?" the response was too often

"You know, qualitative. I conducted interviews." As will be examined below, these are all examples of poor qualitative work.

Many institutions of higher education list critical thinking, using sound criteria on which to base an idea or opinion, as one of the principal goals of student learning (Baxter Magolda, 2001). Judging the merit of inquiry is an outgrowth of the concern with how to distinguish between "true and false appearances" and "belief or opinion," which dates back to ancient Greek philosophers (Smith, 1993, p. 3).

Because criteria for judging the worthiness of an argument or a study have traditionally been grounded in the positivistic paradigm, a conundrum exists related to judging qualitative work. This conundrum revolves around these questions, the exploration of which is the purpose of this chapter:

1. Should qualitative studies be judged on different criteria than quantitative studies? If there are to be criteria for judging the worthiness of a qualitative study, upon what are these criteria based?
2. How should qualitative studies be judged? Does "anything go"? (Smith & Deemer, 2000).
3. Because of the wide array of research traditions in the qualitative paradigm (e.g., grounded theory, case study, phenomenology, ethnography, and narrative), can there be criteria appropriate for all of them?

Let us begin this examination by being clear that, contrary to some criticism of qualitative research, "anything" does not go (Smith & Deemer, 2000, p. 878). According to Smith and Deemer, some poor qualitative work is merely an assertion lacking an articulated grounding that provides a framework for the research design and findings. Even though qualitative work acknowledges relativism, "As individuals, we must make judgments, and as members of social groups, however loosely organized, we must be witness to situations in which our individual judgments are played out with the judgments of other individuals" (Smith & Deemer, p. 887).

According to Smith and Deemer (2000), there has been a demise of objectivism, and consequently no objective "God's-eye view" (p. 880). When it comes to human behavior, even a judgment about a factual account requires a shared framework (Smith, 1993). Judging the worthiness of qualitative inquiry is not determined upon whether or not the researcher conducted the correct procedures as in quantitative research (Smith, 1993). Rather, a study's participants, readers, and discipline all are involved in the judgment process through dialogue centering on criteria. Consensus is reached about judgments of research through reading, dialogue, discourse, and subsequent research. Hammersley (1990) called this a communal assessment. Lincoln (1998) also referred to the community as an arbiter of quality.

WHAT LANGUAGE IS USED IN THIS COMMUNAL ASSESSMENT?

Most readers are probably familiar with terms such as *trustworthiness* and *validity* in determining the quality of a study. Several researchers have advocated for the use of the term *goodness* to indicate quality criteria in qualitative inquiry (Arminio & Hultgren, 2002; Lincoln & Guba, 2000; Marshall, 1990; Smith, 1993). This allows for the "breaking out from the shadow" of quantitative criteria and allows "the *qualis* of qualitative work to be pursued on its own terms" (Arminio & Hultgren, 2002, p. 446). As mentioned in Chapter 2, the word *qualitative* is a derivative of the word *qualis*, meaning "what it is," and is often judged by what it is not—values and criteria from a positivistic paradigm. The etymology of the word *rigor*, often used to depict the criteria of quantitative work, is stiffness, exactness, and severity (Hoad, 1986). Though some qualitative researchers use rigor as a criterion for judging their work, in order to move research in higher education away from using quantitative criteria to judge the worthiness of qualitative work, we promote describing it on its own terms and as such embrace the concept of goodness.

Because qualitative work is grounded on foundations far different from those of quantitative work, it is only reasonable that criteria for evaluating research grounded in different epistemologies be different. Yet, we can also state that some criteria for worthiness cross all research paradigms. Howe and Eisenhart (1990) wrote that there should be both general guidelines that encompass all research and specific criteria for separate "disciplines" of research (p. 6). Regardless of the research paradigm, they believed that the following are criteria for determining the worth of any study.

- First, consistency of epistemology must exist between the research question, data collection, and analysis procedures. The "research question should drive data collection techniques and analysis rather than vice versa" (Howe & Eisenhart, 1990, p. 6).
- Second, collection and analysis procedures must be correctly and "competently" applied.

- Third, researchers must be aware of the background knowledge of the topic (theoretical framework, as discussed in Chapter 1) and background assumptions of the researcher connecting this study with previous studies. "If the results of one study contradict those of another (or several others), then some sort of explanation of why this occurred is in order" (Howe & Eisenhart, p. 6).
- Fourth, the researcher must differentiate why some conclusions were embraced and others discounted.
- Lastly, researchers must articulate the value of this study to practice in a language that is accessible to a wide range of readers. This allows for the necessary opportunity for debate within the discipline (Howe & Eisenhart).

J.K. Smith (1993) believed that all research should provide evidence that it is reasonable, responsive to challenges presented during the process, open to others' points of view, and honest.

We concur that these are appropriate skeletal criteria for determining the worthiness of a study. We also believe, however, that additional specific criteria should be added to these general criteria to more thoroughly address goodness. Figure 6.1 depicts criteria on a continuum from general to more specific. There are criteria for all research as described previously, and then criteria become more specific according to epistemological views and methodological approaches.

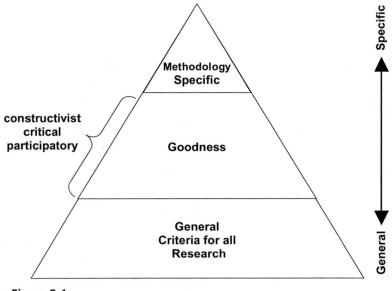

Figure 6.1

A number of authors have written on the criteria for conducting a worthy study. In Table 6.1, we have arranged these references according to the elements of goodness within the chronology of a research design process. We offer these elements of goodness and their characteristics to provide guidance for conducting inquiry as well as for judging the worth of inquiry.

Table 6.1 Elements of Goodness

Epistemology and Theory: The Foundation (Arminio & Hultgren, 2002)
Triangulation of theories (Lather, 2003)

Methodology: The Approach (Arminio & Hultgren, 2002)
Design guided by methodology (Arminio & Hultgren, 2002)

Method (Arminio & Hultgren, 2002; Stage & Manning, 2003)
Triangulation of methods and data sources (Lather, 2003)

Researcher and Participant as Multicultural Subjects: The Representation of Voice (Arminio & Hultgren, 2002)
Autobiographical rendering (Arminio & Hultgren, 2002)
Examining the self-other hyphen (Fine, 1994)

Interpretation and Presentation: The Act of Meaning Making (Arminio & Hultgren, 2002)
Trustworthiness (establishing confidence in the findings, truth value; Glesne, 1999; Lincoln & Guba, 1985; Morse & Richards, 2002)
Reflexive subjectivity (documentation of how the researcher's assumptions have been affected by the data; Lather, 2003)
Prolonged engagement (Glesne, 1999)
Documentation that the research process has led to insight and action (referred to as catalytic validity; Lather, 2003); audit trail (Whitt, 1991)
Peer and/or expert review; human science dialogue (van Manen, 1997)

Triangulation (that interpretations are credible, Lincoln & Guba, 1985; multiple methods to confirm findings, Morse & Richards, 2002)
Recycling of the emerging analysis and conclusions back through at least a subsample of participants (referred to by Lather as *face validity*, and referred to by Glesne, 1999, and Lincoln & Guba, 1985, as *member checking*)
Credibility (Hammersley, 1990)
Plausibility (Hammersley, 1990)
Applicability (Hammersley, 1990)

Recommendations: The Implications for Professional Practice
Documentation that the research process has led to insight and action (referred to as *catalytic validity*; Lather, 2003)
Frame inquiries to prompt action (Lincoln, 1998)
Relevance (Hammersley, 1990)

To meet the criteria of goodness, researchers must embody, discuss, and illustrate the elements of goodness in a language consistent with the philosophical grounding being used (Arminio & Hultgren, 2002). These elements of goodness address epistemology and theoretical perspective, methodology, method, researcher, and participants as multicultural subjects in the representation of voice, analysis and presentation, and recommendations for professional practice. It is important to keep in mind that unlike the objective positivistic paradigm, there is no "mechanical-making procedure" (J. K. Smith, 1990, p. 184) for determining worthiness of the study. Instead, worthiness is determined by the reader and by discussion and debates within the educational community. On the outset, this may seem vague, but it is necessary due to the nature and context of the work itself (J. K. Smith, 1990).

EPISTEMOLOGY AND THEORY: THE FOUNDATION

Studies must be grounded in an epistemological and theoretical stance. Goodness requires that the stance is stated and that evidence is offered that the stance was followed. Unfortunately, we have noticed that some published studies do not state their epistemological and theoretical stance, and no evidence is provided that the study was grounded in such a stance. Ungrounded studies risk running adrift, rambling, becoming lost, and having no direction. Some researchers state that their studies are qualitative, collect data through interviews, but then convert these data into percentages, generalizing the results. Though we recognize the value of mixed methods studies (as discussed in chapter 7), ignoring epistemological and theoretical assumptions is not mixing methods! Some studies are represented as critical inquiry but provide no evidence of the critical nature of the work in their findings.

In a written report of a qualitative study, we would expect to read the researcher's epistemological assumptions. This includes whether the study used a constructivist (interpretive), subjective (critical or participatory), or poststructural epistemological grounding. Studies meeting the criteria of goodness would also state the corresponding theoretical underpinnings, including theoretical perspective (postmodernism, critical, or feminism) and theoretical framework (theories and/or literature that offers suppositions about the phenomenon under study). We would also expect to see references to and quotes from authors from whom the researcher found epistemological and theoretical inspiration and direction.

Evans (2002) described her study as grounded in constructivist epistemology and stated that critical theory "undergirded" the study.

This meets the epistemological element of goodness. Another example is found in Broido's (2000) work on social justice allies. She wrote,

> This study was shaped by my beliefs that people's realities are largely constructed; that is[,] people's perceptions of their experiences are their realities. I also believe that to work effectively with students, understanding how they perceive their world and their experiences is critical. These beliefs and assumptions are congruent with a phenomenological world-view, the paradigmatic orientation underlying this study. (p. 5)

In essence, to meet this criterion of goodness the author must state his or her epistemological stance, theoretical framework, and theoretical perspective and show evidence that all are complementary. Together they harmoniously offer grounding, direction, and insight necessary on which to conduct a study. Furthermore, to meet the criteria of goodness, evidence is necessary to demonstrate that this complementary stance was followed.

METHODOLOGY: THE APPROACH

The methodology selected gives more specific direction to a study, which is in turn grounded in a theoretical perspective and epistemological stance. The methodology is the approach, plan of action, and design. To meet expectations of goodness, there must be a clear question that can be appropriately addressed by the chosen methodology, which offers clarity on how "data are collected and the means for its interpretation" (Arminio & Hultgren, 2002, p. 452). To meet the criteria of goodness, researchers must rely on methodology for study design and provide evidence of that in the written research report. This includes informing the reader of the methodology by introducing the reader to its basic principles and founding experts. We would also expect to see references to contemporary users of this methodology from one's discipline. The researcher must note how the basic principles were followed and applied in the study.

A number of methodologies or research traditions (Maykut & Morehouse, 2001) exist in qualitative inquiry. Some researchers err in combining methodologies without an adequate understanding of any of them. "Superficiality results when researchers use eclecticism in ways that ignore contradictory assumptions, which many times is the result of not devoting sufficient time to learning the knowledge bases or theoretical perspectives from which the various methodologies emanate"

(Arminio & Hultgren, 2002, p. 453). If methodologies are being combined, even those within the same epistemological paradigm, it must be made clear that there is no theoretical contradiction in such a combining. For a more detailed discussion, see Chapter 7.

METHOD

Method, the collection of data, is often confused with methodology. Methodology provides the direction for the method. There must be a clear connection between the methodology, how participants will be recruited and selected, and how data will be collected. Refer to Chapters 2 and 3 for a discussion on how sampling decisions are influenced by methodology.

In the positivist paradigm, the constancy of controlled procedures theoretically offers the promise of objectivity, reliability, and validity and, hence, a quality study. In qualitative research, the procedures themselves are not the criteria on which a study is deemed sound, but rather it is the congruency of the theoretical perspective, methodology, and method. For example, how systematic, structured, or open-ended data collection methods are, again, is determined by the selected methodology. Rather than purportedly being value free, the researcher must be clear about what values he or she is acting upon when collecting data and how the chosen methodology and method support those values.

As the research progresses, the researcher must create an "audit trail" that records the method: who said what, when, where, and under what conditions (Whitt, 1991). The audit trail preserves and makes public the description of a number of aspects of the study, in particular the method. The audit trail provides sufficient information so that the reader can offer a judgment as to the appropriateness and thoroughness of the method.

In qualitative inquiry, the methodology offers a systematic approach, but that approach is also flexible, taking into consideration collaboration with participants (Mishler, 2000; Smith, 1993). Because participants have more of an influence in postmodern research design than in a positivistic or postpositivistic design, it is imperative that researchers ask how it is that researchers are to be with participants.

REFLEXIVITY OF RESEARCHER AND PARTICIPANTS

Smith (1993) advocated for a systematic approach to reflexivity. We propose the following as an appropriate systematic approach to reflexivity for the context of higher education. This approach requires that researchers address the following questions:

1. Why is it that I am engaged in the present study? What is it about me and my experiences that lead me to this study?
2. What personal biases and assumptions do I bring with me to this study?
3. What is my relationship with those in the study?

And that these questions are addressed through the following suggested means:

- Self-reflection
- Reflection with other researchers
- Reflection with participants
- Reflection on the theoretical framework, what we know from previous research and related literature

This provides evidence of reflexivity in the study's written form.

We will explore these questions and offer examples to illustrate how they can meet the criteria of goodness for the researcher and participants as multicultural subjects.

What Is It About Me and My Experiences That Lead Me to This Study?

Researchers must contemplate why it is they are engaged in the study. Arminio and Hultgren (2002) referred to this as "autobiographical rendering" (p. 455). Such rendering illuminates why *I* turn to the question. Because the qualitative researcher is the instrument of analysis, especially in interpretive and constructivist designs, his or her interests, values, experiences, and purpose influence the analysis. Consequently, knowing this autobiographical data is imperative for the user of the research to understand its context and to make judgments about whether the study meets the criteria of goodness. However, this autobiographical rendering should not simply serve to extol one's expertise at the expense of adequately telling participants' stories. "Reflexive accounts . . . demand more than personal tales of research problems and accomplishments. They require thoughts about the researcher's position and how the researcher is affected by the fieldwork and field relationships" (Glesne, 1999, p. 177). This should not be taken as an opportunity for researchers to "make more of themselves than the world around them" (Glesne, p. 177). The researcher's experiences should not supersede the intent of the research, though researcher and findings are connected.

The introduction and literature review sections of a written report offer an opportunity for this autobiographical rendering. Hence, it is no accident that these are written before data are collected. Journaling is another means to reflect on why one turns to these questions. Also before data are collected, researchers need to inform participants as to their connection to the study. For example, in her article regarding the impact of the Safe Zone project for lesbian, gay, bisexual, and transgender (LGBT) students, Evans (2002) noted that she was invited to join the advisory board of the Lesbian, Gay, Bisexual, and Transgender Student Services Office and to conduct the study. She went on to disclose,

> My values clearly supported the project; I was aware that no research had demonstrated the impact of Safe Zone programs, and I was interested in determining the impact of such programs. Being sensitive to the power differential I held as a heterosexual faculty member, I invited three members of the LGBT student population to assist me. (p. 525)

What Personal Biases Do I Bring with Me?

This question seeks to underscore the researcher's preunderstandings by acknowledging one's assumptions. "It is better to make explicit our understandings . . . to hold them deliberately at bay and even to turn this knowledge against itself, as it were, thereby exposing its shallow or concealing character" (van Manen, 1990, p. 47). These assumptions should then be triangulated with literature that confirms the researcher's assumptions and literature that contradicts the researcher's assumptions, stating why the contradiction. Again, journaling and the introduction and literature review sections of a written report offer an opportunity for this clarification of assumptions. In this regard, Davis (2002) wrote,

> For me, this meant being aware that I might try to make the interview data fit my preconceptions (Self) rather than allowing the participants (Other) to speak for themselves. I am drawn to the study of gender and men due to my own curiosity about the impact of gender on men's development, but I also have political, social, and cultural views related to this topic. I also clearly have biases associated with my own development as a White, heterosexual, Italian American male. As I read transcripts and listened to participants, for example, I had to intentionally avoid relying on initial intuitive interpretations rooted in my own experience. (p. 512)

What Is My Relationship with Those in the Study?

Researchers must decide how they are going to negotiate the self-other relationship, and then they must divulge it. For example, in an ethnographic study manuscript submitted for publication in a journal particular to higher education, the author had studied a community-building program in a college residence hall. Yet, the author never divulged what role he or she had in the program. Was the researcher a faculty member who taught in the program, an administrator of the program, a parent of a student in the program, a resident of the program, or unaffiliated with the institution? The role of the researcher and his or her relationship to the program and the students influence whether the user can determine if the findings presented are reasonable. When we do not reveal our role, "Our informants are then left carrying the burden of representations as we hide behind the cloak of alleged neutrality" (Fine, Weis, Weseen, & Wong, 2000, p. 109). For example, Vasti described how her participants' stories reminded her of her own struggles amid clashing cultures while growing up. She managed her subjectivity "through self analysis techniques such as a researcher's journal" (Torres & Baxter Magolda, 2002, p. 479). Through her journaling she was able to "understand how I can balance my own interpretations with the voices of the students, making sure that each of them is able to create his or her own meaning and that I am able to help articulate that meaning" (p. 480).

In another example, Jan (1994) disclosed her position as a "Northern Yankee" when describing an interaction with a participant who brought a mammy doll to one of the data collection conversations.

> I, as Northern Yankee, asked Ann if she felt "okay" having a mammy doll on her shelf. . . . The White South and White North meet here, eyeing the mammy doll, "the Other" (hooks, 1991, p. 23). Whereas I judged the doll as a racist caricature of slavery, Ann saw it simultaneously as a unique gift representing a legacy to the past when life seemed simple to her, and as a representation of an unjust way to be. Both of us had our notions about the doll, "the Other," while "the Other" was speechless to represent herself. (p. 318)

It was by convening a human science dialogue (van Manen, 1990) that Jan was able to understand this interaction. Five informed peers gathered to read the transcript, hear her reflection of the interaction, and listen to what she felt during the interaction. It was through this dialogue that she was able to interpret what was going on for her in her role as researcher as instrument.

Marshall (1990) cautioned qualitative researchers from "going native" (p. 194). This occurs when a researcher goes through the motions of, and takes on, a cultural behavior without knowing, understanding, or embracing the underlying reason for the behavior. The researcher takes advantage of the behavior for his or her own purposes, usually to gain access to participants. When the hyphen between self and other is unfocused, the researcher risks "eating the other" (hooks, 1991, p. 21), behaving inauthentically, and manipulating or even controlling participants. This could be patronizing or, even worse, could lead to harm. The importance of reflecting upon the researcher and participants as intercultural subjects, and its implications for data analysis and presentation, cannot be overstated.

ANALYSIS AND PRESENTATION

The word *analysis* can be traced to the German word *analusein*, meaning to unloosen or undo (Hoad, 1986). This element of goodness requires that the text (or data) is undone according to the methodology. The purpose of analysis is to uncover findings that lead to new and increased understanding. By spending a great deal of time listening and reading the text, "parallel trajectories" (Mishler, 2000, p. 129) emerge that are then coded, placed into categories, or used to create themes as determined by the methodology. From their refinement, interpretation occurs. According to van Manen (1990), "Etymologically, interpretation means explaining in the sense of mediating between two parties . . . it mediates between interpreted meanings and the thing toward which interpretation points. It is this thing toward which interpretation points" (p. 26) that new and beginning qualitative researchers often fail to address. *Novice researchers often merely report what was obvious, rather than interpret what was illuminated.* The latter is much more difficult because it requires a risk or, as Lather (2003) wrote, "credible leaps into the unknown" (p. 205). Maynard (2000) suggested that interpretation calls for going "beyond citing experience in order to make connections which may not be visible alone" (p. 98). To meet this element of goodness, researchers must make obvious the difference between reporting and interpreting. For example, in her article "Identity and Learning: Student Affairs' Role in Transforming Higher Education," Baxter Magolda (2003) offered a lengthy quote from one of her participants. A small portion of it is presented below:

The whole thought process of just taking stock of where you are in your life. It's like putting your life through a sieve, getting the big awkward chunks out of your life, getting the nice finely sifted residue—it is kind of sorting it all out. What is the essence of you and what isn't? (p. 233)

Baxter Magolda provided this interpretation:

Dawn's comments reveal . . . [she] was defining a path to follow until new experiences reshape it, processing each new experience in the context of the essence of who she is. Students using this process during college would be less likely to chose [*sic*] a major because they thought someone (e.g., their parents, their peers, society at large) wanted them to and more likely to choose majors and careers consistent with their own values. Doing so would yield less changing majors and perhaps more effective in-depth learning in areas to which students are committed. Better career decisions would enhance students' education and preparation for careers after college. (p. 233)

Though difficult to illustrate without duplicating the entire article, this excerpt demonstrates that interpretation is not a rephrasing of the text. It embraces the text but broadens and deepens our understanding of what was said, what it means, and its implications. The depth of the interpretation will be determined by epistemology and methodology.

Could other reasonable researchers make these same claims? Would others be able to determine how the findings and interpretations were generated? Would others use these interpretations as a basis for their work? Are these interpretations more probable than other interpretations or conclusions? Was the engagement prolonged, the observation thorough, and the meaning thoughtful? Did the researcher grapple with alternative explanations (Marshall, 1990)? Was there a triangulation of alternative explanations? These are important questions to address in order to comply with criteria of goodness of interpretation. The interpretation must not solely be a restatement of the text. The interpretative approach and depth must fit the methodology.

Though interpretation is never right or wrong, the researcher must offer evidence of how the interpretation was arrived at and that the interpretation is indeed trustworthy. There are a number of components of trustworthiness or "truth value" (Morse & Richards, 2002, p. 168). These components include evidence of

- credibility
- plausibility
- applicability

The researcher must present an abundance of evidence that links the raw data to the interpretation to the real world (Marshall, 1990). Hammersley (1990) offered credibility and plausibility as two means to ensure this link. "No knowledge is certain, but knowledge claims can be judged reasonably accurately in terms of their likely truth" (Hammersley, p. 610). The reader can ask, "Are the findings plausible, and are they credible?" Hammersley defined *credibility* as whether the researcher's judgment is reasonable given the nature of the topic and the circumstances. He defined *plausibility* as whether the interpretation and findings are probable. Furthermore, the researcher must offer evidence sufficient to convince the reader that the findings are credible and plausible. "The researcher must present the best possible case for their claims" (J. K. Smith, 1990, p. 185).

Moreover, researchers must offer verification that they did not reshape the data to merely meet their assumptions. "What the reader should see is evidence that the researcher did not rework the data so that it would be in line with the researcher's preestablished framework or theoretical interests" (Smith, 1993, p. 112). Again, self-reflexivity comes into play here. One's "enthusiasms must be held in check through a systematic self-reflexivity" (Smith, p. 112). The researcher "must document the extent to which theoretical perspectives were altered, revised, or deepened" by the data (p. 113). What were the surprises? Noting changing perspectives between one's early autobiographical rendering and one's findings would be such a means to document altering or deepening perspectives. So, too, could peer reviews, expert reviews, or human science dialogues, where a researcher consults with a knowledgeable peer, an expert in the field, or a group of both. Lather (2003) stressed the importance of ensuring "face validity," which is "recycling categories, emerging analysis, and conclusions back through at least a subsample of the respondents" (p. 206). This is also referred to as *member checking* (Glesne, 1999; Lincoln & Guba, 1985).

As indicated in Figure 6.1, at the beginning of this chapter, some criteria are more closely associated with a particular epistemology than others. There are some ways that criteria can be generalized by epistemology. Methodological interests, values, and purposes can account for differences in interpretation and analysis (J. K. Smith, 1990). The analysis of some methodologies is more interpretive and less structured than others. So, for example, we would expect to see indicated in a written report how a hermeneutic phenomenological study is more interpretive than a grounded theory study. According to J. K. Smith (1990), it is difficult to prove wrong an interpretation in a highly interpretive methodology, "for philosophical hermeneutic interpretations can only be referenced to the interpreter in the sense that the result [is] from a dialogue between the interpreter and that which is interpreted" (p. 176). For example, the reader would expect to see less theoretical triangulation within a phenomenological study because the focus of phenomenology is not theory driven.

In the critical theory paradigm, due to its emancipatory aim (Lincoln & Guba, 2000), users would expect to see more emphasis on a development of increased consciousness through the exposing of false consciousness and distorted communication than an interpretive or constructivist study. According to Hammersley (1990), we would also expect to see an explanation of the social order and ways to transform that order.

How is it that this research is to be presented? Too often, researchers connote deep, rich interpretations of complex phenomena with unclear and imprecise writing. An important aspect of goodness is reader confirmability. If the reader is unclear as to the meaning of the interpretation, then the research does not meet the criteria of goodness. Though the language may be poetic, it should not be implicitly vague as some poetry is, but rather explicitly clear. Marshall (1990) noted that findings must be presented in a readable and accessible form to other researchers, policy makers, and practitioners. We would add that the study should be accessible to participants in the study as well.

Marshall (1990) called for inquirers to continue to search for new ways to uncover meaning. A fine example of a different way to present findings and reflexivity is Lather and Smithies's (1997) work *Troubling the Angels*. Woven into this account of women living with HIV/AIDS is the authors' own experiences with the research process and HIV/AIDS, in addition to HIV/AIDS "fact boxes." This multiple and simultaneous intermingling of stories and information throughout the book presents an integrated representation of the phenomenon for a broader understanding of HIV/AIDS, the experiences of the women living with HIV/AIDS, a critique of society's perceptions of HIV/AIDS, and how the women make meaning of living with HIV/AIDS in light of society's perception.

Once findings have been interpreted, and means taken to ensure that they are credible, plausible, and presented in an accessible manner, it is up to the researcher to provide ideas about how the study is applicable in practice.

RECOMMENDATIONS: IMPLICATIONS
FOR PROFESSIONAL PRACTICE

Arminio and Hultgren (2002) wrote,

> For what purpose do I engage as a researcher in this way? It is not for the sake of research itself that researchers should embark upon this work, but rather to improve the lives of others. Interpretive research is initiated for the purpose of improving the world through more informed action. (p. 457)

Research should not be conducted in an "academic vacuum apart from the outside world" (Lather, 1991, p. xvi). To meet the criteria of goodness, the researcher must convince the reader that the study and its findings are important in bringing about informed action or what van Manen (1990) called "action-sensitive knowledge" (p. 156). This requires that researchers connect their findings to applicable recommendations. These recommendations should allow for the empowerment of people and improvement in the quality of life. "Being conscious of goodness asks that . . . research make connections between self, other, and world and offer reflections on what is right to do and good to be as an inquirer" (Arminio & Hultgren, 2002, p. 458). To meet this criterion of goodness, inquirers must provide reasonable grounds that the results are relevant to their practice.

Besides making recommendations that improve practice and, subsequently, the lives of others, studies should be tied to a larger context (Marshall, 1990). A concern exists that studies too often focus on a "trivial problem" (Smith & Deemer, 2000, p. 879). Researchers should ask themselves questions such as: What are the implications for not just the immediate actors but also a larger circle of others? What are the implications for systems and organizations? Again, it is not for the sake of the inquirer that the study is conducted.

Hammersley (1990) included the concept of "relevance" when considering criteria in qualitative research. He noted that the study should be relevant to issues of public concern, relevant to a range of audiences, and even relevant to a range of topics. He warned researchers to be careful about overestimating the contributions of their research.

Lincoln (1998) called for researchers to "leap from understanding to action" (p. 18). This occurs by not conducting research that exacerbates social ills or takes needed resources from social institutions (e.g., schools and health care). Lincoln directed researchers to frame "inquiries in such a way as to prompt action" (p. 23). This action also includes the discourse between researchers and practitioners in order to promote local efforts of community involvement. The case study of college students involved in a service-learning course conducted by Jones and Abes (2003) is an excellent example of such discourse. Similarly, Carpenter (2003) described such action-oriented research as scholarly practice. Examples of scholarly practice based on research would include the development of LGBT Safe Zones to many campuses, whose benefits were revealed by Evans's (2002) research and the work of ally development that was spearheaded by Broido's (2000) work with LGBT allies and continues with Reason, Roosa Millar, and Scales's (2005) work with racial justice allies.

SUMMARY

J. K. Smith (1990) noted these criteria may seem "loose," but he insisted that this is to be expected due to the dynamic nature of criteria and the relative nature of qualitative inquiry. Emphasis on how much to evaluate criteria is a judgment call according to Marshall (1990), but we believe that this is dependent upon the selected epistemology and methodology. We also believe that consistency between epistemology and methodology and taking measures of reflexivity are the most critical.

As educators, whether faculty members, student affairs staff, or administrators, we must acknowledge, embrace, and integrate the elements of goodness into our research and scholarly practice. In the current era of accountability and assessment, the survival of our programs may depend on it. But, more importantly, we believe that insight can best be gained from studies that follow the criteria of goodness. Arminio and Hultgren (2002) wrote,

> Qualitative research that exemplifies goodness must be an important part of the assessment, research, and evaluation efforts taking place on college campuses, linking [our work] to student learning and offering directions for continuous improvement. Including qualitative research is important not because it might be "trendy," but rather because good qualitative research brings voice and insight forward for all constituents living complex phenomena, including underrepresented people and their experiences. Using good qualitative work to demonstrate effectiveness allows institutions to realize their mission more fully. (p. 458)

Qualitative work must be judged on what it is, rather than upon quantitative research, which it is not. "When we allow those who are powerful to hold all the definitions of what is good and what is useful, we can never get beyond the dominant worldview" (Marshall, 1990, p. 196). Let us be authentic and true to the purpose and intent of qualitative work to find new meaning and understanding, which allow us to better meet our higher education mission.

EXERCISE

Several strategies exist to ensure goodness. Select a couple of strategies for assuring trustworthiness and triangulation that you would like to practice (e.g., audit trail, member checking, peer review, and expert review). To practice, observe and take notes at a meeting, event, or class. Afterward, follow through with the strategy by contacting others who would be considered informed experts, participants, peer reviewers, or human science dialogue members and sharing your notes with them. Be sure to consider carefully who would be informed experts, peers, or human science dialogue team members. How did perceptions differ? How were they similar? Then, write a paragraph or two about what new understandings or insights you gained from this experience concerning data collection and trustworthiness.

7

CHOICES AND CONSEQUENCES OF MIXING METHODS IN QUALITATIVE RESEARCH

The use of mixed method research design is generally accepted as appropriate in many disciplines (Creswell, 2003; Tashakkori & Teddlie, 1998). When the term *mixed methods* is used in this chapter, we refer to the use of qualitative and quantitative methods within a single study. The issue that arises from this mixing of methods is that few researchers take the time to understand the philosophical issues and challenges that occur when methods from different traditions are combined. This avoidance of philosophical issues occurs when researchers focus only on the actual methods (e.g., survey instruments combined with interviews or focus groups) (House, 1994), rather than struggle with the different sets of philosophies the chosen methods should invoke (Guba & Lincoln, 1989, 1994; Jones, 2002). This focus on method alone prompts questions about the quality of the research and the validity or trustworthiness of the design.

Using multiple methods to investigate a research question is common within institutional research and assessment projects in higher education (Paloma & Banta, 1999), yet the expertise seems to be more focused on quantitative methods rather than on the broad spectrum of methods available. The use of qualitative methods is encouraged within the assessment literature, but the discussion has mainly focused on method (e.g., interviews and focus groups) (Paloma & Banta; Upcraft & Schuh, 1996), rather than on the conflicting philosophical foundations that come with the type of methodology associated with the methods. Although the distinction between how knowledge is viewed as well as the role of the researcher is mentioned in these texts, limited attention is given to the paradigmatic issues involved in using qualitative methods in mixed method assessment processes (Paloma & Banta). Baldwin and Thelin (1990) advocated for the fusion of quantitative and qualitative research because, although one can chart change over time (quantitative), the other provides descriptions of the process (qualitative). Rather than grappling with the conflicting philosophical foundations, Baldwin and Thelin advocated for a truce between the quantitative-qualitative feud. Whether conducting institutional assessment or large-scale research studies, when qualitative and quantitative methods are used together in a study, the researcher must consider the unique philosophical, theoretical, and methodological issues that arise in the research process. This chapter will focus on the decisions that should be considered when designing a study that mixes qualitative and quantitative methods. In order to accomplish this task, choices and consequences are explored by investigating perspectives on mixing methods and discussing the role of paradigm, epistemology, and design implications that must be considered when mixing methods.

PERSPECTIVES ON MIXING METHODS

The first step in managing the research process for mixed methods is to understand the terms used in the research literature and the relationship among them. This requires a review of previous chapters and a reminder of the importance that the relationship among research elements plays in all types of research. The techniques or procedures used to gather and analyze data are considered research *methods*. A *methodology* focuses on the strategies used to conduct the research study and necessitates the inclusion of a rationale for the choice of methods within the context of the methodology and research question (Crotty, 1998). And, finally, the *paradigm* describes "the net that contains the researcher's epistemological, ontological, and methodological premises . . . or an interpretive framework" (Denzin & Lincoln, 2000b, p. 19). Each element is related to the other, and attention to each of the elements is critical to a complete research design (Crotty; Jones, 2002) that assures authenticity (Lincoln

& Guba, 2000) or goodness (Arminio & Hultgren, 2002) in the research process.

The second step is to acknowledge certain assumptions that make the discussion of philosophical foundations meaningful to all researchers. Although previous chapters focused solely on qualitative research, it is important to acknowledge that the same issues are involved in mixed method research. There is a dependent connection between paradigms and specific methods, and, therefore, a researcher should not delve into "the business of inquiry without being clear about what paradigm informs and guides his or her approach" (Guba & Lincoln, 1994, p. 116). In addition, many disciplines, including the field of higher education, advance misconceptions about what constitutes mixed methods research, and these misconceptions are fueled by the varied definitions of what "mixing" is actually happening in the research process. This issue is further complicated because many faculty, researchers, and institutional research administrators in higher education have not reinforced the expectation that paradigm orientation be part of the methodology of research or assessment. This results in mixed method research within the field being published with no connection between method, methodology, and epistemology. And, finally, because the concept of paradigmatic orientation is more closely considered in the literature for qualitative research (Denzin & Lincoln, 2000b), it is likely that those trained solely in quantitative methods will pay little attention to the tenets of methodology that are needed to conduct good mixed method research. As a result, when researchers say they conduct mixed method research, it is the qualitative portion of the research that suffers because the focus is placed only on the method (e.g. focus groups and interviews) while paradigmatic issues are neglected. These assumptions about mixed method research in higher education guide the methodological questions considered in this chapter.

Purist quantitative or qualitative researchers may perceive that the differences between the paradigms are too great, and, therefore, mixing cannot occur without compromising philosophical assumptions that are attached to the methodology (Lincoln & Guba, 2000; Tashakkori & Teddlie, 1998). Though the distinctions between the predominant paradigms in quantitative (positivist) and qualitative (constructivist or interpretivist) research must be acknowledged, some researchers believe these distinctions can be managed to create stronger research and evaluation designs (Guba & Lincoln, 1989, 1994; Johnson & Onwuegbuzie, 2004; Lincoln & Guba, 2000; Tashakkori & Teddlie, 1998, 2003). In order to demonstrate how the distinctions can be managed, the historical context of the paradigms will be succinctly presented.

Once a foundation is set for mixed methods, the management of the potential tensions will be addressed by looking at what constitutes mixed method research and understanding the ways researchers ground their worldview during the research process (Tashakkori & Teddlie, 2003). Finally, examples will be provided to illustrate the management of tensions and research decisions that are consistent and congruent with mixed method research designs.

PARADIGMATIC CONTEXT OF MIXED METHOD RESEARCH

Research paradigms tend to be presented in a dichotomous, mutually exclusive manner. What is rarely considered is a "third" type of research that includes both qualitative and quantitative methods (mixed methods). Many authors refer to the distinctions between the tenets of positivist paradigm, used by most quantitative purists, and paradigms like constructivism or critical theory, associated with qualitative purists, as the *paradigm wars* (Denzin & Lincoln, 2000b; Guba & Lincoln, 1994; Tashakkori & Teddlie, 1998, 2003). Although the distinctions between the paradigms are clear on issues like the nature of reality (paradigm), the nature of the relationship between the researcher and participants (epistemology), and the manner in which researchers go about discovering knowledge (methodology) (Guba & Lincoln, 1994; Lincoln & Guba, 2000; Tashakkori & Teddlie, 1998), what is less clear is if mixing methods compromises paradigm distinctions.

In early studies, the use of mixed methods caused little controversy because the discussion of paradigms was neglected (Tashakkori & Teddlie, 2003). It was not until later when mixed method studies were used to illustrate the concept of data triangulation (e.g., data confirmation) that the present discussions emerged. Discussion about the connections between method, methodology, and paradigm (Lincoln & Guba, 1985) seems to have initiated the controversy by asserting that research methodology should articulate the connections between these elements (i.e., method, methodology, and paradigm). The emergence of mixed method studies came during the Blurred Genres Phase (Denzin & Lincoln, 1994) or "the ascendance of constructivism, followed by the paradigm wars" (Teddlie & Tashakkori, 1998, p. 9) era of methodological history.

In Chapter 1, we covered the distinctions between the paradigms involved in quantitative and qualitative research. Before embarking on a mixed method study, a researcher must be clear about those distinctions. Even though mixed methods studies are not new, misconceptions continue to exist over the connection between mixing methods and the paradigmatic issues involved when this type of research design is used.

MISCONCEPTIONS ABOUT MIXING METHODS

The misconceptions that surround mixed methods research revolve around two questions that emerge when researchers understand the connection between methods, methodology, and paradigms. These questions are as follows:

1. Are methods tied to only one paradigm? If so, then should they be used by researchers who prefer, or whose worldview is consistent with, a different paradigm?
2. Can paradigms be combined?

The responses to these questions illustrate the need to be attentive to paradigmatic issues in order to manage the potential tensions in mixed method research.

The first question deals with the notion of what is guiding the research. A common myth exists that researchers who assert themselves as qualitative researchers would never consider the use of quantitative methods. Though many people cite this as the definitive issue in mixed method research, for years Guba and Lincoln (1981, 1989) stated clearly that when using a constructivist paradigm, "there are times, however, when the issues and concerns voiced by audiences require information that is best generated by more conventional methods, especially quantitative methods" (1981, p. 36). In more recent publications, Lincoln and Guba (2000) stressed that the concern is not about the methods used, but rather about the paradigmatic decision that guides the research. Methodology associated with the method provides the technique for analysis; how a researcher interprets those analyses (whether quantitative or qualitative) is related to or determined by the paradigmatic issue. For this reason, certain methods are more closely associated with one tradition of research than the other. It is important to pay attention to the paradigmatic issues inherent in all decisions within the research process. This critical understanding helps researchers manage the challenges in mixed method research.

Many examples of published research studies in higher education exist that do not clearly state the chosen methodology; rather, the authors solely provide information on the methods used in the study. This lack of connection between method, methodology, and paradigm in any research can lessen the validity, goodness, and authenticity of the research and can be particularly problematic in mixed method research. Because many mixed method studies in higher education solely concentrate on the method, the reader is not sure what paradigm guides the research decisions. Though readers of a study may make assumptions about the interpretive paradigm of the researcher, without the explicit declaration of the preferred paradigm, it is impossible to know how the assumptions of each method were managed. Without deliberate connections between method, methodology, and paradigm, the research design will leave the reader wondering about research decisions and, consequently, the quality of the research process. In order to inform the reader, a complete methodology section should explain all research and assessment decisions, making the inclusion of the paradigmatic elements essential.

The custom of not declaring a paradigmatic orientation is more consistent with the training of quantitative researchers, which focuses mostly on the method with less attention paid to paradigmatic concerns. This is distinctly different from courses in qualitative research, which focus on clarifying paradigm (epistemology), methodology (theory and design that guide the research process), and methods (techniques used to gather and analyze data). The different expectations of the two research traditions add to the misconceptions about how to conduct mixed method research and how it is evaluated. Therefore, the way researchers are trained impacts how the research is conducted, and the lack of attention given to mixed method research contributes to these misconceptions.

The second question in conducting mixed method research deals with the concern of whether paradigms can be combined. The question of commensurability (e.g., if one combines paradigms, are methodologies and methods commensurable?) between the paradigmatic, epistemological, and methodological issues among the paradigms causes much confusion for researchers, especially beginning researchers who may tend to oversimplify research. "Commensurability is an issue only when researchers want to 'pick and choose' among the axioms of positivist and interpretivist models because the axioms are contradictory and mutually exclusive" (Lincoln & Guba, 2000, p. 174). Researchers who use mixed methods, but are trained only in quantitative research, are accustomed to thinking about the technical assumptions the data must meet and not about the philosophical assumptions they use. This tendency leads to a misinterpretation of the role of paradigm within the qualitative portion of the research in mixed method studies and thus undermines the goodness or quality criteria of the qualitative findings (Arminio & Hultgren, 2002; Lincoln & Guba, 2000).

When Lincoln and Guba (2000) stated that commensurability between positivist and constructivist worldviews is not possible, they were referring to the paradigmatic, epistemological, and methodological issues—not the methods. The caution offered when combining paradigms deals with the shared elements between the paradigms. For example, it is virtually impossible for a researcher to see reality as both attainable through statistical controls and contextually constructed. This would make combining a phenomenological study with a regression analysis virtually impossible to justify. Once again, it should be noted that Lincoln and Guba made clear that *within* the paradigms, mixed methods can make good sense. An example of this would be to test theoretical concepts that emerged from a constructivist grounded theory study by creating a model and analyzing it for model fit with structural equation modeling. Vasti used this approach to create a new model that considers the intent to persist in college, without using traditional academic achievement measures (Torres, in press). Because Vasti's longitudinal study has many first-generation college students in the sample, she found that few of the Latino/a students felt academically prepared to do college-level work. The issue that emerged during data analysis, using grounded theory techniques, was that students built up their own capacities through other support mechanisms. Seldom did students mention their low academic preparation. This emergent issue became the impetus to consider support issues as strong influences on the intent to persist. Using this insight, Vasti set out to gain a better understanding of this phenomenon. While reading supporting materials on this phenomenon, she began to explore the role of social cognitive theory (Bandura, 1986) in interpreting how students enhanced their capacities within the college environment. The combination of emerging themes in the qualitative data and aspects of social cognitive theory helped conceptualize a new model that considers the impact of environmental and support factors on the intent to persist. Using structural equation modeling, Vasti tested the model to see if it had good model fit. This example respected both traditions by allowing the model to emerge from the data and then using a quantitative technique that tested model fit rather than manipulated or controlled aspects of the data.

SITUATING YOURSELF AS A MIXED METHOD RESEARCHER

In order to identify a preferred research paradigm, a researcher must assess if the values he or she possesses also match the values of the chosen paradigm (Lincoln & Guba, 2000). This is not a simple process and should be seen as part of the evolution of the researcher (Torres & Baxter Magolda, 2002). In an effort to identify the approach that mixed method researchers in the past have taken on this issue, Greene and Caracelli (2003) created stances that illustrate some of the paradigm outcomes that occur when researchers mix methods and paradigms. The stances emerged after reviewing studies that used mixed method approaches in the social science literature. They acknowledged that mixed method studies tended to leave out paradigms as their organizing frameworks; rather, research decisions were based on the nature of the phenomenon. For this reason, they framed the stances around researchers' responses to the question of whether paradigms mattered significantly or not. Though this acknowledges that some mixed method researchers do not place importance on the philosophical bases of paradigms, Greene and Caracelli (2003) stated that if the paradigmatic issues are not attended to, "then the full potential of mixed method inquiry will remain unfulfilled" (p. 107). The possible stances that mixed method researchers can assume are as follows:

- Dialectic: Paradigms have value and contribute to understanding.
- New paradigm: The more recent paradigms are better suited than the traditional ones because they encourage multiple perspectives.
- Pragmatic or context driven: Paradigms are not as important; the critical issue is the responsiveness to research context.
- Concept driven: Paradigms are not as important as the theoretical congruence that promotes the most appropriate study of the phenomenon (Greene & Caracelli, 2003).

The stances of *dialectic* and *new paradigm* indicate the willingness of the researcher to struggle with these issues and find new ways to conduct high-quality mixed method research.

Eventually, paradigmatic issues will influence the inquiry by creating decisions points that are difficult to resolve without consideration of worldview. For example, a researcher creates a series of items to measure a new construct that emerged from a constructivist grounded theory study. Using confirmatory factor analysis (because there is an a priori theory in place), the items are tested to see the reliability of the measurement for this new construct. If the factor loadings are not strong and the overall model-fit indices are not acceptable, the researcher has to make a decision as to what to do with this emerging construct in the qualitative data. Is it discarded because of the quantitative analysis? This is the type of decision that is guided by the paradigmatic orientation of the researcher. These types of decisions include the consistency of research decisions to the methodology and paradigm, as well as placing undue importance on one analysis without regard to the potential of other interpretations. To not consider these paradigmatic concerns is to limit the full potential of the inquiry and to lessen the quality of the analysis. In mixed method research, using a research design that allows for anything to work together without considering commensurability will take away from the goodness of the research and bring into question how the analyses were interpreted. Establishing goodness in research "requires that elements of the meaning making process be illustrated" (Arminio & Hultgren, 2002, p. 459); thus, selecting a stance that does not consider paradigm issues is not managing the issues but is avoiding them and, hence, does not meet the requirements of goodness.

NEGOTIATING THE PARADIGMATIC ISSUES IN MIXED METHOD RESEARCH

Paying attention to paradigmatic concerns is the first strategy in negotiating the methodological issues in mixed methods. Yet there are other issues that need to be clarified in order to negotiate the mixed method research process. Two questions guide the concerns about negotiating the paradigmatic issues in mixed method research.

1. Is there one paradigm that is best suited for mixed method design?
2. What mixing actually occurs in mixed method research, and how should this be identified?

The response to the first question comes from two perspectives. First, there are significant references in the literature on mixed method research advocating for the sole use of pragmatism as a paradigm that accommodates both qualitative and quantitative methods while rejecting the incompatibility thesis (Johnson & Onwuegbuzie, 2004; Maxcy, 2003; Tashakkori & Teddlie, 2003). The second perspective requires a closer look at the notion that a paradigm reflects a researcher's worldview; therefore, the researcher must make an individual choice. Both of these perspectives provide insight into the management of mixed method research.

Addressing the first perspective, the mixed method literature tends to advocate for the use of pragmatism as a single paradigm to guide mixed method studies (Johnson & Onwuegbuzie, 2004; Tashakkori & Teddlie, 1998, 2003). The attractive aspects of pragmatism in mixed method studies include (a) rejection of the need to force a choice between contradicting epistemologies, (b) more importance placed on the research question instead of the method or paradigm, and (c) the acceptance of "a very practical and applied research philosophy" (Teddlie & Tashakkori, 2003, p. 21). Pragmatists avoid the philosophical questions about what is truth and focus on the practical application of the research. As tempting as this pragmatic approach might be, the purpose of identifying a paradigm as a framework is to describe the researcher's worldview. Though some researchers may have this pragmatic worldview, it is probable that not all mixed method researchers see themselves as pragmatists. For this reason, it is difficult to say that pragmatism is the preferred paradigm; it really depends on the researcher and one's own worldview.

The second perspective views paradigms as a choice that relates to the researcher's worldview and therefore can vary depending on the individual investigator. Though Teddlie and Tashakkori (2003) advocated for pragmatism as a better choice to ground mixed method designs, they also acknowledged other paradigms that have been used in mixed method research. If a researcher values the perspective that paradigm choice is relevant to a researcher's worldview, then each investigator must search for his or her own voice within various paradigms. Again, this search becomes part of the evolution of the researcher and is critical to framing the research that uses both quantitative and qualitative methods (Torres & Baxter Magolda, 2002).

The second question deals with the type of mixing that is occurring during the research process and focuses on the confusion that exists in mixed method research. Many researchers do not use consistent language, making it difficult for the reader to understand what mixing is actually occurring. Three terms are most often associated with the different ways in which mixed method research can be conducted: *multimethod, mixed method,* and *mixed model.* Each of these terms has slightly different connotations about the research process. First, multimethod research uses two or more methods or procedures (e.g., observations and oral histories) from the same qualitative or quantitative paradigm (Teddlie & Tashakkori, 2003). Because the methods are from the same tradition, there is little mixing at the paradigm level, and often, when the methods are quantitative, there is little, if any, mention of a paradigm orientation. In multimethod research, mixing methods does not necessarily require mixing research paradigms.

The second term, *mixed method,* includes those studies that use both qualitative and quantitative data collection and analysis (methods) in either a parallel or sequential manner. "The mixing occurs in the methods section of the study" (Teddlie & Tashakkori, 2003, p. 11), and because the analysis of the data is usually done separately, this type of study does not always require the consideration of distinctions between the constructivist or positivist paradigms associated with qualitative and quantitative research (Teddlie & Tashakkori, 2003).

Mixed method research considers four strategies to guide how the research is conducted (Creswell, 2003). The first strategy involves implementation of the data collection. Qualitative and quantitative data can be collected concurrently or sequentially. The second strategy involves deciding if more importance is placed on the data collection and analysis of the qualitative or quantitative data, or if equal importance is given to both. This priority is determined by "the interest of the researcher, the audience for the study, and what the investigator seeks to emphasize" (Creswell, p. 212). This strategy implies an important distinction because it allows for the researcher to express her or his preference toward one tradition of research, yet it does not require the use of a paradigm to guide this decision. The third strategy focuses on the point where data would be integrated or at what point the qualitative and quantitative information are merged. The integration can occur during data collection, data analysis, data interpretation, or some combination of these. Choosing a preference between the quantitative or qualitative tradition would also influence the integration strategy. This strategy could also allow for separate analysis of data. Later in this chapter, in the Doing Mixed Method Research section, a list of strategies for mixed method design is provided.

Finally, the last strategy is that the theoretical perspective can be either explicit or implicit. This strategy considers whether there is a theoretical perspective that guides the research design. Creswell (2003) acknowledged that all research designs have an implicit theoretical perspective, yet it seems unclear if this perspective has to be made explicit at some point in the research process. This strategy is applicable because in a mixed method approach, the level of concern is in the method. Although Creswell's stance constitutes one guideline, we advocate that in order to maintain quality in all aspects of the research process, the theoretical perspective should always be clear. Because the term *mixed method* focuses on the mixing of methods only, it does not deal with the potential paradigmatic tensions between the research traditions, as data integration can be done sequentially. There is an invisible separation (with potential tension) between methods and paradigmatic issues. Though this separation may be attractive to those who do not want to deal with the paradigm challenges, this kind of design would not promote the full integration of all the research elements. Though these strategies may express research decisions, there would still be questions about the larger philosophical (paradigmatic) worldview of the researcher.

The third term used is *mixed model* studies, which have a higher level of mixing of the paradigms (Tashakkori & Teddlie, 1998). The mix is done at all stages of the research process, and therefore mixed model studies have to meet a "much more stringent set of assumptions than [do] multimethod or even mixed method" studies (Teddlie & Tashakkori, 2003, p. 11). Mixed model research can use multiple paradigms in a single study, or it can use a single paradigm to frame the researcher's worldview. There are no exemplary examples of mixed model research in the higher education literature.

This mixing of paradigms can be managed by having multiple research questions each rooted in a different paradigm, or it can make several inferences that correspond to different worldviews (Teddlie & Tashakkori, 2003). In their earlier work, Tashakkori and Teddlie (1998) defined *mixed model* as "studies that are products of the pragmatist paradigm and that combine the qualitative and quantitative approaches within different phases of the research process" (p. 19). The pragmatist paradigm rejects that researchers must force themselves to choose between the quantitative and qualitative approaches and focuses instead on choosing "explanations that produce desired outcomes" (p. 23).

For mixed method researchers who use a single paradigm, pragmatism seems to be the paradigm of choice. Though this paradigm is attractive to researchers for its commonsense approach, it is not the only way that researchers can manage the challenges of mixed method research. Choosing the paradigm and appropriate strategy constitutes the first step in doing good mixed method research.

DOING MIXED METHOD RESEARCH

Although there are several process models within mixed method research literature, this section will focus on three primary decisions that inform the design of a research study. These decisions deal with the implementation (data collection), the priority (which method is given precedence), and integration (process of analysis and incorporation of findings) (Creswell, 2003).

The implementation aspect of the study indicates if the data were collected at the same time (concurrent) or one at a time (sequential). This first aspect of the research process, then, determines the potential strategies that can be used. Although these strategies do not represent all the possible strategies, they do provide insight into the type of design issues that must be considered in this type of research (Creswell).

Strategies for Mixed Method Designs

The following strategies provide terms to illustrate the decisions about data collection, priority, and analysis.

- Sequential explanatory: This design strategy is straightforward in the sense that quantitative data are collected and analyzed, which is then followed by the collection and analysis of qualitative data. "The priority typically is given to the quantitative data, and the two methods are integrated during the interpretation phase" (Creswell, 2003, p. 215). This type of strategy is considered when the qualitative data assumes the role of explaining the quantitative data.
- Sequential exploratory: This design strategy also has data collection in two separate phases, with priority given to whichever type of data is collected first. Generally, this strategy tends to have qualitative data collected first, and the integration of the two types of data (qualitative and quantitative) is done at the interpretation phase. This strategy is used when the goal is to test elements of an emerging theory from the qualitative data (Creswell, 2003).
- Sequential transformative: This design strategy collects data in two separate phases, and priority is given to either qualitative or quantitative methods depending on the theoretical perspective that guides the study. The theoretical perspective would provide the framework as to the manner in which interpretation would be handled. This "strategy may be more appealing and acceptable to those researchers already using a transformative [e.g. critical race theory] framework" (Creswell, 2003, p. 217). This strategy is seldom seen in published research.
- Concurrent triangulation: This strategy collects data at the same time, and the goal is to confirm or substantiate findings within a single study. The goal in this type of strategy tends to offset the weakness of one method with another method. Priority can be given to either, and integration occurs at the interpretation phase by providing convergence in the findings or explaining the lack of convergence (Creswell, 2003).
- Concurrent nested: In this strategy, the data are collected simultaneously, but priority is given to one method that guides the research decisions in the study. This type of strategy can be used to broaden the understanding of a phenomenon by using more than one method (Creswell, 2003). This strategy has much more

potential for researchers, but should be used with care because many research decisions must be justified in the process.

- Concurrent transformative: Although the data are collected at the same time with this strategy, the priority and integration are guided by the researcher's theoretical perspective. Like the sequential transformative strategy, this process is heavily guided by the transformative nature of the research question and theoretical perspective (Creswell, 2003).

The example given earlier in this chapter of Vasti's study on the intent to persist for Latino/a students (Torres, in press) is a concurrent nested strategy because qualitative and quantitative data were gathered concurrently, and the qualitative data took priority in making research decisions about how to view and analyze the quantitative data. The use of specific strategies in mixed method research is relatively new, and therefore examples in the higher education literature are somewhat limited.

MIXED METHOD RESEARCH DECISIONS IN HIGHER EDUCATION

Placing the paradigmatic issues discussed in this chapter within the context of higher education research is somewhat difficult because many researchers attempt to combine methods in their inquiry, but have not necessarily considered the issues illustrated in this chapter.

Some of the most common examples of mixed method research focus on using quantitative methods to make decisions about the research process. As part of a survey development process, researchers from one institution used focus groups to determine the types of questions that should be considered (Torres, Globe, Ketcheson, & Truxillo, 1999). Focus groups were conducted with faculty, first-year students, and peer educators. Decisions about the inclusion of scale items were based on the qualitative data from the focus groups. In this example, there was a sequential use of qualitative and quantitative methods to determine items for survey development, and this resulted in the entering student survey being more practical and useful for its university audience.

Another example of a well-constructed sequential mixed method study is the Documenting Effective Educational Practices (DEEP) project being conducted through the Center for Postsecondary Research at Indiana University. As part of the DEEP project, researchers selected 20 colleges and universities with higher than predicted graduation rates and higher than predicted scores on the National Survey of Student Engagement (NSSE). The institutions were selected for in-depth case studies to discern what these institutions do to attain this level of educational effectiveness (Kuh, Kinzie, Schuh, & Whitt, 2005). Case study methodology was used, and the methods for collecting the qualitative data included interviews, observations, and document analysis. In this example, the quantitative survey (NSSE) was used to determine the sample, and the case study methodology provided the framework for understanding policies and practices that promote educational effectiveness. This is a sequential explanatory strategy, in which the qualitative data were used to explain the results of the quantitative analysis.

A recently defended dissertation used a mixed method approach to explore multicultural competence among community college student affairs practitioners (Martin, 2005). In this dissertation, the student used a pragmatic epistemology to guide research decisions. This epistemology was chosen because there was little information about the topic and the doctoral student wanted to focus on exploring several aspects of the phenomenon. The pragmatic orientation allowed her to concentrate on the research questions rather than on potential philosophical entanglements. In this study, she used scores from a multicultural competence survey to determine the sample of participants who would be interviewed. The integration of the methods was done at the analysis phase, making this a sequential exploratory study.

Considering there are few examples of good mixed method research studies in higher education, the next section provides guidelines for the elements needed to improve mixed method research studies within the higher education context.

IMPROVING MIXED METHOD RESEARCH IN HIGHER EDUCATION

This chapter attempts to frame both the practical and paradigmatic issues involved in mixed method research and provides examples of these concerns in higher education research. As stated previously, the training of higher education researchers needs to be more inclusive of the special concerns that mixed method research brings to the process. In order to accomplish this, it is necessary to combine the methodological suggestions made by constructivist researchers (Lincoln & Guba, 2000) and mixed method researchers (Tashakkori & Teddlie, 2003), and the commonly used guides for doctoral students' research (Creswell, 1994, 2003), into a more inclusive approach toward mixed method research.

This can be done if higher education studies using mixed methods include the following elements:

- Paradigmatic lens: This should be stated along with a statement of how this orientation guides the research. If more than one paradigm is being used, an explanation of the commensurability of the paradigms and why this combination is appropriate should also be included (Lincoln & Guba, 2000).
- Type of mixed method design: This should be articulated along with where mixing is occurring (i.e., only in the methods or throughout the research process). Justification for the design should also be included, illustrating that it is consistent with the paradigmatic orientation. The established terminology (e.g., strategies for mixed method design and the definitions of mixing methods) described in this chapter can serve as a guide (Creswell, 2003; Teddlie & Tashakkori, 2003) for the mixed method research strategies used by the researcher.
- Methodology: This should describe the research design and strategy of inquiry used and the connection the chosen methodology has to the paradigm. The methodology selected provides the approach and process to linking the methods to the desired outcomes of the study (Denzin & Lincoln, 2000b).
- Methods: These describe the techniques used to gather data and how those techniques are appropriate for the phenomenon being studied.

SUMMARY

Mixed method research is complicated and is not appropriate for all studies. Careful attention to the dynamics described in this chapter is warranted before embarking upon mixed method research. The inclusion of the elements outlined in this chapter would help researchers attend to both the paradigmatic issues and concerns for authenticity, thus allowing the study to attain its full potential (Greene & Caracelli, 2003). Faculty who are training mixed method researchers, or those presently conducting mixed method research in higher education, would need to expand their own thinking to include all of the elements suggested. These elements are integral to all research and provide a window into the process and thinking that researchers need to engage in. As stated in the introduction of this chapter, a researcher should not delve into "the business of inquiry without being clear about what paradigm [worldview] informs and guides his or her approach" (Guba & Lincoln, 1994, p. 116).

EXERCISE

All of the exercises listed previously in this book should be considered when conducting mixed method research. As an additional exercise, write out a list of the fundamental tenets of your chosen paradigm, epistemology, and methodology. Now think about the quantitative method and analysis you want to consider. Ask yourself the question "How commensurable are the assumptions of the quantitative method and analysis with the tenets of the qualitative portion of the research?" If they are not, then reconsider combining these in one research study. In these cases, two separate studies may be better suited because the researcher is likely asking two separate questions.

8
ETHICAL ISSUES

> Clearly, researchers need both cases and principles from which
> to learn about ethical behaviors. More than this, they need two
> attributes: the sensitivity to identify an ethical issue and the re-
> sponsibility to feel committed to acting appropriately in regard
> to such issues.
>
> **Eisner & Peshkin (1990, p. 244)**

Qualitative research, like most endeavors involving human relationships,
is replete with ethical issues at every step of the process. Developing the
kind of ethical sensitivity that Eisner and Peshkin refer to in the quote
above involves both knowledge of ethical principles guiding research
decisions and then ample practice in applying principles to the real dilemmas that emerge in a qualitative research context. Knowledge and
practice do not, of course, guarantee that a researcher will then behave
ethically when issues emerge, but paying attention to ethical issues and
making good judgments increase the likelihood of behaving ethically.

An important first step in developing ethical sensitivity is anticipating where and when ethical issues may emerge in the research process.

And indeed, the potential is great for ethical issues to emerge in all areas of the research design, including the statement of purpose and research questions, data collection, data analysis and interpretation, presentation of results, and the role of the researcher (Creswell, 2003). Issues of trust and rapport, as discussed in Chapter 3 on sampling, are ethical issues, as are being clear with the reader about your epistemological, theoretical, and methodological grounding, as discussed in Chapter 1; ways of dem- onstrating participants' historical and cultural situatedness, as stated in Chapter 5; the researcher's personal investments in the research, the various biases a researcher brings to the work, a researcher's surprises in the process of the research endeavor, and/or the ways in which one has avoided or suppressed certain points of view, as explicated in Chapter 5; and developing criteria and integrating strategies for assuring the trust- worthiness of the entire research design, as detailed in Chapters 6 and 7. Nearly every research decision and action carries with it an ethical dimension for which the researcher must be prepared.

The purpose of this chapter is to provide an overview of ethical is- sues that characterize qualitative research designs, principles that guide decision making when resolving ethical dilemmas, and examples from research that illuminate the issues and nature of the dilemmas. As Eisner and Peshkin (1990) appropriately suggested, ultimately, ethical sensi- tivity and behavior depend upon the good judgment of the researcher, which emerges "from the convergence of principle, experience, and re- flection" (p. 245). To that end, every research project requires that the researcher think through the nature of the study and how he or she should behave ethically in a particular set of research circumstances (L. M. Smith, 1990).

ETHICAL PRINCIPLES AT STAKE

[E]thical conduct is not just the simple matter of avoiding plac- ing at risk those whom in our research projects we variously call the researched "others," "subjects," and "respondents." It is the infinitely more complex challenge of doing good, a consid- eration that places researchers at odds with one another as they raise entirely different questions about the location of good in the conduct of research. And it is as well, the identification of what constitutes proper behavior in the range of roles, settings, and circumstances where qualitative researchers are apt to find themselves.

Eisner & Peshkin (1990, p. 243)

The ethical imperative to "do good," rather than to simply avoid risk in the context of qualitative research, significantly increases the obligations of the researcher to understand the ethical principles at stake in conducting research. Although many of these principles hold true for quantitative research as well, the nature of the relationships developed in qualitative studies between the researcher and participants or between the researcher and the research context creates unique dilemmas and issues that must be considered and integrated into research practice. Ethics in qualitative research

> has to do with how one treats those individuals with whom one interacts and is involved and how the relationships formed may depart from the conception of an ideal. At a commonsense level, caring, fairness, openness, and truth seem to be the important values undergirding the relationships and the activity of inquiry. (L. M. Smith, 1990, p. 260)

These ethical imperatives are often safeguarded through principles and promises such as confidentiality, anonymity, informed consent, avoidance of deception, respect, privacy, and "do no harm." Often, researchers remain complacent about ethical issues, thinking that if they simply comply with expectations and procedures dictated by the Institutional Review Board (IRB), then their obligations are met (Magolda & Weems, 2002). The following discussion of these ethical principles and practices demonstrates the considerable elusiveness behind these principles when tested in the complicated contexts of qualitative research.

Confidentiality refers to the treatment of information that an individual has knowingly disclosed in a research relationship, with an expectation that this information will not be disclosed to unauthorized parties without consent. In principle, confidentiality guarantees respondents that the information they provide in the research context will not be shared. *Anonymity* suggests that if and when information is shared, no identifiable data will be disclosed. When personal data are provided, it is only "behind a shield of anonymity" (Christians, 2000, p. 139). Stated differently, Patton (2002) made this distinction: "Confidentiality means you know but won't tell. Anonymity means you don't know, as in a survey returned anonymously" (p. 408). Both confidentiality and anonymity are part of the larger issue of protecting a participant's right to privacy and making promises that disclosure of any kind of information will not occur without a participant's consent.

The principles of confidentiality, anonymity, and privacy are typically operationalized in research through the statement of *informed consent*, which participants must sign before engaging in the research process. For example, following the institutional guidelines provided for human subjects review, a statement of informed consent is prepared and reviewed with each participant prior to the collection of any data. Below is an example of such a statement with excerpted portions that address directly the ethical principles of confidentiality, anonymity, and consent.

Statement of Informed Consent

I agree to participate in the research project entitled "[insert title]" being conducted by [insert researcher's name] of the [insert institutional affiliation]. The purpose of this study is to investigate students' understanding of _____ _____ [insert clear statement of purpose of study].

I understand that my participation in this project, which is expected to take no more than 3 hours, will involve participating in individual interviews and occasionally being observed. I understand that my interviews will be audiotaped. I am aware that some people are uncomfortable talking about themselves, and that any discomfort I might experience should be no more than typically experienced during a small-group discussion [include clear statement of any risks associated with participation]. If I am not comfortable with the discussion and wish to discontinue participation in the study, I will be free to leave without penalty.

The potential benefits of my participation include the opportunity to [insert benefits such as self-knowledge, reflection, and generation of new understanding].

I understand that my participation in this project is strictly voluntary and that information will be treated confidentially. My name will not be connected with any materials produced for this study, although I understand that there is some possibility of someone recognizing me through use of quotations and contextual descriptions. Only [researcher's name] will have access to individual data. Tapes and transcripts will be kept in a locked file and then destroyed 1 year after completion of the study.

I am aware that if I have any questions about my participation in the project, I may contact [researcher's name]. . . .

I may also contact the chair of the Behavioral and Social Sciences Institutional Review Board, [insert name and contact information]. . . .

Participant Name (please print): _____

Signature Date: _____

Investigator Signature Date: _____

By signing this form, the participant signals and verifies that the researcher has met the obligation to inform participants of the nature of the study and their involvement in it, and that the participants understand and agree with what has been communicated to them. Typically, the conversation ends with the signature. More problematically, however, as Weis and Fine (2000) pointed out,

> The consent form sits at the contradictory base of the institutionalization of research. Although the aim of informed consent is presumably to protect respondents, inform them of the possibility of harm in advance, and invite them to withdraw if they so desire, it also effectively releases the institution or funding agency from any liability and gives control of the research process to the researcher. (pp. 41–42)

The issues of control and power in qualitative research are important ones for researchers to consider. On the one hand, most qualitative methodologies emphasize relationship building and reciprocity between researcher and participant as well as the co-construction of meaning in the analysis phases. On the other hand, and important to the integrity of research, more bureaucratic processes such as informed consent seem to serve as subtle—and not so subtle—reminders that, ultimately, power resides with the researcher. Navigating this tension is an important consideration—one that Weis and Fine (2000) reconciled by focusing on informed consent as "a conscience—to remind us of our accountability and position" (p. 42). This idea of informed consent as conscience reminds researchers that there is much at stake for researchers as well as participants in the research process.

CHALLENGES IN APPLYING PRINCIPLES TO PRACTICE

Although nearly all codes of ethics and institutional review board requirements will call for the demonstration of strategies in place to preserve confidentiality, anonymity, privacy, and informed consent, many qualitative researchers stress that these principles and practices are nearly impossible to guarantee (Christians, 2000; Lincoln, 1990; Patton, 2002). Because of the nature of qualitative research, it is very difficult to always disguise the research context or the identity of the respondents participating in the study. Typically, pseudonyms are used, but this does not always guarantee anonymity. When pseudonyms are used, the researcher usually asks participants to choose their own pseudonym, which may make them more likely to be identifiable to those who know them and are reading results of the research. Furthermore, in some cases, participants may choose *not* to disguise information, suggesting that such a practice is inconsistent with the goals of the research project or with participants' needs to fully express who they are. For example, in a study on the importance of the coming-out process to gay, lesbian, bisexual, and transgendered (GLBT) identity, a participant may believe that to disguise one's identity further marginalizes and silences the experiences of GLBT individuals and runs counter to the purpose of the study. This is particularly true in projects with emancipatory goals or when using collaborative approaches.

Several key questions emerge from the realities of actually providing assurances of confidentiality and anonymity. First, as Patton (2002) identified, "What are reasonable promises of confidentiality that can be fully honored?" (p. 408). In some cases, participants may want to be identified or fully described in the setting. In other cases, researchers may inquire about changing certain details of a particular story line (e.g., names, locations, and demographic identifiers), to which a participant may or may not agree. The most important principle in thinking about this question is to promise only those assurances and guarantees that the researcher is confident can be delivered and to always honor and respect the wishes of participants. This requires a process of negotiation between the researcher and participants and may continually evolve as the research progresses.

This issue relates to the second question—are there ever any circumstances in which the researcher would not honor a participant's request for confidentiality or not promise confidentiality (Patton, 2002)? Examples of such circumstances might include a researcher learning from a participant about significant substance abuse, domestic violence, or theft. In some situations, for example, the reporting of child abuse or sexual assault, a researcher may be legally obligated to disclose information. It behooves the researcher to consider her or his research in the context of these situations and to evaluate the likelihood of any of these issues emerging. If there is any likelihood that these situations might, the researcher should consider discussing these issues in advance rather than waiting until a situation occurs and risking the perception of violating what was promised at the outset of the study. If any legal obligations may become a factor, these too should be included in the consent form.

In an investigation of lesbian identity development, the researcher listened as one of her young college student participants described suicidal thoughts and ideation. In consultation with her dissertation advisor, the decision was made to call the director of counseling services at the university where the research was conducted. The director had agreed, prior to the beginning of the research, to serve as a consulting psychologist to the researcher if the need arose. The researcher was then able to talk through with a highly skilled professional, in a confidential environment, the nature of the suicidal talk from her participant and make a decision about how to best handle the situation. These situations call for a researcher to think about ethical obligations to participants as well as to the research. If, in the above example, the researcher had simply "turned the student in," then any relationship of trust would most likely have been violated and the participation of this student in the research ended. On the other hand, if the researcher had chosen to ignore the participant's suicidal talk and considered it as data for her study, the risks she assumed were great and the potential consequences disastrous.

Another example that illustrates the tension in providing assurances of confidentiality, anonymity, and privacy focused on location of research. Despite the promise of anonymity, much research is conducted in public spaces or in office settings with public waiting areas. Although the "coffee shop interview" was suggested by a participant, the researcher should take care to think through all possible consequences of interviewing in a highly trafficked area. Despite a researcher's inquiry about a participant's comfort and perception of safety in a certain research space, anonymity cannot always be guaranteed.

Patton (2002) aptly summarized some of the tensions inherent in a promise of confidentiality in qualitative research:

> These are examples of how the norms about confidentiality are changing and being challenged as tension has emerged between the important ethic of protecting people's privacy and, in some cases, their desire to own their story. Informed consent, in this regard, does not automatically mean confidentiality. Informed consent can mean that participants understand the risks and benefits of having their real names reported and choose to do so. Protection of human subjects properly insists on informed consent. That does not automatically mean confidentiality. (p. 412)

Even the ethical imperatives of "do no harm" (Kitchener, 1985) and respect in the research relationship carry with them challenges and tensions. As Magolda and Weems (2002) aptly suggested, a sole reliance on meeting the requirements of IRB procedures can provide the researcher with a misguided sense of security with regard to harm. Furthermore, they wrote, "Because the IRB narrowly defines harm as physical or mental abuse, blatant violation of privacy, and ill-informed consent, the review process implicitly communicates that qualitative inquiry is relatively innocuous on the harm continuum" (p. 492). However, given the nature of the relationships between researchers and participants, which is at the core of qualitative research, even the best intentions can lead to the unintended consequences of harm or disrespect. For example, interview questions that are culturally inappropriate and insensitive may constitute a microassault on a participant's self-esteem, or interpreting results in an unfavorable light may bring further harm to a group already experiencing marginalization in their setting.

In their provocative article entitled "Doing Harm: An Unintended Consequence of Qualitative Inquiry?" Magolda and Weems (2002) argued, through the use of confessional tales from their own research, that the potential for harm is present for those serving as gatekeepers in qualitative studies and for participants in a study, the cultural communities of interest in a particular study, and researchers themselves. In summary, their tales suggest that although it is incumbent on the researcher to fully disclose and discuss the potential for harm in a study, it is not possible to ever fully anticipate the complexities, and therefore harm, that may emerge as the research progresses. Likewise, although participants often quickly provide consent to participate in a study, which signifies that they understand the risks involved and potential for harm, "safeguard measures . . . cannot ensure that respondents will fully understand (or care about) potential harm to themselves" (Magolda & Weems, p. 498).

As results of research are prepared, interpreted, and disseminated, issues of harm are also associated with how results will be received and perceived. And finally, the researcher runs the risk of harm in qualitative research through exposing oneself to others, bumping up against strongly held notions that are counter to research findings, and entertaining compromises to negotiate the complicated terrain of qualitative research contexts. Because the influence of social identities is omnipresent in qualitative studies, researcher self-disclosure can also be a difficult ethical issue. In an ethnographic study on the postsecondary pathways of rural high school students, conducted by a doctoral student for her dissertation research, this issue became soul-wrenching. The researcher wrote,

> I quickly put to rest any question of "being out" while completing my field work in a place where "people like to talk . . . when they find something, if someone does something wrong, they latch onto it and it just spreads like fire. . . . It's HORRIBLE. Horrible" [interview quotation]. Still, I struggle with the question of

coming out to any high school student who might identify as gay, lesbian, or bisexual. To disclose my own sexual orientation may well jeopardize my research, in terms of access to the school and the students. Disclosure might also put me in jeopardy. Not to disclose butts up against the principle of integrity with which I strive to live my life in a not-always-gay-friendly world. Having survived the trials and tribulations of my own queer adolescence with no assistance from nearby adults who clung to the hinges of their own closet doors, I have been particularly committed to being out to young people who might benefit from a lesbian role model the same way I might have benefited all those years ago. (T. L. Maltzan, personal communication, April 15, 2005)

Thus, the personal ethics involved in negotiating such tensions in the research process are both central to and complicated by the ethical dimensions inherent in qualitative research projects.

PHASES OF THE RESEARCH PROCESS AND ETHICAL ISSUES

The ethical principles of confidentiality, anonymity, informed consent, privacy, respect, and do no harm are central to the process of conducting qualitative research and emerge as dilemmas throughout the research process. An understanding of these principles is important in the development of ethical sensitivity but is not enough to effectively anticipate and resolve ethical dilemmas. As Eisner and Peshkin (1990) suggested, principles must be interwoven with practice and reflection for the development of good judgment. In this section of the chapter, phases of the research process are examined in concert with ethical principles at stake. Examples from research projects are offered as a pathway for reflection upon the ethical issues involved and how a researcher might think about and deal with such issues. It is important to note that these examples are illustrative in nature and that every research project is unique and contextual; thus, there are no simple templates or recipes to follow when working through ethical issues. Ethical principles provide helpful guidelines for thinking about issues—they do not offer answers. Individual researchers, then, must learn to recognize ethical issues, discern what is most important in the situation, and act accordingly.

To drive home the ubiquitous nature of ethics in qualitative research, L. M. Smith (1990) stated,

At the most microlevel, every decision and every act in a qualitative research project can be placed against one's ethical standards. From the very conception of the problem to the entry procedures to the kind and place of sampling and data collecting on through to publication—the entire research process can be viewed in terms of its implications for the people involved. (p. 273)

Statement of Purpose and Research Questions

The statement of purpose and guiding research questions provide the organizing framework for a study. They provide participants and researcher alike with guideposts for what it is the researcher would like to learn more about. Although nearly every text on qualitative research design offers statements such as "[p]articipants' rights include . . . the right to be fully informed about the study's purpose and about the involvement and time required for participation" (Morse & Richards, 2002, p. 205), this is not always easily accomplished because what is clear to the researcher may not be so clear to participants. The importance of clarity in the writing of these statements of purpose and in direct communication to participants about the goals of the researcher cannot be underestimated because participants do need to know something about the nature of their contributions and participation and what it is the researcher will ask of them. However, this communication must be ongoing because some aspects of the research design may shift as the study unfolds.

Embedded in the need for clarity in the statement of purpose and research questions are two related ethical issues: the ethical imperative to "do good" and the need to create a purpose statement that is consistent with the chosen methodology. "Doing good" suggests that care must be taken to assure that the focus of a study does not in any way contribute to the marginalization or disempowerment (Creswell, 2003) of participants and that, in fact, there exists the potential for benefit to participants. Doing good is more than simply "doing no harm" in that striving for goodness suggests that the research works toward participant authority, fulfillment, and social change. This is particularly crucial when conducting research with or about traditionally underrepresented or disenfranchised individuals and/or communities. Weis and Fine (2000) articulated this ethical responsibility well: "Because we write between the poor communities and social policy and because we seek to be taken seriously by both audiences, we know it is essential to think through the power, obligations, and responsibilities of social research" (p. 33). These commitments are first articulated in the statement of purpose and research questions for a study.

In a doctoral dissertation exploring the perceptions of the parents of first-generation college students, the researcher was careful not to further marginalize a population (first-generation college students and their parents), more typically characterized as unknowledgeable and unsupportive, in his statement of purpose and in the language he used to describe his focus. In further describing his interest, he wrote,

> In my literature review on first-generation college students, I was struck by how frequently researchers constructed parents as unable to support their children at college. Researchers often explained that parents without college experience could not advise their children about what happens there. Because my study utilized parents as participants, I felt obligated to those parents to consider whether my work might further contribute to the construction of *them* as deficient, or obstacles to their children's success. This could suggest to policy makers and administrators that to help first-generation students succeed, the students must be somehow separated from their parents. Did I want to contribute to that? (A. Delong, personal communication, May 5, 2005)

We, then, see his commitment to the parents reflected in both the statement of purpose and research questions for this study:

> The purpose of this study was to examine the perceptions of first-generation college students' parents about college attendance, and how they came to form these perceptions. . . . Two primary research questions guided this study:
>
> 1. How do parents view the role and significance of college attendance?
> 2. How do families define and exhibit "support" for their first-generation college student in both the college selection process and once the student is enrolled? (Delong, 2003)

In the writing of the statement of purpose and research questions, we see an intentional effort to avoid harm to participants through the use of marginalizing and devaluing language. This also conveys the respect the researcher has for understanding the experiences of parents and their understandings of the college choice and experience processes.

A second ethical issue connected to the statement of purpose and research questions rests in the relationship between the focus of the study and the chosen methodology. This issue has an ethical dimension to it because if a researcher presents in the statement of purpose, for example, that a study is a critical ethnography, then this suggests a certain relationship between the researcher and participants as well as an emancipatory goal for the research. In essence, the methodological approach, which is reflected in the statement of purpose, communicates to participants important information about how they will be interacting with the researcher and about promised outcomes from the participation. A good example of such a connection is found in Patti Lather and Chris Smithies's (1997) *Troubling the Angels: Women Living with HIV/AIDS*:

> This book explores the cultural meanings and cultural ramifications of the experiences and understandings of a particular group of women who live with the disease. . . . As witnesses to the women's courage and struggle, our hope is that this book will support, inform, and trouble its various readers as well as make visible the work of living with HIV/AIDS. . . . By moving from inside to outside, across different levels and a multiplicity and complexity of layers that unfold an event which exceeds our frames of reference, we hope to create a book that does justice to these women's lives, a book that exceeds our own understandings, some widened space to speak beyond our means. (pp. xiii, xvi)

Similarly, an ethnographic inquiry suggests to participants the inclusion of participant observation and prolonged engagement. No shortcuts for meeting these methodological criteria are acceptable. In addition, a stated purpose of an ethnographic approach should alert participants to the nature of their involvement with the researcher and their roles in data collection and analysis. Regardless of methodological approach, the researcher must be able to deliver on the promises communicated implicitly or explicitly in the statement of purpose and research questions.

One last issue related in a more indirect way to the statement of purpose and research questions is that of scope and timing. As noted in earlier chapters, the focus of a study must be defined enough to be not only clear but also realistic. Once a study is initiated, the purpose communicated to participants, and consent granted, the researcher then has an ethical responsibility and obligation to follow through on the project. Although many projects often take longer than initially planned due to a variety of factors that may not be anticipated at the early stages of planning, failure to complete a project once initiated is a breach of trust, respect, and the commitment made to participants, as well as an abuse of the power in the researcher–participant relationship. Researchers must be cognizant of the fact that following through on research projects is not just a function of—or reaction to—one's own commitments and time considerations, but also an obligation owed to participants who shared their time and expertise at the request of the researcher.

DATA COLLECTION

Ethical issues may emerge in the data collection phases of research because of how data are collected, where data are collected, and why data are collected. Once again, these factors are guided by methodological choice so that, for example, ethical issues related to participant observation will emerge more potently in ethnographic studies than in narrative inquiry. More importantly, these decisions must be anchored in a fundamental respect for research participants and research sites. Although researchers are deeply invested in and very familiar with the phenomenon they are investigating, participants may be less so and therefore vulnerable to what might be perceived as intrusions on their space—both physical and psychological. Whether collecting data via interviews or observations, researchers must be sensitive and attuned to how participants might receive and perceive interview questions and the scrutiny of observation. Any signs of discomfort, resistance, or other indications of emotional distress must be recognized and appropriately negotiated. Some studies may elicit the revelation of painful memories or experiences that require the researcher to both respond empathically and know when consultation or referral to counseling is warranted. For example, in a study that Susan conducted on college women's identity development, one participant, in talking about formative experiences to her construction of self, conveyed the influence of an eating disorder (Jones, 1997). Clearly central to her understanding of herself as a woman and the development of positive self-esteem, the memories evoked were painful and elicited tears as she told her story. In this particular situation, Susan utilized her counseling skills and made a professional judgment that consultation or referral was not necessary. She did, however, have access to a professional counselor willing to serve in a consultant role should the need arise during the course of the study.

Another potential ethical issue related to data collection revolves around the collection of data that the researcher *hopes* to gather. The researcher necessarily frames the focus of the study through the statement of purpose and research questions and then goes out to ask questions and/or observe the phenomenon under investigation in order to elicit some answers and responses to these questions. Interview questions, for example, then have the potential to lead participants in a certain direction in their responses. Although some of this is unavoidable by the sheer construction of questions, care must be taken not to direct participants so much that they are telling your story rather than their own. Weis and Fine (2000) referred to this as the "voyeuristic search for 'good' stories" (p. 48). They went on to explain how these stories got constructed among their research team:

> While engaging in interviewing, the research assistants would gather informally and share stories. We talked about respondents not showing up for interviews, the lives of interviewees, "funny things that happened along the way," our pain, and our early understanding of the material. The words and phrases thrown around included: "interesting," "boring," "nothing out of the ordinary," "you should have heard this," and "this one has great stories." (p. 48)

These somewhat natural and human reactions to what has been heard also assign judgment to the stories told that reflect the researcher's perspective and point of view and must be checked because they could lead to bias in analysis.

One of the reasons these reactions occur is because the researcher erroneously constructs data collection only through a one-way conversation, leaving no room for reciprocal conversations with participants. Opportunities for reciprocal dialogue and conversations, even in those methodologies that call for a more structured approach to interviewing, create the space for researchers and participants to reflect on the meaning-making process together. In reflecting on her own research process in relation to interviewing, a recent doctoral graduate wrote,

> One of the ethical principles that guided me through the study was that I should not expect the participants to discuss anything with me that I would not discuss with them. Although in the context of teaching, this quote from bell hooks (1994) about engaged pedagogy is very prominent in my thinking on this matter. "Empowerment cannot happen if [professors] refuse to be vulnerable while encouraging students to take risks. . . . " (p. 21). While this was not a critical/emancipatory study, I did want it to be empowering for them. But even more so, it felt like I was using them if I asked them to talk about things I wouldn't talk about (and it reinforced the power difference). While this was usually very comfortable for me, there were some times when it was less comfortable. And I shied away from their questions of me. (E. S. Abes, personal communication, May 1, 2005)

The issue of researcher disclosure in the data collection process is an important one to consider. Some research contexts or cultures may make this decision even tougher. For example, in Susan's research with young college women students, she was aware that several participants clearly saw her in the role of "friend" rather than researcher as the research process evolved (Jones, 1997). Because of the nature of the questions being explored, participants let Susan know that she knew more about them than almost anyone else in their lives. In another example of blurred boundaries between the purpose of the study, researcher, and participants, Jan reported,

> I had a student who was conducting a study on the experience of male Asian American students in a same sex, same race mentoring program. During her study, two of her participants stopped participating in the mentoring program because they said that they saw her as a mentor. (J. L. Arminio, personal communication, January 14, 2005)

In this case, the research process itself became an intervention, which is actually quite a common occurrence in qualitative studies, particularly when participants are invited to talk about topics that are important to them and about which they rarely have occasion to discuss. Torres and Baxter Magolda (2002) discussed this phenomenon as an enduring characteristic of constructivist studies and as emblematic of the trust and respect that evolve in qualitative research. This phenomenon is not in and of itself harmful or unethical, except when it prevents or dissuades participants from experiencing positive benefits from the research process. Blurred boundaries in qualitative research are fairly typical, and, although they are often unavoidable, they must be negotiated carefully.

Data Analysis and Interpretation

Analyzing and interpreting data carry with them a significant ethical responsibility to tell the story of the research and the participants who are a part of a study in a way that participants themselves recognize as their story (Jones, 2002). As noted in Chapter 4, data analysis is a more or less structured process (depending on the researcher's methodological approach) and is integrally related to interpretation of the analyses (see Chapter 5 for a more thorough discussion of interpretation and representation). In fact, data analysis is essentially an interpretive process.

The important point is that data analysis is much more than simply reading transcripts and describing what is there. Novice qualitative researchers often identify this as "looking for themes." Data analysis is a time-consuming and labor intensive process that requires immersion in the data and continual reading and rereading of transcripts as codes, themes, patterns, and categories are generated. The more time (both in terms of quantity of time and quality of time) the researcher is immersed in the data, the stronger the analyses and interpretation will be. This time is required to meet the ethical obligations the researcher has to the participants and to the research project. Respecting participants and assuring the integrity of the research process are ethical imperatives that guide analysis and interpretation.

Several strategies exist to check the researcher's analyses and interpretations. Building on the theme of continuity and congruence, which is fully discussed in Chapter 4, the readers of qualitative studies must see a clear connection between what are presented as data and what are offered as interpretations of the data. Most typically, rich description and many quotations from transcripts are offered so that the reader may join the researcher on the *inside* of the data. It is not acceptable to simply offer one quote for each theme because this does not provide the kind of evidence that a reader needs to trace the claims that the researcher makes back to the data itself. "Evidentiary inadequacy" (Erickson, 1986) is in fact an ethical issue because it relates to the integrity of data analysis and interpretation. Erickson detailed five types of evidentiary inadequacy that come from both data collection decisions and analytic strategies:

1. *Inadequate amounts of evidence.* The researcher has too little evidence to warrant certain key assertions.
2. *Inadequate variety in kinds of evidence.* The researcher fails to have evidence across a range of different kinds of sources (e.g., direct observation, interviewing, and site documents) to warrant key assertions through *triangulation.*
3. *Faulty interpretive status of evidence.* The researcher fails to have understood the key aspects of the complexity of action or of meaning perspectives held by actors in the setting due to inadequate time in the field or interviewing that was not intensive enough.
4. *Inadequate disconfirming evidence.* The researcher lacks data that might disconfirm a key assertion and lacks evidence that a deliberate search was made for potentially disconfirming data (leading to the critique that the researcher only looked for evidence to support his or her own interpretations).
5. *Inadequate discrepant case analysis.* The researcher did not scrutinize the set of disconfirming instances, examining each instance (i.e., discrepant case) and comparing it with the confirming instances to determine which features of the disconfirming

case were the same as or different from the analogous features of the confirming cases. Such comparative feature analysis often reveals flaws in the original assertion (Erickson, 1986, p. 140).

Implicit in a discussion of the importance of providing sufficient evidence for the claims the researcher makes is that evidence of an analytic process is also provided. Data analysis typically involves a process of moving from concrete words and categories to more abstract ones. This process results in the naming of themes intended to capture what is going on in the data. Therefore, these themes should offer a glimpse into the richness of the data rather than simply convey a nondescriptive, generic name. For example, in a master's thesis exploring the experiences of allies to GLBT students, an early draft of the presentation of results included theme names such as *awareness of self* and *advocacy as allies*. Neither of these theme names gives the reader any idea of the texture of awareness or advocacy—was it increased awareness? Shifting awareness? Highly visible advocacy? Limited advocacy? Subsequent versions, after going back into the data and taking a more critical and analytical look, included a much more nuanced and complex picture of what was really going on for these allies. The resulting analysis included theme names such as *perceived consequences to self, rationalizing non-ally behavior,* and *influences of religious and political contexts.* This is the truth-telling dimension in the ethics of qualitative research—the researcher must spend significant time with the data and the analytic process to get the interpretation of the data close to participants' meaning.

Accurate interpretations are advanced through the use of trustworthiness strategies (see a more detailed discussion in Chapter 6). One central strategy is to involve the participants in the data analysis and interpretation. This is often referred to as *co-construction*. The mechanics of truly accomplishing co-construction are both time consuming and complicated. Abes captured these dynamics:

> In thinking about how I use the interview transcripts, it's important to me that I consider them to be life stories, rather than only "data." As I write, I'm invested in co-constructing these stories. But as well-intentioned as I might be, I fear I'm beginning to take ownership of the participants' stories for my own research agenda. As I interpret, reinterpret, and rewrite the stories, they become less co-constructed. . . . Co-constructing the stories told in this manuscript requires, at the very minimum, asking the participants to review and discuss my interpretations. Needing them to be part of this process raises several ethical concerns.

First, some analysis that shapes how I tell their stories focuses on my understandings of the students' cognitive complexity. Some of my interpretations are grounded in inconsistencies within and omissions from their stories. Students cannot provide any check on interpretations that exceed their cognitive capacity. These interpretations are thus ultimately based on my own biased understanding of how they make meaning of their identity. Second, I question how much time I ethically can expect participants to invest in the study. These busy young adults have already given much of their time through data collection. Asking for additional time is beginning to feel selfish, and even exploitive, knowing that whatever personal benefits they initially reaped from this research are diminishing. Yet not working with them to co-construct the story also feels unethical. I'm still processing these dueling ethical concerns. At a minimum, I believe I need to invite them to review and discuss the analysis and manuscript and trust that they will not do so only out of a sense of obligation. Third, I cannot locate one of the participants. Is it ethical for me to continue using her stories? It feels wrong, but still I am doing so because I believe she has an important story to tell that can benefit others, which was her motivation for participating in the study. I hope I am telling a version of her story that captures her understandings. (E. S. Abes, personal communication, April 28, 2005)

The ethics of data analysis (which are related to the ethics and politics of representation as discussed in Chapter 5) are at the heart of good qualitative research. Reflection on the ethical obligations to fully engage in the analytic process is crucial before, during, and after the research process. As summarized well by Soltis (1990), "Description is not neutral. It is the interpretive result of an interpersonal engagement with others and as such has the potential to be ethically sensitive, especially with regard to the principle of respect for persons" (p. 252).

WRITING AND PUBLICATION

Lamott (1994) connected ethics and the writing process with this cogent passage:

Becoming a writer is about becoming conscious. When you're conscious and writing from a place of insight and simplicity and real caring about truth, you have the ability to throw lights on for your reader. He or she will recognize his or her life and truth in what you say, in the pictures you have painted. . . . Tell the truth as you understand it. If you're a writer, you have a moral obligation to do this. (pp. 225–226)

Although writing is central to the communication of results and discussion in both qualitative and quantitative studies, writing and rewriting are the primary means of communication in qualitative research. It is in and through the writing process that meaning takes shape and insights are sharpened. Therefore, excellent writing skills are crucial to qualitative research in order to "throw the lights on" for readers. Good writing requires significant practice and benefits from multiple perspectives. We never submit anything for publication that several others have not read and proofed for us and for which they have not offered feedback and commentary. This not only improves our writing but also assures that we are communicating clearly and succinctly. The use of an "inquiry auditor" (Lincoln & Guba, 1985) provides a check on the content of what is written because the person in this role has read all the transcripts and, in essence, provides verification that what is written truly comes from the data. What becomes known about your research comes through what is written, and, therefore, the writing process carries with it a great responsibility. Telling and not telling are equally powerful, and this power most often resides with the researcher. What one writes—or withholds—has significant consequences for the research and to the participants. This can get complicated if, for example, what the researcher writes is not received well by the participants. They might not quibble with what is written but might be more concerned that it does not reflect well on them. Related, if the research is funded by an external source and/or by individuals with specific expectations about the findings, the researcher may experience pressure to soften or suppress certain findings (Creswell, 2003; Soltis, 1990). This dilemma may be a test of the researcher's integrity if continued funding is in jeopardy and should be negotiated in the initial stages of the research process.

Ethical issues also exist as researchers consider the dissemination of results. For example, is there an ethical obligation to share results and publish findings in a reasonable amount of time? We would suggest that the answer is yes because herein lies the public good in research. However, researchers cannot always control what consumers of research actually do with the results. It is important for researchers to consider the possible uses for their results and the potential consequences for their participants or the setting in which the research was conducted.

STRATEGIES FOR WORKING
THROUGH ETHICAL ISSUES

No simple recipes or templates exist for definitively anticipating and responding to ethical issues in qualitative research. However, the combination of knowledge, reflexivity, and experience (action) increases the likelihood that researchers will be sensitive to the ethical dimensions of research and respond appropriately. Lincoln (1990) offered this overarching principle, which she referred to as a "categorical imperative" to guide action:

> Behave as if the principle underlying your action were to become—by your will alone—a universal law of nature. That is, act in such a way that you would not be distressed to discover that the principle undergirding your own action were now a law that could be enacted by others upon you. (p. 291)

Using this underlying principle, we offer the following strategies as a beginning place:

- Anticipate ethical issues that may come up, and integrate these into the research design process (Magolda & Weems, 2002).
- Develop rapport with participants, and work on sustaining relationships through ongoing and honest communication and dialogue about the research process.
- Identify an ethical "mentor" or those with whom you can consult as issues emerge.
- Join a writing group or research team so that you can learn from others' ethical dilemmas and gain experience in resolving them.
- Familiarize yourself with and adhere to ethical codes (e.g., ACPA) and ethical guidelines provided in style manuals (e.g., American Psychological Association [APA], 2001) and for professions such as the APA, Association for the Study of Higher Education (ASHE), and the American Educational Research Association (AERA).
- Take seriously the reflective process on ethical issues, which helps connect ethical sensitivity to action.
- Your greatest ethical commitment must be to the participants in your study. All research decisions must be evaluated against the likelihood of avoiding harm and doing good to them. This is the ethical injunction to *care*, which is not simply, as Noddings (1984) wrote, putting yourself in others' shoes, but instead receiving the other into oneself such that their reality "becomes a real possibility" for you (p. 14).

SUMMARY

No researcher can escape the ethical dilemmas posed by qualitative inquiry. The purpose of this chapter was to highlight some of the overarching ethical principles at work in qualitative research as well as particular issues that emerge at each stage of the research process. Our hope is that such knowledge will increase the ethical sensitivity of researchers and improve the skills needed to connect sensitivity to action. Ultimately, both sensitivity and skill depend upon respect—for the research process, the research setting, and the people in it. When respect is diligently and deliberately practiced, all involved in the research process benefit because, as Lawrence-Lightfoot (1999) noted, "Respectful relationships also have a way of sustaining and replicating themselves" (p. 10).

EXERCISE

You are involved in teaching a leadership course for first-year African American students at your large, public, predominantly White campus. Midway through the course, you think, "Wow, this course is a great little case study. I think I am going to turn it into a research project." You know that you still have reflective journals from the students, which were written at the beginning of the semester, and you have been in class each session so you have heard what students have been saying in the class.

- Identify the ethical issues in this scenario and the principles at stake.
- If you were to go ahead and design this research, what specific steps would you need to take to conduct the study in an ethical manner?
- Is there another (better) alternative than conducting the study?

9

WHAT IS IT TO WORK QUALITATIVELY?

While writing this book, we would periodically come together to work on the revisions of chapters and revisit our progress. As a collective, composed of individual insights and experiences, we listened to each other's descriptions of and perspectives on qualitative research and made decisions that eventually created a common understanding. As we emphasize throughout this book, understanding one's worldview and researcher reflexivity are essential elements of good qualitative inquiry. Thus, we want to structure this last chapter through our own individual stories and reflections about our evolution as qualitative researchers and our collective understanding about how qualitative work is done. As we acknowledged in the Preface, we came to this project from different life experiences and prior knowledge of qualitative inquiry. However, we were in agreement in our commitment to providing a good and helpful resource on qualitative inquiry and had some ideas about what needed to be included in such a text. As we toiled on this book, we came to a mutual understanding about what constitutes good qualitative work. However, we recognized that this understanding emerged from our discussions about the disparate pathways and experiences that significantly influenced our current knowledge and practice of qualitative inquiry. We want now to share the paths that led us to this understanding.

In sharing our stories, we are also offering reflections on our writing and our beginnings as qualitative researchers. What follows is each of our stories about how we came to learn about qualitative research and become qualitative researchers. Then, utilizing an approach modeled on the principles of narrative analysis, we examine our stories to illuminate the various pathways to doing qualitative work and the lessons we have learned. Because we are using a narrative approach to analysis, it is important for us to acknowledge the importance of context and how context impacts our individual stories and the interpretations we make of these stories. This is a tension to be navigated in narrative analysis because of the "problem of context or the embeddedness of a text or story within personal or group experience" (Manning & Cullum-Swan, 1994, p. 474). With this caution in mind, we proceed in sharing the lessons we learned in the process of doing qualitative research.

OUR STORIED LIVES

Susan's Story

Some set great value on method, while others pride themselves on dispensing with method. To be without method is deplorable, but to depend on method entirely is worse. You must first learn to observe the rules faithfully; afterwards, modify them according to your intelligence and capacity.

Lu Ch'ai, *The Tao of Painting* **(1701)**

I first encountered this quotation on the first page of the syllabus for a course entitled Qualitative Research Methods which was my initial introduction to qualitative research. The course was taught by Corrine Glesne (who at the time was working on the first edition of *Becoming Qualitative*, 1999, with A. Peshkin) at the University of Vermont. I was working as a dean of students, but was actively questioning whether or not I wanted to leave the security of a full-time job I loved for life as a full-time doctoral student. A friend had recommended this course because Dr. Glesne had a reputation as a wonderful teacher. I had no idea what I would be learning, or the influence of this one class on my future work in higher education and student affairs. I did like that the entire syllabus included quotations from a wide variety of literature because I often used quotations from other sources to orient and locate my written work.

We spent the semester engaged in voluminous reading (or so I thought at the time) *about* qualitative research, while also *engaging in* the practice of qualitative research by designing and conducting a study. My study explored students' decisions to leave college after their first year. I began my final paper reporting on my study with an orienting quote to set the context for what followed:

> Far into the night, while the other creatures slept, Charlotte worked on her web. First she ripped out a few of the orb lines near the center. She left the radial lines alone, as they were needed for support. As she worked, her eight legs were a great help to her. So were her teeth. She loved to weave, and she was an expert at it.

This, of course, is a quotation from E. B. White's *Charlotte's Web*. Although perhaps not the source of most academic and scholarly renderings of great research, at the time it helped me situate the results of my study not as a single explanation for departure, but more so as a *web* of decision making.

My next transformative experience with qualitative research occurred in a course at the University of Maryland with Dr. Francine Hultgren. This course focused specifically on the methodology of phenomenology. Two dimensions of this course profoundly impacted my development, I think, as a qualitative researcher. First, I developed an appreciation of the importance of understanding philosophical traditions that undergird specific methodologies. In essence, I began to *weave* the more philosophically oriented qualitative methodological approaches with traditional qualitative methods and understand the importance for doing so. Second, this course was extremely writing intensive. We wrote reflections (some of which we were asked to read aloud to the other students in the class) every week of the semester. I have always loved to write, but I believe this experience with writing enabled me to write with a depth and clarity that are hard to now, ironically, put words to. However, I did put words to the experience of *becoming* a qualitative researcher in my final phenomenology reflection for the class:

> In reflecting on the actual experience of phenomenological writing, I marvel as that which I had inside of me which took new shape through my writing. Or that which was called forth through the readings and discussions we had in class. I basked in the experience of letting my writing go, having on several occasions looked back at something I had written and wondered where it had come from. And in letting the writing take its own

shape, I experienced the sensation of describing some piece of my core and the essence of a particular phenomenon. . . . Phenomenological inquiry, it seems to me, is a vehicle for entering into the lives of others who help us make their lives a part of our own, which then offers us the opportunity-responsibility-to be-in-the world in more thoughtful ways.

Enlivened by the philosophical ideas of Jacques Derrida (1985), my research project for the phenomenology class explored the lived experience of *difference*. I was interested in how the perception of, or experience with, difference or otherness touched a core sense of self. Phenomenological research enabled me to explore the entanglements of self-other without dichotomizing these realities of lived experience, but more so by inhabiting the space in between. Of course, what drew me to this inquiry was my own experience with *othering*, so this research connected me not only to others but also to myself in new and significant ways. As a student of student development theories in my graduate programs, I failed to see myself in what I was reading. I was tired of placing myself into stages, quadrants, phases, types, statuses, or what seemed an endless repertoire of possible categories that would name and claim me for who I was (or not). Perhaps a bit unfair in my critique of pioneering work at the time, I kept thinking that development is more complicated than this—and I wanted to grapple with the complexities and figure out how best to study complex phenomena like "development" and "identity." These interests have served as the foundation for my teaching and research since that phenomenology class.

I believe that, as Patti Lather (1992) has written, we need to work against the "one best way approach to the generation and legitimization of knowledge about the world" (p. 1). I was not eager to take doctoral statistics classes—and in fact (confessional tale) spent some amusing time (to me) in my classes inventing new definitions for words like *categorical variable, degrees of freedom, disordinal interaction, homoscedasticity, kurtosis,* and *platykurtic distributions*. I do think it is important to understand both traditions well enough to be good evaluators of research (e.g., consumers of research in educational journals) and, as qualitative researchers, to defend this approach to skeptical quantitative researchers. I have been in a number of dissertation defenses or editorial boards where feedback is given that conveys a lack of respect for qualitative research. "How can you say anything about this topic with so few participants?" "Wouldn't a control group help?" "This paper reads like a chatty little monograph." "Would you want your daughter taking medication tested on an *N* of 10?" Usually not mean-spirited questions, they emerge from a lack of exposure to and understanding of good qualitative research. We need to be able to demonstrate that certain questions are best explored through qualitative methodologies and rigorous methods, and that this produces empirical work. Hence, the purpose of this book.

As I reflect now on my evolution as a qualitative researcher and how that has influenced the creation of this book, I am once again taken by the idea of the web and, perhaps more significantly, the *weaving* of a web. I am also more firmly committed than when I wrote the words above to the idea—necessity—of putting research to good use. I came to the writing of this book with an interest in weaving together the pieces of qualitative research in meaningful ways so that greater numbers of researchers would engage with the research process in more thoughtful ways. My experience writing this book has only underscored the importance of thinking through these connections and relationships—not so much to snap them neatly into place, but to inhabit the gaps and navigate the tensions. As Lu Ch'ai suggested long ago, you must first understand the "rules" before pushing their boundaries.

I also appreciate the process of creating and weaving together this book with two others. Although we certainly knew this intellectually before embarking on this project, the process of writing the book brought to the surface our individual histories, writing styles, and points of view. We came to the book with a common interest, intent, and understanding of what the outcome might look like, but the process of getting there was quite different. We joked that Jan's writing—and outlook on life—was always phenomenological, Vasti's very direct, and I was the storyteller who wrote the effusive metaphorical opening paragraph that Vasti never liked! Nonetheless, the weaving together of our past histories and experiences with different approaches to communicating our message is a strength of the book. It has also greatly contributed to my development as a qualitative researcher. I *know* a whole lot more about qualitative research now, and I *understand* more fully the complexities and tensions inherent in this work—which reminds me of a quote: "Understanding involves intimacy and equality between self and object, while knowing implies separation from the object and mastery over it" (Belenky, Clinchy, Goldberger, & Tarule, 1986, p. 101).

Jan's Story

I knew as I sat in Dr. Saddlemire's office at the end of my master's oral comprehensive examination when he asked, "Is a doctorate in your future?" that I could not complete a statistical analysis worthy of a doctoral dissertation. My preparation in statistics had been poor. This, combined with years of previous messages that assumed I had a poor ability in math, made succeeding in a doctoral program my impossible dream. Nonetheless, I found myself 12 years later contemplating a research topic in an interview for a doctoral program with Dr. Marylu McEwen. She offered qualitative means as an option for conducting a study. Qualitative research became my doctoral Dulcinea. Not considered "hard" science, it was the prostitute of research epistemologies. "How is this any different from therapy?" I once was asked. But it offered an opportunity to engage in something important.

Assuming incorrectly that qualitative research was the sole purview of anthropology, as a doctoral student I registered for the qualitative research course in that department. I soon found out that my chances of actually taking the course were slim because anthropology students had first priority in enrolling for the course. When my place on a long waiting list was determined, my advisor, Marylu, suggested a qualitative course in the College of Education with a professor she knew and recommended. Marylu directed me to consult flyers that had been posted advertising the course, Phenomenology and Pedagogy. Though thrilled that I could register and actually get into the course, I was dismayed at taking a course the name of which I could not pronounce. Driving to campus on the first day of class, I repeatedly practiced saying the course title out loud, hoping I wouldn't be identified as a first-generation college student fraud unworthy of being there. How could I succeed in a course I could not pronounce?

My fears were misguided. On the first day of the class, friendly signs pointed the way through the hallways to the "P and P" classroom. Muffins and a sincere teacher scholar met us. My first impression of Dr. Francine Hultgren was of a middle school home economics teacher I wish I would have had. She was a blessing.

I was blessed also with fellow doctoral students from a variety of disciplines (teacher education, nursing, vocational technology, and exercise science) who were talented writers willing to struggle with what it meant to allow phenomenology to influence pedagogy. We wrote in class and shared our musings into and about phenomenology. I heard a nurse contemplate what care meant when patients are connected to machines, not to human touch. A man who worked for a large corporation contemplated how his life lived him rather than he lived his life. A student with a physical disability, who was told she would never drive, wrote how her beautiful red sports car with a black interior and Delta Sigma Theta vanity plates was a reminder not to believe others' limitations of her. A drama teacher questioned why nuns at his elementary school admonished him for saying he understood that the Trinity was three Gods in One. What is there not to understand, Father, Son, and Holy Spirit? Where is the mystery? They insisted that it be a mystery for him.

Including the self into one's research was poignant and powerful. Having grown up in rural Ohio in an all-White community, I naïvely wondered what it was like for people of color to have a race and live the history of the implications of race. During readings and critiques of our wonderings, Francine reminded me that phenomenology is the lived experience. Why was I compelled to wonder so much about what, as a White woman, I could not experience? Why was I turning away from my own experience of race and privilege? That was a watershed moment for me. Other incidents supported the watershed—the racial identity development workshop for my assistantship, the assigned readings on race and White privilege in doctoral classes, and discussions with classmates and colleagues more thoughtful than I about the realities of the world. It was then that I turned to questions about race, as it is possessed and experienced by White people, as my scholarly passion.

Phenomenology and Pedagogy ended with my creating the concept of "waking up White." A survey course covering a variety of qualitative methodologies ensued, followed by the course Communication in the Curriculum. It was in this last class that a fellow student and I sat on the steps outside the classroom building contemplating why it is that eyes cry—Michael Levin's (1988, 1989) "breaking down" and "breaking through"—and why the ears hear. These courses, and the thoughts, ideas, and discussions they prompted, embraced a worldview that was not positivist or objective but nonetheless vibrant, rich, in-depth, poetic, and explicit.

The concept of waking up White turned into a hermeneutic phenomenological dissertation about the lived experience of White graduate students trying to live a life of racial justice. This inquiry exposed myths about what it means to be White. This investigation also led me to explore the nature of race-related guilt for White people and how guilt has the potential to teach people authentic ways of being. I also have explored the legacy that White people leave to subsequent generations. For example, the following questions now press upon me: How is the historical legacy of your people a part of who you are now? Who might you become again, and under what circumstances? Would asking for forgiveness of those individuals whom we have wronged bring us to a more authentic way to be with each other? Like a fan where one insight blossoms into adjacent ones, I also sought insight into how race and privilege influence perspectives on leadership, counseling, involvement, and teaching.

My work at a teaching institution has been enhanced by being a qualitative researcher and doing qualitative research. My teaching, but more so my lived experience of learning with my students, has prompted insight into unexplored issues. How is it that we should teach about justice? How is it that students learn about justice? How do we understand this learning? It also has prompted me to honor and respect language. Word choice certainly influences learning and barriers to learning. I have learned to try to be deliberate with word choice. With each reading of what I have written, I debate and then change words that during a previous reading I was so sure captured the appropriate meaning. My weaving of hermeneutic phenomenological stories necessitates deliberate attention that includes the frustration of searching for words that adequately convey meaning and settling for some that almost, but do not quite, fit. Yet, some words so easily convey meaning. I have come to realize not only the potential power of words, but also the inadequacy of some words, or even all words at some times. My preparation in qualitative research and in negotiating what to write in this book has made me more respectful of the skills involved in the choosing and placement of words—both when writing and also when speaking. This demonstrates how the knower and known struggle to become merged. Who are we as individuals and as professionals? How does where we are in our life's journey and our worldview influence the studies we are compelled to conduct, how we conduct them, how we write about them, and how we teach about them? Qualitative work has become a vehicle on which to journey to become a more informed and authentic teacher, researcher, writer, and advocate.

Vasti's Story

Unlike my coauthors, I was not groomed as a qualitative researcher. I was taught to have respect for both traditions, but to remember that qualitative research took a lot of time. During my doctoral studies I took a course in qualitative research that provided a foundation, but I was encouraged to have much more training in quantitative methods. By the time I finished my doctoral work, I had taken nearly the complete offering of statistics courses, as well as classes in measurement and research design. What this training also taught me was that numbers are not as constant as some people make them out to be. The more understanding one has of quantitative analysis, the more one can manipulate the findings; this all depends on your worldview and the impact that view can have on the interpretation of data. (Sound familiar?)

In spite of my strong quantitative training, there was always one question that kept creeping into my research. Because my research has always been on Latino/a college students, I often questioned why I should pay attention to these quantitative studies if most of them only tell me about the deficiencies among Latino/as. According to many quantitative (mostly regression) studies in higher education, a series of characteristics determines the likelihood that a student will be retained and graduate from college. Because I do not have the demographic characteristics of students who succeed, I should not have graduated from college (especially in four years), not completed my master's, and certainly not completed my Ph.D. Although I did possess some of the characteristics that predict college retention, there were only a few characteristics that matched the statistical formula for success in higher education. I knew these studies were not expressing my experiences as an immigrant, second language learner, Latina who wanted an education and wanted to maintain my cultural roots. It is difficult for quantitative research to capture the complexity of real life.

After completing a quantitative dissertation that validated a bicultural orientation model for Latino college students, I immediately began to express that a major shortcoming of this research study was that it could only place the student within the cultural orientation quadrant, but the model could not say anything about the process (choices) that occurred for the student to attain the cultural orientation. I knew I had to conduct a qualitative study to explore the choices between two cultures that influence how Latino/a students (and I) express their culture.

My introductory course in qualitative research taught me enough to know that I needed to do much more reading about the act of doing qualitative work before I could begin a study with any confidence. I spent 6 months reading about different paradigms and methodologies in order to decide what matched my own worldview and the goals of my future longitudinal research study. The time I spent learning and reflecting on the process of research was critical and was one that I think many researchers skip. I know I am a better researcher for having spent this time reflecting and exploring. In hindsight, I make this sound like an idyllic process, but in reality I was frustrated! I agreed with some aspects of one methodology, but would disagree with others' tenets. Finally, I was so frustrated with the whole process that I wrote out my reactions and sent the ramblings to two qualitative researchers I respected. It was not until others expressed that they understood my concerns that I felt comfortable situating myself as a constructivist qualitative researcher who uses grounded theory methodology.

My search to claim my own worldview and methodology also forced me to decide what role my quantitative training would take within my research agenda. I struggled with this question and reflected on the limitations

I saw in quantitative research. During this internal struggle, I was also reading more research articles in the area of minority student retention and found some interesting research designs using structural equation modeling. The process of testing models based on the theoretical understanding of a phenomenon was intriguing to me. This type of quantitative research seems to be more precise in what could be said about the data and created a clear place for theory to impact and shape the quantitative technique. This exploration coincided with a department chair who was an expert in structural equation modeling. The ability to use him as a listening board for my ideas and to ask questions that dealt with paradigm and methodology allowed me to explore my own ideas about the nature of knowledge and how I saw the tension between these types of methodologies as both complementary and contradictory. Although I could rule out certain types of quantitative analyses as being too much of a fishing expedition to be consistent with my own worldview, I could not rule out all of the quantitative techniques available. At this point I knew I had to make a decision about how I wanted to be seen as a researcher. Doing good work in both areas is difficult to do and even more difficult to explain.

The defining issue for me became the research question or, as I prefer to call it, the question of interest. The question I was interested in was complex and required multiple methods to attempt to answer. I also knew that I was likely to spend the rest of my career attempting to answer this question: What are the choices Latino/a students make that help them succeed in college?

For the past 6 years, I have been conducting a mixed method study looking at the choices to stay in college for Latino/a students. Each summer I spend my time deciding what analysis I will conduct and how it fits with my stated paradigm, methodology, and strategies. I know I drive my research assistants crazy with these questions about process and purpose, but I also know they appreciate watching me struggle with the tensions inherent in research and are better equipped for their own struggles with research.

I recognize that because I use mixed methods, some purists (from both qualitative and quantitative traditions) will always question me. This is also the reason that mixed method studies are difficult to publish. At the same time, I see the benefit and hope that with time and understanding, more people will understand the process of mixing methods and how it can be done with respect for both traditions.

I have also recognized that as a person, I tend to order my thoughts before I ever spill them out on paper. This was highlighted during the writing of this book. This writing style is different from that of many qualitative researchers and can seem less "emergent"—in reality, it is the way I organize myself as a human being, and it naturally spills into my qualitative research. The systematic analysis process in grounded theory matches my style of organizing my thoughts. Yet, other aspects of the qualitative research process (like trustworthiness) help to balance organization with a constructivist worldview. I will always use inquiry auditors as a part of a research design. This provides both a mechanism to achieve goodness in my research and the check I need to make sure that I am not too orderly in my thinking. The role that inquiry auditors play for me is to address my own biases and to help me out of my organized thinking and branch out into unconsidered areas. It takes a while for graduate students to recognize that I want them to question me, but when they do, the analysis process is both challenging and rewarding.

I am often asked which research tradition I "really" prefer. To this question I respond by saying that it is important to respect both traditions and to recognize which tradition will truly answer the research question. Perhaps what I learned as a doctoral student really did teach me a good lesson. I came to this project knowing that I was not a purist and was curious to see how this would impact the process and how tensions would emerge. Perhaps the best example of multiple perspectives is found in a project where people are so different that almost everything has to be negotiated. In many ways, our book project illustrates this process. Foremost, what carried me through this process is what also helps me keep participants involved in my longitudinal process—we respect each other and trust each other to do good work.

ANALYZING OUR STORIED PATHS AS QUALITATIVE RESEARCHERS

To provide an analytic snapshot of how qualitative researchers arrive at themes and interpretations, we offer a brief summary of how we individually and collectively approached our data set—our three individual stories. More typically, discussions of data analysis would not include results at the initial stages of analysis. We present several of our individual codes from that first phase of data analysis in order to illustrate both the process in action and the individual differences that present themselves as a researcher reads and analyzes data. This illustrates a major emphasis throughout the book—the significant role of the researcher in all phases of the research process. Indeed, every decision a researcher makes influences the process and outcome of a particular study.

To gain meaning of the lessons our narratives might offer, we each read and reread the three narratives thoroughly, individually noting key words, themes, and interpretations in the margins; disassembling the interpretations from the text; and reassembling them into emerging themes. Despite a relatively small data set, we mirrored an analytic process that takes apart several stories, delving into what lies beneath the words, and then putting the story back together in a way that tells one story while also honoring the individual stories that give shape, form, and meaning to the whole. As noted above, it became clear how our diverse worldviews, prior knowledge and experiences, and methodological approaches shaped how we *read* and interpreted our stories. For example, our first slice of data analysis and interpretive work for the three narratives looked something like this:

Jan

- Learning, modifying the learning to become informed in new ways, not learning
- Knower–known connection and disconnection
- Quotations—quoting others, the making of quotes, the hearing of quotes, inability to quote
- Web, weaving, and complexity
- Being called and compelled

Vasti

- Exploration of assumptions
- Desire to have research that is inclusive of our own experiences
- Wanting to explore the complexity of the lived experience

Susan

- Presence of self in research
- Value of multiple perspectives
- The evolving question begins with one "abiding concern"
- Standing outside, getting inside: navigating the self-other dynamic
- Importance of writing and rewriting

In addition to the differences present in these themes, we also begin to see spaces of convergence in the themes we individually identified. The next phase of analysis was to try to understand these differences to see where commonalities, if any, presented themselves; and to move the analysis and interpretation to a slightly more abstract conceptualization of what was going on in the data. To accomplish this phase, we went back to the individual stories, read and reread the texts, and asked questions of the data—what is really going on here, and how can we best capture this phenomenon? We compared our themes to the data and to each other. Out of this "constant comparison," common emerging themes were then identified and are briefly described below.

Exploration of Assumptions

We each spent considerable time exploring our own assumptions about research in general and our beliefs about how we come to know and understand. This included studying the philosophical underpinnings of qualitative research. All of this is an ongoing process, but we believe this kind of thinking needed to take place before we could settle into our own paths as qualitative researchers. This exploration included "voluminous reading," "writing intensive[ly]," "read[ing] aloud," "being critiqued," "reflecting," and "writing out my reactions." Furthermore, this exploration also resulted in an acknowledgment of how we, as the "human instruments" of the research, influence the manner in which we proceed with our research.

The exploration of assumptions is not an action item that quickly gets checked off a list of "things to do before I initiate a qualitative study." Instead, the very nature of qualitative inquiry (which hopefully has become very evident in the preceding chapters) squares the researcher off with his or her assumptions each and every time a study is conducted. Taken-for-granted assumptions surface as well as those integral to the researcher's worldview. As we have suggested throughout this book, researcher reflexivity is an important skill to be developed and one that is integral to conducting good qualitative work.

Centrality of the Research Question

For each of us, the questions we were asking and the phenomena we wanted to know more about or understand better were the guiding force in our pathways to qualitative research. We each had a desire to research something that was not fully explored in existing literature. We also were interested in illuminating the complexity of the phenomenon we were compelled to study, which at once took us to broader views of a phenomenon while also engaging the phenomenon at greater depth. This theme emerged through our use of words and phrases such as *inhabiting the space in between, weaving relationships and connections, navigate the tensions, a fan where one insight blossoms into adjacent ones, prompted insight into unexplored issues, capture the complexity of real life, the question I was interested in was complex,* and *one question kept creeping in.* Our research questions, then, represented our abiding concerns. These were not stagnant, but continued to evolve, just as we did as qualitative researchers.

We offer this as a lesson learned because our understanding of the importance and influence of the research question has evolved over our years as researchers. Writing a clearly stated research question is much harder than one might suspect at first blush. If you need an entire paragraph to describe what you are after in a study, then most likely your study is not focused enough and your research question is not clear enough to give you the direction you need. Furthermore, we have learned that it is tempting to move into qualitative research projects seeking answers, so research questions are written with this in mind. However, we have discovered that good research questions actually lead to more questions that elicit greater theorizing and understanding, at greater depth and sophistication, about the phenomenon under inquiry. This is the ambiguity—and beauty—of qualitative inquiry: A good research question is clear and focused and, if so, then brings forth greater complexity and lack of clarity. A love of engaging with these kinds of tensions and ambiguities will serve qualitative researchers well.

Influence of Our Lived Experience

Our personal experiences influenced the choices we made about what to study (the abiding concern) and how to study the phenomenon (methodological approach). Our interests in considering depth and complexity come from understanding our own lived experiences, and our curiosity as researchers tapped into what we had experienced. We see this theme surfacing in descriptive stories such as the following:

> "I was tired of placing myself into stages, phases, types, statuses, or what seemed an endless repertoire of possible categories that would name and claim me for who I was (or not)."

> "Why was I compelled to wonder so much about what, as a White woman, I could not experience? Why was I turning away from my own experience of race and privilege? That was a watershed moment for me."

> "Why should I pay attention to these quantitative studies if most of them only tell me about the deficiencies among Latino/as? . . . I knew I had to conduct a qualitative study to explore the choices between two cultures that influence how Latino/a students (and I) express their culture."

We were never far from our own experiences, motivated in part by something we did not understand about ourselves or by a part of our own experience that had not been investigated before, but was very present in our own lived experience.

LESSONS LEARNED

From the analysis and interpretations of our stories about our pathways to becoming qualitative researchers, we developed overlapping themes. Now, in the spirit of putting research to use, we offer these lessons learned. We hope these will be helpful to you as you embark upon your future research endeavors, conducting qualitative inquiries consistent with carrying out good qualitative research.

1. Consider your own experience as something that provides inspiration—or consternation—and situate your research in that dynamic. Tap into an abiding concern you carry with you. If you can't figure this out, talk with trusted friends and colleagues about their perceptions of your patterns of interest and curiosities. Reflect on and analyze your past experiences—where do your commitments lie? What stirs you or gets you fired up? What aspects of your professional practice need improvement or just don't make sense to you? Research is too often experienced as a burden rather than as the possibility of illuminating practice and providing direction for improved practice.

2. Identifying your abiding concern also requires that you acknowledge the presence of self in the research process. The tendency to avoid our own experiences in research is a remnant of a more quantitative objectivist stance and is contrary to the tenets of qualitative research. We believe that all research, quantitative and qualitative alike, comes out of the subjectivity and worldview of the researcher. Placing this in the foreground of research is a strength of qualitative inquiry. However, truly understanding how one's positionality influences the research process requires constant attention and thoughtfulness.

3. Another strength of qualitative research is the opportunity to delve into the complexities of life. This includes the possibility of illuminating multiple perspectives or an intensive look at one perspective. Qualitative research, when conducted congruently with philosophical and methodological elements, and when it meets the criteria of goodness and ethical considerations, offers

insight beyond what is obvious, assumed, or floating on the surface of phenomena. Researching a complex phenomenon is not easy. Rarely do we engage in qualitative research to prove a point or affirm what is known. Rather, qualitative research questions provoke, illuminate, complicate, surprise, and emancipate that which we are coming to know and understand. This more dynamic process calls for both flexibility and clarity of focus. The lesson we offer here is not to be content with obvious or expected interpretations, but rather to push yourself to stretch and work toward what is interrelated, webbed, complicated, and difficult to put into words. Unfortunately, there are plenty of examples of published qualitative research that are merely descriptive and barely skim the surface of what is going on in the data. The challenge is to go deeper than what a casual read would provide—to delve into greater meaning making and interpretation.

4.   We know our work benefits from the perspectives of others who read and provide feedback to our interpretations and writing. So, too, this book is the result of three different individuals coming together to write one book. We conceptualized the book together, but wrote chapters individually. We read, reviewed, and edited each other's work over and over again. As you conceptualize and design studies, and then as you write the results of your work, always consult with others. These should be individuals both familiar and unfamiliar with your area of focus because all perspectives contribute to the overall strength of research. We would never submit anything for publication without first having it reviewed by trusted colleagues and then responding to their feedback. Identify individuals who have strengths in different areas to read and evaluate your work: someone who writes better than you do and can edit and proof your work, someone who you know will challenge your ideas and interpretations, someone with greater knowledge of the context of your research than you have, and someone who has no background in your focus to ascertain how clear your work is to those reading about this area for the first time. Qualitative research benefits from multiple perspectives in all phases.

CONCLUSION

We shall not cease from exploration
And the end of all our exploring
Will be to arrive where we started
And know the place for the first time.

T. S. Eliot

As we come to the place where concluding this chapter, and the book, makes sense, we are as clear as we were when we started the book that our worldviews and experiences are different and that these influence the process of research. However, we were reminded as we tried to model in this concluding chapter "what it is to work qualitatively" that this is indeed the process a qualitative researcher engages in when interpreting the voices and experiences of participants in a study. The process of understanding—and ability to understand—is closely tied to how we understand ourselves.

We tried to write a book that was both accessible and useful, while raising questions and navigating the complexities of qualitative research. Furthermore, we wanted it to become clear that "the self" is always lurking in qualitative research, and, indeed, this is what brings tension and ambiguity to the research process. We did not want to provide a simplistic rendering of the steps involved in conducting qualitative inquiry, although we recognize the importance of understanding these before one steps out in a different direction. In this last chapter, we hoped to model some of what we have learned over the years *about* qualitative research and *as* qualitative researchers.

REFERENCES

Abes, E. S., & Jones, S. R. (2004). Meaning-making capacity and the dynamics of lesbian college students' multiple dimensions of identity. *Journal of College Student Development, 45,* 612–632.

American Psychological Association. (2001). *Publication manual of the American Psychological Association* (5th ed.). Washington, DC: Author.

Apple, M. (1991). Series editor introduction. In P. Lather, *Getting Smart* (vii–xi). New York: Routledge.

Arminio, J. L. (1994). *Waking up White: A phenomenological journey into racial being.* Unpublished doctoral dissertation, University of Maryland, College Park.

Arminio, J. L. (2001). Exploring the nature of race-related guilt. *Journal of Multicultural Counseling, 29,* 239–252.

Arminio, J. L., & Hultgren, F. H. (2002). Breaking out of the shadow: The question of criteria in qualitative research. *Journal of College Student Development, 43,* 446–460.

Arminio, J. W., & McEwen, M. K. (1996). White connections of family, place, race, and ethnicity: Implications for student affairs. *Journal of College Student Development, 3,* 315–323.

Ashworth, P. (1999). "Bracketing" in phenomenology: Renouncing assumptions in hearing about student cheating. *Qualitative Studies in Education, 12,* 707–721.

Ayala, J. (2000). Across dialects. In L. Weis & M. Fine (Eds.), *Speed bumps: A student-friendly guide to qualitative research* (pp. 102–105). New York: Teachers College Press.

Baldwin, R. G., & Thelin, J. R. (1990). Thanks for the memories: The fusion of quantitative and qualitative research on college students and the college experience. In J. C. Smart (Ed.), *Higher education: Handbook of theory and research* (Vol. 6, pp. 337–360). New York: Algora.

Ballard, K. (1996). Finding the ghost in the machine and giving it back to the body. In L. Heshusius & K. Ballard (Eds.), *From positivism and interpretivism and beyond* (pp. 100–107). New York: Teachers College Press.

Bandura, A. (1986). *Social foundations of thought and action: A social cognitive theory*. Englewood Cliffs, NJ: Prentice Hall.

Baxter Magolda, M. B. (1992). *Knowing and reasoning in college: Gender-related patterns in students' intellectual development*. San Francisco: Jossey-Bass.

Baxter Magolda, M. B. (2001). *Making their own way: Narratives for transforming higher education to promote self-development*. Sterling, VA: Stylus.

Baxter Magolda, M. B. (2003). Identity and learning: Student affairs' role in transforming higher education. *Journal of College Student Development, 44*, 231–247.

Belenky, M. F., Clinchy, B. M., Goldberger, N. R., & Tarule, J. M. (1986). *Women's ways of knowing: The development of self, voice and mind*. New York: Basic Books.

Berube, M. S. (Ed). (1995). *Webster's II new collegiate dictionary*. Boston: Houghton Mifflin.

Bhaskar, R. (1979). *The possibility of naturalism*. Atlantic Highlands, NJ: Humanities Press.

Brightman, E. S. (1964). *An introduction to philosophy* (3rd ed.). New York: Holt Rinehart Winston.

Broido, E. M. (2000). The development of social justice allies during college: A phenomenological investigation. *Journal of College Student Development, 41*, 3–18.

Broido, E. M., & Manning, K. (2002). Philosophical foundations and current theoretical perspectives in qualitative research. *Journal of College Student Development, 43*, 434–445.

Bronner, S. E. (1999). *Ideas in action: Political tradition in the twentieth century*. Lanham, MD: Rowman & Littlefield.

Butler, J. D. (1957). *Four philosophies: And their practice in education and religion* (Rev. ed.). New York: Harper & Row.

Caputo, J. D. (1987). *Radical hermeneutics: Repetition, deconstruction, and the hermeneutic project*. Bloomington: Indiana University Press.

Carpenter, S. (2003). Student affairs scholarship (re?) considered: Toward a scholarship of practice. *Journal of College Student Development, 42*, 301–318.

Charmaz, K. (2000). Grounded theory objectivist and constructivist methods. In N. K. Denzin & Y. S. Lincoln (Eds.), *Handbook of qualitative research* (2nd ed., pp. 509–535). Thousand Oaks, CA: Sage.

Christians, C. G. (2000). Ethics and politics in qualitative research. In N. K. Denzin & Y. S. Lincoln (Eds.), *Handbook of qualitative research* (2nd ed., pp. 133–155). Thousand Oaks, CA: Sage.

Clandinin, D. J., & Connelly, F. M. (2000). *Narrative inquiry: Experience and story in qualitative research*. San Francisco: Jossey-Bass.

Clarke, A. E. (2005). *Situational analysis: Grounded theory after the postmodern turn*. Thousand Oaks, CA: Sage.

Coles, R. (1993). *The call of service: A witness to idealism*. Boston: Houghton Mifflin.

Coomer, D. L. (1989). Introduction to critical inquiry. In F. H. Hultgren & D. L. Coomer (Eds.), *Alternative modes of inquiry in home economics research* (pp. 167–184). Peoria, IL: Glencoe.

Coomer, D. L., & Hultgren, F. H. (1989). Introduction, considering alternatives: An invitation to dialogue and question. In F. H. Hultgren & D. L. Coomer (Eds.), *Alternative modes of inquiry in home economics research* (pp. xv–xxiii). Peoria, IL: Glencoe.

Creswell, J. W. (1994). *Research design: Qualitative and quantitative approaches*. Thousand Oaks, CA: Sage.

Creswell, J. W. (1998). *Qualitative inquiry and research design: Choosing among five traditions*. Thousand Oaks, CA: Sage.

Creswell, J. W. (2003). *Research design qualitative, quantitative and mixed method approaches* (2nd ed.). Thousand Oaks, CA: Sage.

Crotty, M. (1998). *The foundations of social research: Meaning and perspective in the research process*. Thousand Oaks, CA: Sage.

Davis, T. L. (2002). Voices of gender role conflict: The social construction of college men's identity. *Journal of College Student Development, 43*, 508–521.

Deaux, K. (1993). Reconstructing social identity. *Personality and Social Psychology Bulletin, 19*, 4–12.

Delgado, R. (1995). Introduction. In R. Delgado (Ed.), *Critical race theory* (pp. xiii–xvi). Philadelphia: Temple University Press.

Delgado, R., & Stefancic, J. (2001). *Critical race theory: An introduction*. New York: New York University Press.

Delong, A. (2003). Perceptions of parents of first-generation college students about college attendance and enrollment. Unpublished doctoral dissertation, Ohio State University, Columbus.

Denzin, N. K. (2001). *Interpretive interactionism*. Thousand Oaks, CA: Sage.

Denzin, N. K., & Lincoln, Y. S. (2000a). (Eds.). *Handbook of qualitative research* (2nd ed.). Thousand Oaks, CA: Sage.

Denzin, N. K., & Lincoln, Y. S. (2000b). Introduction: The discipline and practice of qualitative research. In N. K. Denzin & Y. S. Lincoln (Eds.), *Handbook of qualitative research* (2nd ed., pp. 1–28). Thousand Oaks, CA: Sage.

Derrida, J. (1985). *The ear of the other: Texts and discussions with J. Derrida*. Ed. C. V. McDonald, trans. Peggy Kamuf. New York: Schocken Books.

Dey, I. (1995). *Qualitative data analysis: A user-friendly guide for social scientists*. London: Routledge.

Doll, W., Jr. (1993). *A post-modern perspective on curriculum*. New York: Teachers College Press.

Duneier, M. (2004). Finding a place to pee and other struggles of ethnography: Reflections on race and method. In M. Fine, L. Weis, L. Powell Pruitt, & A. Burns (Eds.), *Off White: Readings on power, privilege, and resistance* (2nd ed., pp. 206–214). New York: Routledge.

Durant, W. (1961). *The story of philosophy*. New York: Touchstone.

Durham, M. G. (1998). On the relevance of standpoint epistemology to the practice of journalism: The case for "strong objectivity." *Communication Theory, 8*, 117–140.

Eisner, E., & Peshkin, A. (Eds.). (1990). *Qualitative inquiry in education*. New York: Teachers College Press.

Ellis, C., & Bochner, A. P. (2000). Autoethnography: Personal narrative, reflexivity; researcher as subject. In N. K. Denzin & Y. S. Lincoln (Eds.), *Handbook of qualitative research* (2nd ed., pp. 733–768). Thousand Oaks, CA: Sage.

Ellsworth, E. (1997). *Teaching positions: Difference, pedagogy, and the power of address*. New York: Teachers College Press.

Ely, M. (1991). *Doing qualitative research: Circles within circles*. London: Falmer.

Erickson, F. (1986). Qualitative methods in research on teaching. In M. C. Wittrock (Ed.), *Handbook of research on teaching* (3rd ed., pp. 119–161). New York: Macmillan.

Erikson, E. (1968). *Identity: Youth and crisis*. New York: Norton.

Evans, N. J. (2002). The impact of an LGBT safe zone project on campus climate. *Journal of College Student Development, 43*, 522–539.

Ewell, P. T. (2002). A brief history of assessment. In T. W. Banta (Ed.), *Building a scholarship of assessment* (pp. 3–23). San Francisco: Jossey-Bass.

Fine, M. (1994). Working the hyphens: Reinventing self and other in qualitative research. In N. K. Denzin & Y. S. Lincoln (Eds.), *Handbook of qualitative research* (pp. 70–82). Thousand Oaks, CA: Sage.

Fine, M., Weis, L., Weseen, S., & Wong, L. (2000). For whom? Qualitative research, representations, and social responsibilities. In N. K. Denzin & Y. S. Lincoln (Eds.), *Handbook of qualitative research* (2nd ed., pp. 107–131). Thousand Oaks, CA: Sage.

Flew, A. (1984). *A dictionary of philosophy* (2nd rev. ed.). New York: St. Martin's.

Fontana, A., & Frey, J. H. (2000). The interview: From structured questions to negotiated text. In N. K. Denzin & Y. S. Lincoln (Eds.), *Handbook of qualitative research* (2nd ed., pp. 645–672). Thousand Oaks, CA: Sage.

Gadamer, H. G. (1989). *Truth and method* (2nd rev. ed.) (J. Weinsheimer & D. G. Marshall, Trans.) New York: Crossroad. (Original work published 1960.)

Gamson, J. (2000). Sexualities, queer theory, and qualitative research. In N. K. Denzin & Y. S. Lincoln (Eds.), *Handbook of qualitative research* (2nd ed., pp. 347–365). Thousand Oaks, CA: Sage.

Geertz, C. (1973). *The interpretation of cultures: Selected essays*. New York: Basic Books.

Gergen, M. M., & Gergen, K. J. (2000). Qualitative inquiry: Tensions and transformations. In N. K. Denzin & Y. S. Lincoln (Eds.), *Handbook of qualitative research* (2nd ed., pp. 1025–1046). Thousand Oaks, CA: Sage.

Gitlin, A. D. (2000). Educative research, voice, and school change. In B. M. Brizuela, J. P. Stewart, R. G. Carrillo, & J. G. Berger (Eds.), *Acts of inquiry in qualitative research* (pp. 95–118). Cambridge, MA: Harvard Educational Review.

Glaser, B. G. (1978). *Theoretical sensitivity*. Mill Valley, CA: Sociology Press.

Glaser, B. G., & Strauss, A. L. (1967). *Discovery of grounded theory: Strategies for qualitative research*. Chicago: Aldine.

Glesne, C. (1999). *Becoming qualitative* (2nd ed.). New York: Longman.

Glesne, C., & Peshkin, A. (1992). *Becoming qualitative researchers.* White Plains, NY: Longman.

González, K. P., Marin, P., Figueroa, M. A., Moreno, J. F., & Navia, C. N. (2002). Inside doctoral education in America: Voices of Latinas/os in pursuit of the PhD. *Journal of College Student Development, 43,* 540–557.

Greene, J. C. (2000). Understanding social programs through evaluation. In N. K. Denzin & Y. S. Lincoln (Eds.), *Handbook of qualitative research* (2nd ed., pp. 981–999). Thousand Oaks, CA: Sage.

Greene, J. C., & Caracelli, V. J. (2003). Making paradigmatic sense of mixed methods practice. In A. Tashakkori & C. Teddlie (Eds.), *Handbook of mixed methods in social & behavioral research* (pp. 91–110). Thousand Oaks, CA: Sage.

Gribbin, K. M. (2005). *Understanding the experiences of gay, lesbian, bisexual, and transgender (GLBT) allies: The influence of perceived consequences to self and others.* Unpublished master's thesis, Ohio State University, Columbus.

Guba, E. G., & Lincoln, Y. S. (1981). *Effective evaluation: Improving the usefulness of evaluation results through responsive and naturalistic approaches.* San Francisco: Jossey-Bass.

Guba, E. G., & Lincoln, Y. S. (1989). *Fourth generation evaluation.* Thousand Oaks, CA: Sage.

Guba, E. G., & Lincoln, Y. S. (1994). Competing paradigms in qualitative research. In N. K. Denzin & Y. S. Lincoln (Eds.), *Handbook of qualitative research* (2nd ed., pp. 107–117). Thousand Oaks, CA: Sage.

Habermas, J. (1984). *The theory of communicative action: Vol. 1. Reason and the rationalization of society* (Trans. Thomas McCarthy). Boston: Beacon. (Original work published 1981.)

Hammersley, M. (1990). *Reading ethnographic research: A critical guide.* New York: Longman.

Hammersley, M., & Atkinson, P. (1983). *Ethnography principles and practice.* New York: Routledge.

Hamrick, F. A. (1998). Democratic citizenship and student activism. *Journal of College Student Development, 39,* 449–460.

Heidegger, M. (1996). *Being and time* (Trans. J. Macquarrie & E. Robinson). New York: Harper & Row. (Original work published 1926)

Hidalgo, N. (1998). Toward a definition of a Latino family research paradigm. *Qualitative Studies in Education, 11,* 103-120.

Hittleman, D. R., & Simon, A. J. (2002). *Interpreting educational research: an introduction for consumers of research* (3rd ed.). Upper Saddle River, NJ: Pearson Education.

Hoad, T. F. (1986). *The concise Oxford dictionary of English etymology.* Oxford: Oxford University Press.

Hodder, I. (2000). The interpretation of documents and material culture. In N. K. Denzin & Y. S. Lincoln (Eds.), *Handbook of qualitative research* (2nd ed., pp. 703–716). Thousand Oaks, CA: Sage.

Honderich, T. (Ed.). (1995). *The Oxford companion to philosophy.* New York: Oxford University Press.

hooks, b. (1990). *Yearning: Race, gender, and cultural politics.* Boston: South End.

hooks, b. (1991). *Black looks: Race and representation*. Boston: South End.

hooks, b. (1994). *Teaching to transgress*. New York: Routledge.

House, E. R. (1994). Integrating the quantitative and qualitative. In C. S. Reichardt and S. F. Rallis (Eds.), *The qualitative-quantitative debate: New perspectives* (New Directions for Program Evaluation, No. 61, pp. 13–22). San Francisco: Jossey-Bass.

Howe, K., & Eisenhart, M. (1990). Standards for qualitative (and quantitative) research: A prolegomenon. *Educational Researcher, 19,* 2–9.

Hultgren, F. (1989). Introduction to interpretive inquiry. In F. H. Hultgren & D. L. Coomer (Eds.), *Alternative modes of inquiry in home economics research* (pp. 37–59). Peoria, IL: Glencoe.

Husserl, E. (1970). *Logical investigation*. Atlantic Highlands, NJ: Humanities Press.

Johnson, R. B., & Onweugbuzie, A. J. (2004). Mixed method research: A research paradigm whose time has come. *Educational Researcher, 33,* 14–26.

Jones, S. R. (1997). Voices of identity and difference: A qualitative exploration of the multiple dimensions of identity development in women college students. *Journal of College Student Development, 38,* 376–386.

Jones, S. R. (2002). (Re)writing the word: Methodological strategies and issues in qualitative research. *Journal of College Student Development, 43,* 461–473.

Jones, S. R., & Abes, E. S. (2003). Developing student understanding of HIV/AIDS through community service-learning: A case study analysis. *Journal of College Student Development, 44,* 470–488.

Jones, S. R., & Hill, K. (2001). Crossing high street: Understanding diversity through community service-learning. *Journal of College Student Development, 42,* 204–216.

Kezar, A. (2002). Expanding notions of leadership to capture pluralistic voices: Positionality theory in practice. *Journal of College Student Development, 43,* 558–578.

Kezar, A. (2004). Wrestling with philosophy: Improving scholarship in higher education. *Journal of Higher Education, 75,* 42–55.

Kitchener, K. S. (1985). Ethical principles and ethical decisions in student affairs. In H. J. Canon & R. D. Brown (Eds.), *Applied Ethics in Student Services* (New Directions for Student Services, No. 30, pp. 17–30). San Francisco: Jossey-Bass.

Kuh, G. D., Kinzie, J., Schuh, J. H., & Whitt, E. J. (2005). *Student success in college: Creating conditions that matter*. San Francisco: Jossey-Bass.

Kuhn, T. S. (1962). *The structure of scientific revolutions*. Chicago: University of Chicago Press.

Kuhn, T. S. (1970). *The structure of scientific revolutions* (2nd ed.). Chicago: University of Chicago Press.

Kvale, S. (1987). Validity in the qualitative research interview. *Methods: A Journal for Human Science, 1,* 37–72.

Ladson-Billings, G. (1998). Just what is critical race theory and what's it doing in a nice field like education? *Qualitative Studies in Education, 11*(1), 7–24.

Lamott, A. (1994). *Bird by bird: Some instructions on writing and life*. New York: Doubleday.

Lather, P. (1986). Research as praxis. *Harvard Educational Review, 56,* 257–277.

Lather, P. (1991). *Getting smart: Feminist research and pedagogy with/in the postmodern.* New York: Routledge.

Lather, P. (1992). Critical frames in educational research: Feminist and post-structural perspectives. *Theory Into Practice, 31,* 1–13.

Lather, P. (2003). Issues of validity in openly ideological research: Between a rock and a soft place. In Y. S. Lincoln & N. K. Denzin (Eds.), *Turning points in qualitative research: Tying knots in a handkerchief* (pp. 185–215). Walnut Creek, CA: AltaMira.

Lather, P., & Smithies, C. (1997). *Troubling the angels: Women living with HIV/AIDS.* Boulder, CO: Westview.

Lawrence-Lightfoot, S. (1999). *Respect: An exploration.* Reading, MA: Perseus.

Levin, M. (1988). The opening of vision: Seeing through the veil of tears. In K. Hoeller (Ed.), *Heidegger & psychology* (pp. 113–146). Seattle, WA: Review of Existential Psychology & Psychiatry.

Levin, M. (1989). *The listening self.* London: Routledge.

Lincoln, Y. S. (1990). Toward a categorical imperative for qualitative research. In E. Eisner & A. Peshkin (Eds.), *Qualitative inquiry in education* (pp. 277–295). New York: Teachers College Press.

Lincoln, Y. S. (1997). Self, subject, audience, text: Living at the edge, writing in the margins. In W. G. Tierney & Y. S. Lincoln (Eds.), *Representation and the text: Reframing the narrative voice* (pp. 37–55). Albany: State University of New York Press.

Lincoln, Y. S. (1998). From understanding to action: New imperatives. *Theory and Research in Social Education, 26,* 12–29.

Lincoln, Y. S., & Guba, E. G. (1985). *Naturalistic inquiry.* Beverly Hills, CA: Sage.

Lincoln, Y. S., & Guba, E. G. (2000). Paradigmatic controversies, contradictions, and emerging confluences. In N. K. Denzin & Y. S. Lincoln (Eds.), *Handbook of qualitative research* (2nd ed., pp. 163–188). Thousand Oaks, CA: Sage.

Locke, J. (1975). *An essay concerning human understanding.* Oxford: Clarendon. (Original work published 1690)

Madriz, E. (2000). Focus groups in feminist research. In N. K. Denzin & Y. S. Lincoln (Eds.), *Handbook of qualitative research* (2nd ed., pp. 835–850). Thousand Oaks, CA: Sage.

Magolda, P. M., & Weems, L. (2002). Doing harm: An unintended consequence of qualitative inquiry? *Journal of College Student Development, 43,* 490–507.

Manning, P. K., & Cullum-Swan, B. (1994). Narrative, content, and semiotic analysis. In N. K. Denzin & Y. S. Lincoln (Eds.), *Handbook of qualitative research* (2nd ed., pp. 463–477). Thousand Oaks, CA: Sage.

Marshall, C. (1990). Goodness criteria: Are they objective or judgment calls? In E. G. Guba (Ed.), *The paradigm dialogue* (pp. 188–197). Newbury Park, CA: Sage.

Marshall, C., & Rossman, G. B. (1999). *Designing qualitative research* (3rd ed.). Thousand Oaks, CA: Sage.

Martin, S. (2005). A pragmatic exploration of the multicultural competence of community college student affairs practitioners. Unpublished doctoral dissertation, George Washington University, Washington, DC.

Maxcy, S. J. (2003). Pragmatic threads in mixed methods research in the social sciences: The search for multiple modes of inquiry and the end of the philosophy or formalism. In A. Tashakkori & C. Teddlie (Eds.), *Handbook of mixed methods in social & behavioral research* (pp. 51–89). Thousand Oaks, CA: Sage.

Maykut, P., & Morehouse, R. (2001). *Beginning qualitative research: A philosophic and practical guide.* Philadelphia: Routledge/Falmer.

Maynard, M. (2000). Methods, practice, and epistemology: The debate about feminism and research. In J. Glazer-Raymo, B. K. Townsend, & B. Ropers-Huilman (Eds.), *Women in higher education: A feminist perspective* (pp. 89–100). Boston: Pearson Custom Publishing.

Merchant, B. M. (2001). Negotiating the boundaries and sometimes missing the mark: A White researcher and a Mexican American research assistant. In B. M. Merchant & A. I. Willis (Eds.), *Multiple and intersecting identities in qualitative research* (pp. 1–18). Mahwah, NJ: Lawrence Erlbaum.

Merriam, S. B. (1998). *Qualitative research and case study applications in education.* San Francisco: Jossey-Bass.

Merriam, S. B., & Associates. (2002). *Qualitative research in practice: Examples for discussion and analysis.* San Francisco: Jossey-Bass.

Miles, M. B., & Huberman, A. M. (1994). *Qualitative data analysis: An expanded sourcebook* (2nd ed.). Thousand Oaks, CA: Sage.

Mishler, E. G. (2000). Validation in inquiry-guided research: The role of exemplars in narrative studies. In B. M. Brizuela, J. P. Stewart, R. G. Carillo, & J. G. Berger (Eds.), *Acts of inquiry in qualitative research* (pp. 119–146). Cambridge, MA: Harvard Educational Review.

Moffatt, M. (1989). *Coming of age in New Jersey: College and American culture.* New Brunswick, NJ: Rutgers University Press.

Moos, R. H. (1979). *Evaluating educational environments.* San Francisco: Jossey-Bass.

Morse, J. M., & Richards, L. (2002). *README FIRST for a user's guide to qualitative methods.* Thousand Oaks, CA: Sage.

Nathan, R. (2005). *My freshman year: What a professor learned by becoming a student.* Ithaca, NY: Cornell University Press.

Noddings, N. (1984). *Caring: A feminine approach to ethics and moral education.* Berkeley: University of California Press.

Padover, S. K. (Ed.). (1977). *The Karl Marx library* (Vol. 7). New York: McGraw-Hill.

Paloma, C. A., & Banta, T. W. (1999). *Assessment essentials: Planning, implementing, and improving assessment in higher education.* San Francisco: Jossey-Bass.

Parker, L. (1998). Race is . . . race ain't: An exploration of the utility of critical race theory in qualitative research in education. *Qualitative Studies in Education, 11*(1), 43–55.

Pascarella, E. T., Pierson, C. T., Wolniak, G. C., & Terenzini, P. T. (2004). First-generation college students: Additional evidence on college experiences and outcomes. *Journal of Higher Education, 75*, 249–284.

Patton, M. (1990). *Qualitative evaluation and research methods* (2nd ed.). Newbury Park, CA: Sage.

Patton, M. (2002). *Qualitative research and evaluation methods* (3rd ed.). Newbury Park, CA: Sage.

Peshkin, A. (1988). In search of subjectivity: One's own. *Educational Researcher, 17*(7), 17–21.

Phallas, A. M. (2001). Preparing education doctoral students for epistemological diversity. *Educational Researcher, 30*, 6–11.

Pinar, W. F., Reynolds, W. M., Slattery, P., & Taubman, P. M. (1995). *Understanding curriculum.* New York: Peter Lang.

Radhakrishnan, R. (2003). *Theory in an uneven world.* Malden, MA: Blackwell.

Reason, R. D., Roosa Millar, E. A., & Scales, T. C. (2005). Toward a model of racial justice ally development. *Journal of College Student Development, 46*, 530–546.

Reinharz, S. (1992). *Feminist methods in social research.* New York: Oxford University Press.

Rhoads, R. A. (1994). *Coming out in college: The struggle for a queer identity.* Westport, CT: Bergin & Garvey.

Richards, T. J., & Richards, L. (1994). Using computers in qualitative research. In N. K. Denzin & Y. S. Lincoln (Eds.), *Handbook of qualitative research* (pp. 445–462). Thousand Oaks, CA: Sage.

Ryan, G. W., & Bernard, H. R. (2000). Data management and analysis methods. In N. K. Denzin & Y. S. Lincoln (Eds.), *Handbook of qualitative research* (pp. 769–802). Thousand Oaks, CA: Sage.

Schlossberg, N. K. (1989). Marginality and mattering: Key issues in building community. In D. C. Roberts (Ed.), *Designing campus activities to foster a sense of community* (New Directions for Student Services, No. 48, pp. 5–15). San Francisco: Jossey-Bass.

Silverman, D. (2000). Analyzing talk and text. In N. K. Denzin & Y. S. Lincoln (Eds.), *Handbook of qualitative research* (pp. 821–834). Thousand Oaks, CA: Sage.

Sipe, L., & Constable, S. (1996). A chart of four contemporary research paradigms: Metaphors for the modes of inquiry. *Taboo: The Journal of Culture and Education, 1*, 153–163.

Smith, J. E. (1978). *Purpose and thought: The meaning of pragmatism.* New Haven, CT: Yale University Press.

Smith, J. K. (1990). Alternative research paradigms and the problem of criteria. In E. G. Guba (Ed.), *The paradigm dialogue* (pp. 168–187). Newbury Park, CA: Sage.

Smith, J. K. (1993). *After the demise of empiricism: The problem of judging social and educational inquiry.* Norwood, NJ: Ablex.

Smith, J. K., & Deemer, D. K. (2000). The problem of criteria in the age of relativism. In N. K. Denzin & Y. S. Lincoln (Eds.), *Handbook of qualitative research* (2nd ed., pp. 877–896). Thousand Oaks, CA: Sage.

Smith, L. M. (1990). Ethics in qualitative field research: An individual perspective. In E. Eisner & A. Peshkin (Eds.), *Qualitative inquiry in education* (pp. 258–276). New York: Teachers College Press.

Soltis, J. F. (1990). The ethics of qualitative research. In E. Eisner & A. Peshkin (Eds.), *Qualitative inquiry in education* (pp. 247–257). New York: Teachers College Press.

Spradley, J. (1979). *The ethnographic interview*. New York: Holt, Rinehart and Winston.

Spradley, J. (1980). *Participant observation*. New York: Holt, Rinehart and Winston.

Stage, F. K., & Manning, K. (2003). *Research in the college context: Approaches and methods*. New York: Brunner-Routledge.

Stake, R. E. (1995). *The art of case study research*. Thousand Oaks, CA: Sage.

Stake, R. E. (2000). Case studies. In N. K. Denzin & Y. S. Lincoln (Eds.), *Handbook of qualitative research* (2nd ed., pp. 435–454). Thousand Oaks, CA: Sage.

Stewart, D. L. (2002). The role of faith in the development of an integrated identity: A qualitative study of Black students at a White college. *Journal of College Student Development, 43*, 579–595.

Strauss, A., & Corbin, J. (1990). *Basics of qualitative research: Grounded theory procedures and techniques*. Thousand Oaks, CA: Sage.

Strauss, A., & Corbin, J. (1998). *Basics of qualitative research techniques and procedures for developing grounded theory* (2nd ed.). Thousand Oaks, CA: Sage.

Sue, D. W., Ivey, A. E., & Pedersen, P. B. (1996). *A theory of multicultural counseling and therapy*. Pacific Grove, CA: Brooks/Cole.

Talburt, S. (2004). Ethnographic responsibility without the "real." *Journal of Higher Education, 75*, 80–103.

Tashakkori, A., & Teddlie, C. (1998). *Mixed methodology: Combining qualitative and quantitative approaches* (Applied Social Research Methods Series, Vol. 46). Thousand Oaks, CA: Sage.

Tashakkori, A., & Teddlie, C. (2003). *Handbook of mixed methods in social & behavioral research*. Thousand Oaks, CA: Sage.

Teddlie, C., & Tashakkori, A. (2003). Major issues and controversies in the use of mixed methods in the social and behavioral sciences. In A. Tashakkori & C. Teddlie (Eds.), *Handbook of mixed methods in social & behavioral research* (pp. 3–50). Thousand Oaks, CA: Sage.

Tedlock, B. (2000). Ethnography and ethnographic representation. In N. K. Denzin & Y. S. Lincoln (Eds.), *Handbook of qualitative research* (2nd ed., pp. 455–486). Thousand Oaks, CA: Sage.

Thelin, J. R. (2003). Historical overview of American higher education. In S. R. Komives & D. Woodard Jr. (Eds.), *Student services: A handbook of the profession* (pp. 3–44). San Francisco: Jossey-Bass.

Torres, V. (2003). Influences on ethnic identity development of Latino college students in the first two years of college. *Journal of College Student Development, 44*, 532–547.

Torres, V. (2004). Familial influences on the identity development of Latino first year students. *Journal of College Student Development, 45,* 457–469.

Torres, V. (in press). A mixed method study testing data-model fit of a retention model for Latino students at urban universities. *Journal of College Student Development.*

Torres, V., & Baxter Magolda, M. (2002). The evolving role of the researcher in constructivist qualitative studies. *Journal of College Student Development, 43,* 474–489.

Torres, V., Globe, J., Ketcheson, K., & Truxillo, D. (1999). Development of an entering student survey for urban institutions. *Metropolitan Universities: an International Forum, 10*(3), 41–50.

Torres, V., Howard-Hamilton, M., & Cooper, D. L. (2003). *Identity development for diverse populations: Implications for teaching and practice* (ASHE/ERIC Higher Education Report, Vol. 26, No. 6). San Francisco: Jossey-Bass.

Upcraft, M. L. (2003). Assessment and evaluation. In S. R. Komives & D. B. Woodard (Eds.), *Student services: A handbook of the profession* (pp. 555–572). San Francisco: Jossey-Bass.

Upcraft, M. L., & Schuh, J. H. (1996). *Assessment in student affairs: A guide for practitioners.* San Francisco: Jossey-Bass.

Upcraft, M. L., & Schuh, J. H. (2002, March–April). Assessment vs. research: Why we should care about the difference. *About Campus, 7,* 16–20.

van Manen, M. (1990). *Researching lived experience: Human science for an action sensitive pedagogy.* Albany: State University of New York Press.

van Manen, M. (1997). *Researching lived experience: Human science for an action sensitive pedagogy* (2nd ed.). London, Ontario: Althouse Press.

Weber, M. (1958). *Essays in sociology* (Ed. & Trans. H. H. Gerth & C. Wright Mills). New York: Galaxy. (Original work published 1946)

Weis, L., & Fine, M. (2000). *Speed bumps: A student friendly guide to qualitative research.* New York: Teachers College Press.

Weitzman, E. A. (2000). Software and qualitative research. In N. K. Denzin & Y. S. Lincoln (Eds.), *Handbook of qualitative research* (2nd ed., pp. 803–820). Thousand Oaks, CA: Sage.

Whitt, E. (1991). Artful science: A primer on qualitative research methods. *Journal of College Student Development, 32,* 406–415.

Wittgenstein, L. (1953). *Philosophical investigations.* Oxford: Basil Blackwell.

Wolcott, H. F. (1994). *Transforming qualitative data description, analysis, and interpretation.* Thousand Oaks, CA: Sage.

Wolcott, H. F. (2002) Writing up qualitative research . . . better. *Qualitative Health Research, 12*(1), 91–103.

Woozley, A. D. (Ed.). (1964). *John Locke: An essay concerning human understanding.* New York: Meridian.

Yin, R. K. (1994). *Case study research: Design and methods.* Thousand Oaks, CA: Sage.

Yin, R. K. (2004). *The case study anthology.* Thousand Oaks, CA: Sage.

Zurita, M. (2001). La mojada y el coyote: Experiences of a wetback researcher. In B. M. Merchant & A. I. Willis (Eds.), *Multiple and intersecting identities in qualitative research* (pp. 9–32). Mahwah, NJ: Lawrence Erlbaum.

INDEX

A

Advocacy as research aim, 5
African-American students, 173
AIDS
    case study example, 54–56
    reflexivity and, 131
    sampling and, 64, 68, 73, 76
Analysis of data, *see* Data analysis and interpretation
Anonymity of participants, 158
Assessment as research aim, 29–31
Auditor/mentor
    benefits of, 100, 190
    ethical issues and, 172
    inquiry, 110–111, 171, 185
Autonomy and social identities, 110–111
Axial coding in data analysis, 45, 89–90

B

Bias, 2, 126, 166; *see also* Researchers, positionality
Bisexual community, *see* Gay, lesbian, bisexual, and transgendered (GLBT) community

Boundedness in case studies, 55–56
Bracketing in phenomenology, 48–49

C

Case study methodology, 53–56, 90–91
Catalytic validity, 27, 121
Categories in open coding, 44–45
Co-construction and ethical issues, 169–170
Coding in data analysis, 44–45, 89–90
Co-investigators, *see* Researcher-participant relationship; Sampling
Collective case study, 55
College men's identity study, 48–52, 64, 68–69, 73, 96–97
Coming clean at the hyphen, *see* Working the hyphen of self-other
Commensurability and mixing methods, 140–141
Compelling question, 37, 187–188; *see also* Research question
Computer software use, 97–98
Conditions in axial coding, 45, 90
Confidentiality, 155, 158
Constant comparative method, 43–45, 90

D